Representative Bureaucracy

Representative Bureaucracy

Classic Readings and Continuing Controversies

Julie Dolan and
David H. Rosenbloom

Editors

M.E.Sharpe
Armonk, New York
London, England

Library of Congress Cataloging-in-Publication Data

Representative bureaucracy : classic readings and continuing controversies / edited by
Julie A. Dolan and David H. Rosenbloom.
    p. cm.
  Includes bibliographical references and index.
  ISBN 0-7656-0960-6 (cloth: alk. paper) — ISBN 0-7656-0961-4 (pbk.: alk. paper)
  1. Bureaucracy—United States. 2. Representative government and
representation—United States. I. Dolan, Julie, A., 1968– II. Rosenbloom, David H.

JK421 .R47 2003
352.6'3'0973—dc21

2002030855

Printed in the United States of America

The paper used in this publication meets the minimum requirements of
American National Standard for Information Sciences
Permanence of Paper for Printed Library Materials,
ANSI Z 39.48-1984.

BM (c) 10 9 8 7 6 5 4 3 2 1
BM (p) 10 9 8 7 6 5 4 3 2 1

To Kenneth J. Meier and Samuel Krislov,
in appreciation of their contributions to knowledge
about representative bureaucracy

Contents

List of Tables and Figures

Tables

Figures

Preface

Democracies throughout the world face substantial challenges in reconciling the basic principles of representative government with the powerful roles that unelected civil servants collectively play in the formulation and implementation of public policies. "Representative bureaucracy" is the body of thought and research examining the potential for government agencies to act as representative political institutions if their personnel are drawn from all sectors of society. In the United States, the goal of achieving a representative federal civil service was written into the Civil Service Reform Act of 1978 and popularized by former president Bill Clinton's call for a government that "looks like America." Elsewhere, especially in contemporary democracies, representative bureaucracy has also emerged as a major component of public human resources policy.

In the 1990s, academic research on representative bureaucracy coalesced on a standard model for tracking the impact of social background on the performance of civil servants, particularly those who exercise considerable discretion. The model focuses on the linkages between social origins, life experiences, attitudes, and administrators' decision making. It deals with many of the main concerns of contemporary politics, including diversity and equal opportunity policy, democratic control of administration, administrative performance, and "reinventing government."

Representative Bureaucracy: Classic Readings and Continuing Controversies provides a comprehensive guide to the established knowledge and current issues regarding public policies and research on democratizing public administration by making it socially representative of the populations it ostensibly serves. Each chapter begins with a brief overview by the editors and includes excerpted readings that efficiently highlight and draw students into the key controversies. Discussion questions at the end of each chapter help students to integrate the material and appreciate its importance.

The readings were chosen for a variety of reasons. First, we hope to provide readers with a sound foundation for understanding representative bureaucracy as an area of study. Chapter 1 includes excerpts from some of the classic theoretical works on the subject, explaining the main theoretical tenets, the conditions under which they are likely to hold true, and competing theories for understanding bureaucratic behavior in representative democracies. Throughout the entire text, we reprint excerpts that showcase some of the most widely cited works in the field: some of the first empirical tests of the links between social origins and administrative decision making; some of the earliest criticisms of the contention that bureaucrats' social background is significant; and additional writings that have simply withstood the test of time.

Second, we hope to expose the reader to the vast range of scholarly research spawned by the early theoretical works on representative bureaucracy. The quantity of that research precludes reprinting all of the substantively relevant articles and books available, but we have tried to provide readers with a general sense of the depth and breadth of the scholarly research that guides contemporary thinking. To this end, we focused our efforts in a couple of ways. First, we attempt to provide balance by covering bureaucracies at all three levels of U.S. government: federal, state, and local. In the late 1960s and throughout the 1970s, when representative bureaucracy emerged as an area of study in American public administration, the vast majority of scholarship concentrated on the federal bureaucracy. Since then, scholars have increasingly turned their attention to examining state and local government bureaucracies. Second, we strive for some balance between the number of studies dealing primarily with race and ethnicity and those considering gender. Most early research and theory building focused entirely on race and ethnicity, whereas a growing body of more contemporary scholarship assesses the relevance of gender in public administration.

Our overall goal is to encourage more students and scholars alike to familiarize themselves with representative bureaucracy's existing terrain so that they will be able to pose new questions, fill in existing gaps, and generally continue to advance the state of our knowledge in the field. While there are numerous additional studies we would have liked to include had space permitted, *Representative Bureaucracy: Classic Readings and Continuing Controversies* presents a balanced range of material that provides a good introductory grasp of both the older and more contemporary literature. Many of the selections included in the text contain comprehensive bibliographies that can serve as guides for additional reading. Ultimately we hope the book will help spur new thinking, research, and policy perspectives on an old question: How can the large-scale administrative components of modern governments be made more representative?

Julie Dolan
David H. Rosenbloom

Acknowledgments

As always, we have many colleagues, friends, and students to thank for their support and assistance in preparing this manuscript. Special thanks go to Yana Sokolenko at Virginia Commonwealth University, who provided much needed assistance in the early phases of the project. Thanks also to Provost Dan Hornbach at Macalester College for his most generous financial support. The entire Department of Political Science at Macalester College also deserves thanks for their constant support, encouragement, and good cheer. They are a wonderful group of colleagues who make academic life more fun and rewarding than seems legally permissible. Roxanne Fisher expertly supervised the tedious chore of scanning and double-checking the original text of many of the excerpts contained in the text. Without her, we would still be typing everything by hand! We would also like to extend our sincerest thanks to the many Macalester students who contributed their time and energies, including Michael Gelardi, Rena Karipidis, Simone King, Katie LaZelle, Auyana Orr, and Jill Polson. All their efforts are greatly appreciated. Thanks also go to American University's School of Public Affairs for providing a highly supportive environment; Tanya Garcia for assisting with preparation of the manuscript; and Suzanne J. Piotrowski, who did much to shape and improve chapters one and five, obtain publishers' permissions to reprint the book's materials, and finalize the work. Although we were unable to include any of Norma Riccucci's or Gregory B. Lewis' own works on representative bureaucracy, we greatly appreciate the support and guidance they provided at several points along the way. Finally, thanks go to Elaine Cummins and Marni Ezra Goldberg for their years of friendship and their willingness to house, feed, transport, and entertain coeditor Dolan whenever she finds herself in Washington, DC.

Representative Bureaucracy

Chapter 1

Theoretical Underpinnings

Why Does the Social Background of Public Administrators Matter?

All modern governments have large-scale administrative components. The units within them—departments, ministries, agencies, bureaus, and so forth—are routinely called "bureaucracies," regardless of how they are organized. These units make some public policies and participate in the development of others. They also affect the impact of many governmental programs and initiatives by making choices when implementing or enforcing them. American bureaucracies make more rules, which are the functional equivalent of legislation, than Congress and the state legislatures make laws. More disputes are adjudicated in administrative hearings than civil matters decided by the courts. In one way or another, bureaucracies are the part of government most responsible for executing laws, rules, judicial and other governmental decisions, and foreign and domestic policies. This raises some obvious questions to which this chapter is devoted: Can public bureaucracies be representative institutions? That is, can they represent the public, or portions of it, in terms of policy preferences or interests, ideologies, characteristics such as race, ethnicity, gender, and social class, or other dimensions? If so, how and with what limitations? Is it important for democracies to promote bureaucratic representativeness? These and related questions are subsumed under the label, "representative bureaucracy."

Since 1944, when J. Donald Kingsley coined the term, representative bureaucracy has become a major concern in the study and practice of public administration and administrative policy making. The idea that public bureaucracies should or can be representative has been hotly contested, as the selections in this chapter explain.

One key issue is whether public administrators, aside from those at the very top levels, have the opportunity or flexibility to do anything other than strictly follow dictates from above. In the chapter's first selection, Max Weber sets forth the classic view of the bureaucrat as a discretionless, "single cog in an ever-moving mechanism which prescribes to him an essentially fixed route of march" (1958, 228). But Weber is describing a theoretically constructed "ideal type" or "pure type" of bureaucracy that intentionally extrapolates bureaucratic tendencies to formulate a clear, if extreme, portrayal of bureaucratic organizations. In his ideal type, bureaucracies are very hierarchical and highly specialized, formalistic, and impersonal. For him, the "special virtue" of bureaucracy is that it is "dehumanized" by "eliminating from official business love, hatred, and all purely personal irrational, and emotional elements" (1958, 216). Nevertheless, he notes that bureaucracies do have a tendency to represent themselves by promoting their own interests in obtaining and retaining power.

Weber's model is important because it is the very antithesis of representative bureaucracy. For Weber, the idea that government bureaucracies and bureaucrats can independently represent the public is self-contradictory. Weber's bureaucracy is tightly controlled from the top down. Bureaucrats in the middle and lower levels have insufficient discretion or independence to represent anyone. A cog is a cog, whether Democrat or Republican, black or white, male or female, from this region or that, or from a poor or wealthy family. If Weber is correct with regard to real-world bureaucracies, as many have believed him to be, then representative bureaucracy is a nonstarter. His model is often invoked by those who argue that bureaucracies simply cannot be politically representative institutions. They contend that if unelected, specialized, hierarchical, politically powerful bureaucracies are to operate compatibly with democracy, it will be by other means, such as external controls. By contrast, contemporary representative bureaucracy scholars emphasize that individual bureaucrats can have a significant impact on administrative choices and their acceptance by the general population or specific segments of it.

In the next selection, Kingsley presents a major challenge to Weber's conclusions. Without directly confronting the notion that bureaucracies are impersonal and staffed with "cogs," Kingsley contends that the civil service as a whole can have a particular outlook, set of values, and overall culture. In studying British national administration, he finds that "administrators are drawn overwhelmingly from the upper and middle classes of the population and that they have been educated according to the traditional pattern of the ruling class" (1944, 151). He then asks questions that underlie a great deal of the interest in representative bureaucracy: "What does this mean in terms of Civil Service mentality? What are its effects upon the outlook and orientation of the Administrative Class?" (1944, 151) After searching for answers—some of which are not happy—Kingsley concludes that "bureaucracies, to be democratic, must be representative of the groups they serve" (1944, 305).

Kingsley is primarily concerned with the consequences of the British bureaucracy's social class composition, but he also addresses another central concern of representative bureaucracy—equal opportunity to obtain positions in the civil service. In this context, he focuses on overt legal and implicit social discrimination against women. This not only deprives women of equal rights and full citizenship, it also denies the state the benefit of their full participation in government: "The democratic State cannot afford to exclude any considerable body of its citizens from full participation in its affairs. It requires at every point that superior insight and wisdom which is the peculiar product of the pooling of diverse streams of experience. . . . In a democracy competence alone is not enough. The public service must also be representative if the State is to liberate rather than to enslave" (1944, 185). It follows that public personnel practices, that is, recruitment, selection, promotion, and retention, are closely related to democratic governance as well as to technical administrative performance in the Weberian sense.

Writing in the 1940s, Kingsley did not develop the theoretical links among his claims or test them empirically the way contemporary social scientists would. Greater analytical clarity was brought to the study of representative bureaucracy by Frederick C. Mosher. In the chapter's next selection, he straddles the competing interpretations of Weber and Kingsley. Mosher agrees with Kingsley that making the public service compatible with democracy is a central administrative and political problem. However, siding more with Weber, he doubts representative bureaucracy is an answer. Mosher demands empirical evidence of the linkage between the social backgrounds of civil servants, which he calls "*passive* (or sociological)" representation, and their "*active* (or responsible) *representativeness* wherein an individual (or administrator) is expected to press for the interests and desires of those whom he is presumed to represent, whether they be the whole people or some segment of the people" (1968, 11–12).

Mosher's distinction between passive and active representation has informed subsequent analysis and theoretical development of representative bureaucracy. Today, there is growing consensus among researchers that there are links between the two. A general contemporary model would assume that social groups with distinctive status or identities (such as women and minorities) have life experiences that lead them to adhere to outlooks and values differing from those of other groups. Given the opportunity, when civil servants drawn from such groups are confronted with issues of high salience to their group's welfare they *tend* to become active representatives. Just what affects this tendency is the subject of both chapters 3 and 4.

In the next and final selection, Samuel Krislov further develops the theoretical underpinnings of representative bureaucracy in five ways. First, he emphasizes that passive representation is not only a question of equal rights and opportunity. It is directly related to administrative legitimacy and therefore to performance: "A major task of governance is to gain support for policies. No matter how brilliantly conceived, no matter how artfully contrived, government action usually also requires societal support. And one of the oldest methods of securing such support is to draw a wide segment of society into the government to convey and to merchandise a policy" (1974, 4–5). Second, he reminds us that neither passive nor active bureaucratic representation needs to be perfect in order to be valuable: "the bureaucracy is still at least potentially more representative than other arms of government and . . . in at least some senses it does in fact manage to be just that—more representative than other units" (1974, 63).

Third, Krislov confronts Weber head on in arguing that trying to turn bureaucrats into impersonal cogs is a mistake: "the human potentialities brought by bureaucrats to their jobs are inevitable and advantageous. Far from being solely liabilities they may have advantages that far outweigh the alleged— and exaggerated—benefits of neutrality. . . . The qualities of judgment, information, and fervor that bureaucrats do bring as they aid decision-makers are in fact resources of immense social advantage" (1974, 81). This insight has very substantial implications. If active representation is to be encouraged, "ideal type" bureaucracies are undesirable. Instead, hierarchical authority and impersonality should be diminished in order to promote more participatory and collegial decision making. Moreover, rather than detracting from efficiency, as Weber argued, many believe that employee empowerment and team building promote it (Osborne and Gaebler 1992; Gore 1993).

Fourth, Krislov argues that because public bureaucracies are large and powerful, their employment practices can "effect change with spillover into the broader society" (1974, 130). A public bureaucracy that prizes passive representation may serve as a model for private firms; one that discriminates against women or minorities can exacerbate inequality in the society at large.

Finally, taken as a whole, Krislov places a normative value on representative bureaucracy. Representative bureaucracy is desirable because it makes government as a whole more representative, can help counteract defects in the representativeness of other institutions, such as legislatures and courts, and it symbolizes as well as promotes equal opportunity and equality.

The selections in this chapter raise central questions about the role of the individual bureaucrat in governance. In Weber's ideal type model, bureaucrats do not bring any individuality to the job. Krislov, by contrast, argues that as individuals, bureaucrats make important contributions to public policy and administrative decision making. Mosher's view lies somewhere in between. He is skeptical about the interest and capacity of individual bureaucrats to represent the groups from which they are drawn. However, he does not rule out the possibility that an individual bureaucrat may sometimes act in a representative capacity. Kingsley has little to say about bureaucrats as individuals. His focus is overwhelmingly on them as members of social groups whose values and outlooks have a major impact on the overall culture of bureaucracies.

Weber, Kingsley, Mosher, and Krislov frame the key components and issues associated with representative bureaucracy. Their ideas are complex and full of insights that have become the basis of much research and discussion. Unfortunately, for all their brilliance, the reader must be forewarned that they are not all easy reads. Mosher and Krislov present no problem. However, Weber is no page-turner and Krislov referred to Kingsley as "somnambulistic" (1974, 13). Nonetheless, investing effort in them will yield a rich return.

References

Gore, Al. 1993. *From Red Tape to Results: Creating a Government that Works Better & Costs Less: Report of the National Performance Review.* Washington, DC: U.S. Government Printing Office.

Kingsley, J. Donald. 1944. *Representative Bureaucracy.* Yellow Springs, OH: Antioch Press.

Krislov, Samuel. 1974. *Representative Bureaucracy.* Englewood Cliffs, NJ: Prentice-Hall.

Mosher, Frederick C. 1968. *Democracy and the Public Service.* New York: Oxford University Press.

Osborne, David and Ted Gaebler. 1992. *Reinventing Government.* Reading, MA: Addison-Wesley.

Weber, Max. 1958. *Essays in Sociology.* Trans. and ed. by H.H. Gerth and C. Wright Mills. New York: Oxford University Press.

Bureaucracy

Max Weber

Technical Advantages of Bureaucratic Organization

The decisive reason for the advance of bureaucratic organization has always been its purely technical superiority over any other form of organization. The fully developed bureaucratic mechanism compares with other organizations exactly as does the machine with the non-mechanical modes of production.

Precision, speed, unambiguity, knowledge of the files, continuity, discretion, unity, strict subordination, reduction of friction and of material and personal costs—these are raised to the optimum point in the strictly bureaucratic administration. . . . As compared with all collegiate, honorific, and avocational forms of administration, trained bureaucracy is superior on all these points. And as far as complicated tasks are concerned, paid bureaucratic work is not only more precise but, in the last analysis, it is often cheaper than even formally unremunerated honorific service. . . .

Bureaucratization offers above all the optimum possibility for carrying through the principle of specializing administrative functions according to purely objective considerations. Individual performances are allocated to functionaries who have specialized training and who by constant practice learn more and more. The "objective" discharge of business primarily means a discharge of business according to *calculable rules* and "without regard for persons." . . .

. . . When fully developed, bureaucracy also stands in a specific sense under the principle of *sine ira ac studio* [without either resentment or favoritism]. Its specific nature . . . develops the more perfectly the more the bureaucracy is "dehumanized," the more completely it succeeds in eliminating from official business love, hatred, and all purely personal, irrational, and emotional elements which escape calculation. This is the specific nature of bureaucracy and is appraised as its special virtue. . . .

From *Max Weber: Essays in Sociology*, trans. and ed. by H.H. Gerth and C. Wright Mills (New York: Oxford University Press, 1958), pp. 214–216, 228–229, 231–234. Copyright © 1946, 1958 by H.H. Gerth and C. Wright Mills. Used by permission of Oxford University Press, Inc.

8

The Permanent Character of the Bureaucratic Machine

Once it is fully established, bureaucracy is among those social structures which are the hardest to destroy. Bureaucracy is *the* means of carrying "community action" over into rationally ordered "societal action." Therefore, as an instrument for "societalizing" relations of power, bureaucracy has been and is a power instrument of the first order—for the one who controls the bureaucratic apparatus.

Under otherwise equal conditions, a "societal action," which is methodically ordered and led, is superior to every resistance of "mass" or even of "communal action." And where the bureaucratization of administration has been completely carried through, a form of power relation is established that is practically unshatterable.

The individual bureaucrat cannot squirm out of the apparatus in which he is harnessed. In contrast to the honorific or avocational "notable," the professional bureaucrat is chained to his activity by his entire material and ideal existence. In the great majority of cases, he is only a single cog in an ever-moving mechanism which prescribes to him an essentially fixed route of march. The official is entrusted with specialized tasks and normally the mechanism cannot be put into motion or arrested by him, but only from the very top. The individual bureaucrat is thus forged to the community of all functionaries who are integrated into the mechanism. They have a common interest in seeing that the mechanism continues its functions and that the societally exercised authority carries on.

The ruled, for their part, cannot dispense with or replace the bureaucratic apparatus of authority once it exists. For this bureaucracy rests upon expert training, a functional specialization of work, and an attitude set for habitual and virtuoso-like mastery of single yet methodically integrated functions. If the official stops working, or if his work is forcefully interrupted, chaos results, and it is difficult to improvise replacements from among the governed who are fit to master such chaos. This holds for public administration as well as for private economic management. More and more the material fate of the masses depends upon the steady and correct functioning of the increasingly bureaucratic organizations of private capitalism. The idea of eliminating these organizations becomes more and more utopian. . . .

The objective indispensability of the once-existing apparatus, with its peculiar, "impersonal" character, means that the mechanism—in contrast to feudal orders based upon personal piety—is easily made to work for anybody who knows how to gain control over it. A rationally ordered system of officials continues to function smoothly after the enemy has occupied the area; he merely needs to change the top officials. This body of officials continues to operate because it is vital to the interests of everyone concerned, including above all the enemy. . . .

. . . The mere fact of bureaucratic organization does not unambiguously tell us about the concrete direction of its economic effects, which are always in some manner present. At least it does not tell us as much as can be told about its relatively leveling effect socially. In this respect, one has to remember that bureaucracy is such a precision instrument which can put itself at the disposal of quite varied—purely political as well as purely economic, or any other sort—of interests in domination. . . .

The Power Position of Bureaucracy

Everywhere the modern state is undergoing bureaucratization. But whether the *power* of bureaucracy within the polity is universally increasing must here remain an open question.

The fact that bureaucratic organization is technically the most highly developed means of power in the hands of the man who controls it does not determine the weight that bureaucracy as such is capable of having in a particular social structure. The ever-increasing "indispensability" of the officialdom, swollen to millions, is no more decisive for this question than is the view of some representatives of the proletarian movement that the economic indispensability of the proletarians is decisive for the measure of their social and political power position. If "indispensability" were decisive, then where slave labor prevailed and where freemen usually abhor work as a dishonor, the "indispensable" slaves ought to have held the positions of power, for they were at least as indispensable as officials and proletarians are today. Whether the power of bureaucracy as such increases cannot be decided *a priori* from such reasons. The drawing in of economic interest groups or other non-official experts, or the drawing in of non-expert lay representatives, the establishment of local, inter-local, or central parliamentary or other representative bodies, or of occupational associations—these *seem* to run directly against the bureaucratic tendency. How far this appearance is the truth must be discussed in another chapter rather than in this purely formal and typological discussion. In general, only the following can be said here:

Under normal conditions, the power position of a fully developed bureaucracy is always overtowering. The "political master" finds himself in the position of the "dilettante" who stands opposite the "expert," facing the trained official who stands within the management of administration. This holds whether the "master" whom the bureaucracy serves is a "people," equipped with the weapons of "legislative initiative," the "referendum," and the right to remove officials, or a parliament, elected on a more aristocratic or more "democratic" basis and equipped with the right to vote a lack of confidence, or with the actual authority to vote it. It holds whether the master is an aristocratic, collegiate body, legally or actually based on self-recruitment, or whether he is a popularly elected president, a hereditary and "absolute" or a "constitutional" monarch.

Every bureaucracy seeks to increase the superiority of the professionally informed by keeping their knowledge and intentions secret. Bureaucratic administration always tends to be an administration of "secret sessions": in so far as it can, it hides its knowledge and action from criticism. . . .

. . . In facing a parliament, the bureaucracy, out of a sure power instinct, fights every attempt of the parliament to gain knowledge by means of its own experts or from interest groups. The so-called right of parliamentary investigation is one of the means by which parliament seeks such knowledge. Bureaucracy naturally welcomes a poorly informed and hence a powerless parliament—at least in so far as ignorance somehow agrees with the bureaucracy's interests.

Representative Bureaucracy

J. Donald Kingsley

*"... bureaucracies, to be democratic, must be representative of
the groups they serve."* (p. 305)

The New Aristocracy

One need not be surprised . . . to discover that the Civil Service also reflects
the basic inequalities of the social structure and the prevailing temper of the
nation. For the Civil Service is only in the loosest sense democratic. It is
divided into a series of compartments which, after two generations of democratic assault, remain surprisingly water-tight. Each of these compartments
or classes is articulated to a stage in the educational system. Thus, in the non-
specialist Civil Service, the Clerical Class is recruited from boys and girls
who, at sixteen or seventeen, have completed the intermediate stage of a
secondary school course; the Executive Class from those who, at eighteen to
nineteen, have completed a secondary school course; and the Administrative
Class from those who at twenty-two to twenty-four have graduated from the
Universities. There are, to be sure, some promotions, particularly from the
Clerical Class to the Executive. But in terms of the numbers involved, recruitment from outside the Service is in all cases the more usual procedure.

The effects of this articulation to the educational system are interesting
and important. In the first place, it is obvious that opportunity in the Civil
Service will be to a large extent a reflection of educational opportunity.
The boy who has been unable to proceed to a university can scarcely hope
to become an administrator. The question, then, of how far educational
opportunities are related to abilities is one of very great importance. It is,
moreover, a question not easily answered in view of the chaotic and hap-
hazard educational structure and of the absence of comprehensive educational statistics. Nevertheless, it is possible to reach a number of important
conclusions.

Reprinted from J. Donald Kingsley, *Representative Bureaucracy: An Interpretation of the British Civil Service* (Yellow Springs, OH: Antioch Press, 1944), pp. 141–
142, 148–158, 181–185, 305.

Perhaps the most striking characteristic of British education is the squatness of the educational pyramid. It rests upon a nearly universal pupil base at the elementary level, but tapers off sharply in the higher reaches. In comparison with American conditions, pupil mortality is extreme as one moves up the educational ladder. Thus, of the children in elementary schools, only about one in ten continues to a secondary school. In the United States, the corresponding figure is better than one in two. Even more striking are the comparative data for university attendance. In England no more than one child in one hundred forty-five continues his education all the way to the university. In the United States the proportion is approximately one in ten. . . .

I have already indicated the existing articulation between the educational system and the Civil Service. I have shown, also, that educational opportunity is pretty directly related to economic status; more closely related to it, in fact, than to ability. I wish now to undertake a more specific analysis of the effects of this upon the Civil Service.

Because equality of educational opportunity does not exist in England, the fact that the Service classes are linked to various rungs of the educational ladder means that each is drawn pretty largely from a distinct stratum of society. It is as unusual for the son of a working class parent to find his way into the Administrative Class as it is for a son of the well-to-do to become a clerk at the bottom. Both cases may, in fact, occur, but such exceptions do not imperil the generalization. To a remarkable degree each Service class is also a social class—a caste—and the Service hierarchy pretty accurately mirrors the economic and social hierarchies outside.

It is controlled at the top by a small Administrative Class the members of which are drawn from the universities and thus overwhelmingly from a narrow social stratum closely identified with the historic ruling class. Selected on the basis of competitive examinations in academic subjects, the 1300 members of this group comprise a tiny fraction of the public service. But their importance cannot be gauged by their numerical strength. The richest rewards and the highest service responsibilities are reserved to them, and they constitute an upper caste separated by a broad social gulf from the rest of the Service. This fact is the cause of continual complaint by the more ambitious of the rank and file and the social pretensions of the Administrative Class have been known to frighten even cabinet ministers.

In contrast to the rank and file, the training of this elite is that traditional with English gentlemen. In educational background they have conformed, in large measure, to the pattern of the well-to-do. The predominance of the more select public schools and of the ancient universities in their educational histories is, indeed, remarkable. This is particularly true of the universities.

"Only an old civil servant, himself of the upper caste," Sir Albert Flynn observed after nearly forty years in the public service, "knows how firmly the Heads of Departments regard the ruling class as the peculiar property of the resident universities." To have been up at Oxford or Cambridge is almost a *sine qua non* for the aspiring administrator. . . .

The process through which young men and women ultimately become eligible to compete for admission to the Administrative Class is, then, rigidly selective from the social and economic points of view. But the group from which Britain's administrators are chosen is even narrower than might be suggested by university statistics. For the members of the Administrative class [*sic*] are still, typically, educated also at the better public schools. . . .

. . . Nevertheless, upon the basis of all available data the conclusion is inescapable that Britain's administrators are drawn overwhelmingly from the upper and middle classes of the population and that they have been educated according to the traditional pattern of the ruling class. What does this mean in terms of Civil Service mentality? What are its effects upon the outlook and orientation of the Administrative Class? These questions have several facets which deserve exploration. The answers to them depend in part upon assumptions regarding the relationship of training to later behavior and of early environment to philosophies of life. Like most fundamental questions, they cannot, perhaps, be resolved with certainty. But one may be permitted some tentative inferences.

The question of the influence of the public schools is, in itself, a large and interesting one. That that influence has been profound, few observers would deny. "These schools have been the chief reservoirs of our statesmen," observed the Public Schools Inquiry Commission in 1861, "and they have had perhaps the largest share in moulding the character of an English gentleman." . . . Conformity is deeply rooted in English society, but nowhere more deeply than in the public schools. They are, indeed, the institutional personification of this quality. What we are looking for, said Dr. Arnold of the system he instituted at Rugby, is "first, religious and moral principle; secondly, gentlemanly conduct; thirdly, intellectual ability." Noting the order in which these qualities were listed, Professor Ernest Barker found it characteristic not only of the public schools, but of England as well. Everywhere a higher value is place upon good form than upon intelligence. Such an attitude is, of course, a vestige of aristocratic rule, but most observers are agreed that it is fostered by the public schools. The spirit of these institutions Bertrand Russell finds to be one of "contempt for intelligence." They strive, he says, "to turn out a finished product so imbued with the worship of good form as to be incapable of learning anything important throughout the rest of life. . . ." (Ellipsis, *sic*) . . .

There is, too, a quality of snobbishness about the public school, antipathetic to the democratic spirit. These are class institutions. They are not of, by, or for the people. They serve the few. So far as they stand for any social philosophy it is a paternalistic one, like that represented by Thring's famous dictum: "the rich boys must learn to help the poor boys." . . .

Finally, there is some evidence to suggest that the atmosphere of the public school stimulates a thirst for power, a desire for people to govern. Such an attitude is . . . encouraged by . . . the whole artificial boarding school environment. The school is, itself, a State in miniature, with a ruling class of its own. Prestige attaches to the exercise of trivial authority, as in all institutions erected upon a foundation of discipline. Thus the boy comes to seek such authority and to continue to seek it in his later life. . . .

But not all British administrators are educated in the great public schools. Are there, then, any tendencies in secondary education generally which are of significance from the standpoint of Civil Service mentality? I think that there are. Secondary education in England is exceptionally academic. The schools, even today, reflect the aristocratic contempt for useful knowledge. There is a deep-rooted feeling that knowledge which is useful cannot be cultural and vice versa. . . .

. . . Special prestige attaches to those subjects which comprised the medieval curriculum: the ancient languages, theology, pure mathematics. In these areas there is the most intense specialization, particularly on the part of those who look forward to scholarships at Oxford or Cambridge. It is not unusual for a boy to devote almost all of his time between the age of fifteen and his entrance to the university to one or two subjects—usually Latin and Greek, or mathematics and physics. . . .

British secondary education is, then, academic, formal, and narrowly specialized. To a disturbing extent it neglects instruction in the social sciences and in the history and cultures of modern nations. It is, essentially, a training which faces backwards rather than forwards and is adapted to the conditions of a static rather than a changing world. It is more concerned with manners and morals than with stimulating the intellect and it still reflects, to a surprising degree, the centuries of aristocratic dominance.

To a considerable extent, university education may be similarly characterized. The ancient universities still labor under the humid influence of medieval conceptions. . . .

The results of this are frequently unhappy. Men trained in the familiar group of mathematics, physics, and chemistry are often amazingly ignorant of the most elementary social conditions and problems, while those trained in the humanities frequently possess no knowledge of general scientific principles. There is an absence of integration, a failure to see the world as a whole which, under present conditions of interdependence, is dangerous. . . .

Thus, emphasis on good form runs like a silken thread through the educational tapestry woven by the well-to-do and even assumes the magnitude of a national trait. A Civil Service deeply imbued with this notion has obvious disabilities. It is not, for example likely to look with favor upon suggested innovations. It is likely to reflect some degree that traditional resistance to change which has characterized British higher education. But it also enjoys a rather special advantage. The worship of good form goes far, it seems to me, to explain the comparative ease with which Civil Service neutrality has so far been maintained. A body of officials imbued with such spirit is likely to nurture a particular regard for conventions; to disregard them only when fundamentals are at stake and provocation is extreme. . . .

Forgotten Men—and Women

. . . The large-scale employment of women is a phenomenon of even more recent origin than that of specialists and their relative standing is considerably lower. They are discriminated against in three principal directions. In the first place, they are still wholly excluded from certain branches of the service, such as the Foreign Office and the three defense departments. There are also large numbers of specific posts in other departments, usually of a directing or controlling nature, reserved to men. The result is that the area of opportunity is much smaller for women than for men.

In the second place, women, with negligible exceptions, are forced to retire upon marriage. To be sure, the Treasury may lift this marriage bar in exceptional instances for the "good of the service." But in the years between the two World Wars it did so only three times and the rule is, for practical purposes, absolute in normal times. Women, therefore, are forced to choose between marriage and a career. They cannot have both.

Thirdly, the pay of women is very much lower than that of men engaged in comparable work. Women's scales average only seventy-five to eighty percent of men's scales and the women are being exploited by the State. The fact that women are exploited everywhere in England is no answer to this fact. A progressive government might be expected to set a standard, not follow existing practice.

Discrimination in these three directions is a matter of established policy. There are additional disabilities in practice which follow from unwritten rules. There is, unquestionably, prejudice against women in controlling posts. Of the more than 75,000 women employed in the non-industrial Civil Service, only about one percent are found in the higher classes. In the Administrative

Class women are employed in only a dozen of the seventy-seven government departments and in 1938 there were less than fifty in the whole administrative corps. Such conditions seriously limit the opportunities for promotion and contribute to a state of chronic discontent. . . .

. . . In England the bureaucracy was perfected in a period before the emancipation of women. When at length women began to seek careers they found themselves, like all other submerged groups struggling toward power, confronted by a firmly entrenched class who would not willingly abandon their position. This, it seems to me, is the crux of the whole matter. The rise of women challenged the traditional supremacy of the men and it made no difference that the cleavage was along sex lines. What was at stake was nonetheless power and economic advantage and to maintain them the men have struggled. Thus it has happened that despite numerous proclamations by Parliament of the principle of sex equality, that principle has not yet been accepted in the Civil Service. The entrenched officials have proved on this point more powerful than the House of Commons. . . .

. . . That there are undoubted differences between the sexes, I should be the first to admit. But it is increasingly evident that many of those differences which we once regarded as rooted in the nature of things are really the products of differing environments. It is increasingly evident that many of those universal laws of human nature (which, of course, no one could change), were merely projections of our own blind prejudice.

It may be true, for example, that at the present time women would be generally less successful in administration than men, for reasons similar to those advanced by Mr. G. T. Hankin before the Tomlin Commission. "At the present moment," he said, "I feel that the education of women, as a whole, has not given them the chance to acquire the power of doing the sort of semi-administrative work that I have been trying to describe, with the same ease as men. As things are at present it is very much easier for me, than it is for a women, to go and smoke a pipe with the director . . . [ellipsis sic] and discuss matters with him in an informal way."

Questioned as to the indispensability of the pipe "for interchange of thought," Mr. Hankin replied that it was a "symbol of the sort of way one does discuss matters with the director." Many men, he added, "do not find it so easy to sit down and gossip with a woman as they do with a man. The training of the woman has in the past been more formal. She takes her work more seriously and in a more rigid way than a man, and this informal work I am speaking about is distinctly easier for a man than for a woman."

I have no doubt at all that what Mr. Hankin says is true. What I do question is whether such a condition should be much longer tolerated. For it is precisely because the female administrator is so exceptional and because women do not enjoy with men equality of opportunity inside, or outside, the service that Mr. Hankin's observations are correct. The continuance of such a condition is, it seems to me, antipathetic to political democracy. The democratic State cannot afford to exclude any considerable body of its citizens from full participation in its affairs. It requires at every point that superior insight and wisdom which is the peculiar product of the pooling of diverse streams of experience. In this lies the strength of representative government. Upon it depends the superiority of the democratic Civil Service over its totalitarian rivals. In a democracy competence alone is not enough. The public service must also be representative if the State is to liberate rather than to enslave.

Democracy and the Public Service

Frederick C. Mosher

The Issues

Reliance upon popularly elected representatives is one step removed from direct participative democracy. A second step occurs when officers so chosen select and delegate powers to other officers, appointed and removable by them. As the dimensions of the administrative tasks of government grew these came greatly to outnumber the elective officers; and for a period in U.S. history, a substantial part of the public service were politically appointive and removable officers and employees. A third step away from direct democracy is taken with the designation of personnel who are neither elected nor politically appointive and removable, but rather chosen on the bases of stated criteria—social class or caste, family, general competence, specialization in given tasks and skills, etc.—and, once appointed, are protected from removal on political grounds. It is now of course clear that in every developed country in the world the vast majority of public officers and employees are in this category; that many of them command specialized knowledges and skills which give them unique competence in some subject-matter fields—competence that neither the people nor their elected or appointed political officers possess. It is also obvious that they influence—or make—decisions of great significance for the people, though within an environment of constraints, controls, and pressures which itself varies widely from one jurisdiction to another, from one field or subject to another, and from one time to another.

The accretion of specialization and of technological and social complexity seem to be an irreversible trend, one that leads to increasing dependence upon the protected, appointive public service, thrice removed from direct democracy. Herein lies the central and underlying problem to which this volume is addressed: how can a public service so constituted be made to operate in a manner compatible with democracy? How can it be assured that a highly differentiated body of public employees will act in the interests of all the people, will be an instrument of all the people? . . .

From Frederick C. Mosher, *Democracy and the Public Service*, 2d ed. (New York: Oxford University Press, 1968), pp. 1, 3–5, 11–14, 94–95. Copyright © 1968 by Oxford University Press. Used by permission of Oxford University Press, Inc.

... How does one square a permanent civil service—which neither the people by their vote nor their representatives by their appointments can replace—with the principle of government "by the people"? . . .

. . . [T]here has been rather little articulation of a theory of "representative bureaucracy" until quite recently. Some writers have, in the last thirty years, endeavored to promote such a concept as an antidote or a supplement to legislative inadequacies and as a substitute for the shaky dichotomy of policy-politics and administration. . . . And it may well be that, ere too long, some of the avowed political theorists will find room to discuss it in their larger discourses on political philosophy.

But there is a confusion of at least two quite different meanings of representativeness. . . . First, there is an *active* (or responsible) *representativeness* wherein an individual (or administrator) is expected to press for the interests and desires of those whom he is presumed to represent, whether they be the whole people or some segment of the people. Some hold that, like objective responsibility, assurance of continuing active representativeness requires some degree of answerability for decisions made and actions taken to those who are being represented. And answerability implies the possibilities of rewards for jobs well done and sanctions for failures. For the career public servant, of course, the ultimate sanction of political representatives—removal from office—is seldom available. But other and more subtle rewards and sanctions are possible: unfavorable publicity, reassignment, reduction of responsibilities, withholding of promotion, etc.

It may be noted that active representativeness run rampant within a bureaucracy would constitute a major threat to orderly democratic government. The summing up of the multitude of special interests seeking effective representation does not constitute the general interest. The strengths of different private interest groups within administration are vastly unequal, and the establishment of anything approaching equity would be nearly impossible. And the dangers of interest representation are reflected—perhaps excessively—in the conflict of interest laws. Thus there are real problems in the development of a rounded concept of representative bureaucracy within our democratic framework.

The *passive* (or sociological) meaning of representativeness concerns the source of origin of individuals and the degree to which, collectively, they mirror the total society. It may be statistically measured in terms, for example, of locality of origin and its nature (rural, urban, suburban, etc.), previous occupation, father's occupation, education, family income, family social class, race, religion. A public service, and more specifically the leadership personnel of a public service, which is broadly representative of all categories of the population in these respects, may be thought of as satisfying Lincoln's prescription of government "by the people" in a limited sense. At least, such a breadth of characteristics and origins suggest the absence of any single ruling class from which public personnel are drawn or of any single perspective and set of motivations. But this does not necessarily mean that a public servant with given background and social characteristics will *ipso facto* represent the interests of others with like backgrounds and characteristics in his behavior and decisions. A man born and brought up in Ohio who takes a job in Washington is not bound to represent the interests of Ohioans; in fact vigorous disciplinary measures may be invoked to prevent such partiality. The same might be said of a farmer's son or a farmer representing the interests of farmers; or of a business man, or college graduate, or a poor man.

I lay stress on the distinction between active and passive representativeness because it seems to me there has been a good deal of confusion on the matter in the recent literature about public executives. The fact is that we know too little about the relationship between a man's background and pre-employment socialization on the one hand, and his orientation and behavior in office on the other. Undoubtedly, there are a good many other intervening variables: the length of time in the organization, or the time-distance from his background; the nature and strength of the socialization process within the organization; the nature of the position (in some, particularly among political appointees, incumbents are expected to represent actively; in others, active representation may be expressly forbidden and incumbents encouraged to "lean over backwards" to avoid the appearance of partiality); the length and content of preparatory education; the strength of associations beyond the job and beyond the agency; etc.

While passive representativeness is no guarantor of democratic decision-making, it carries some independent and symbolic values that are significant for a democratic society. A broadly representative public service, especially at the level of leadership, suggests an *open service* in which access is available to most people, whatever their station in life, and in which there is *equality of opportunity*. . . . The importance of passive representativeness often resides less in the behaviors of public employees than in the fact that the employees who are there are there at all. Negatively, its significance rests on the absence, or conspicuous underrepresentation, of certain categories of people, suggesting or reflecting barriers to their entry or advancement. Severest among the violations of passive representativeness in this country today [United States] are the shortages of minority races in middle and upper levels of service in most public (as well as private) agencies.

The Evolution of American Civil Service Concepts

It may be noted in passing that any theory of truly representative bureaucracy in a highly pluralistic society must also contemplate conflict within the administration as the milieu for decision-making. Administration would mirror all of the conflict and competition between and among the various interests and elements in the private sector. To a degree that might surprise a good many citizens, including political theorists, this has already developed in large sectors of our national administration, though not by conscious design. It is interesting that advocacy of representative bureaucracy, seen as a response to the dilemma posed by the collapse of the dichotomy of policy-politics and administration, should lead full circle to the argument that administration should be built upon internal conflict rather than a single, consistent, administrative hierarchy headed by the President.

Finally, it may be noted that representative bureaucracy, in theory at least, introduced quite a new dimension to personnel administration, at least for some positions. If individual officers are to be chosen to represent certain interests and points of view, clearly a merit system premised on efficiency and mastery of knowledges and skills appropriate to specific jobs is not adequate. In fact, it is pretty hard to accommodate the concept of representativeness within the bedrock core of [position] classification and examinations. Furthermore, can one reasonably expect an appointee, recruited early with the expectation of spending most of his working life in the public service, to continue to represent and respond to outside interests and points of view for twenty or thirty or forty years? The idea suggests a drastic modification of the career concept itself to take care of "in-and-outers" so that fresh "representatives" may be injected continuously into the flow of public administrative decisionmaking.

Representative Bureaucracy

Samuel Krislov

Bureaucracy and Representation

. . . [T]he public sector has explicit need for extrinsic validation. A major task of governance is to gain support for policies. No matter how brilliantly conceived, no matter how artfully contrived, government action usually also requires societal support. And one of the oldest methods of securing such support is to draw a wide segment of society into the government to convey and to merchandise a policy. . . .

Who writes the directive—his or her style, values, concept of role—is as significant as who gets to be president, congressman, senator, member of parliament, or cabinet minister. The notion of representative bureaucracy is that broad social groups should have spokesmen and officeholders in administrative as well as in political positions. The issue of the composition of a country's civil service is a basic one for political analysts and students as well as for citizens anxious to understand and activists interested in reform. . . .

Legitimizing the American Bureaucratic State

The notion that the bureaucracy is in fact representative is advanced in two separate ways: (1) it is seen as such in composition and in the manner of its selection; (2) it is judged in terms of substantive product, and the quality of its decisions is evaluated in the light of their accord with what is assumed to be public opinion. The two arguments are intertwined, and it is clear that results alone would not justify the defense without certain assumptions about the validity of the first claim. [Roger] Davidson suggests the theme as well: "Analytically, the test of representation is whether, in public policy-making, the demands or interests of every relevant definable public have been effectively articulated" [Davidson 1967, 366]. However, weaknesses in each of the arguments often go unnoticed, at least in part, because evidence for one is confused with evidence for the other.

23

The representativeness of the American bureaucracy can be asserted in simple, factual terms. A broad range of talents, types, and social and ethnic backgrounds is to be found in the operative portions of government. Given these facts, the method of selection is subordinated to results. Objective, nondiscriminatory testing can, it is argued, perform selection and retain legitimate representational aspects; we can regard the Athenian selection by lottery as a form of such "objective" selection in much the same manner.

Nor is the purely electoral process free from chance or from designed-in elements involving distortion of popular will. Gerrymandering and less overt systematic efforts to pervert electoral systems are omnipresent; a leading study finds a universal bias in election systems always favoring the largest party in two-party systems, and even more so in multiple-party systems. There are good functional reasons for this; election systems are designed to provide viable governments as well as mirror opinion. Insofar as it succeeds in subtly—or even openly—beefing up the majority, an electoral system necessarily departs from puristic representativeness. When a small popular majority produces a larger legislative majority—or complete control of the executive—the governmental advantages seem to outweigh the costs of distortion. However, other modifications of popular will may be less subtle, less justifiable, less based on popular choice, and yet probably inevitable. The committee structure of Congress necessarily entrusts policies to a substructure which must seriously distort broad opinion. Specialization of committees means precisely that those most involved in an issue are most decisive. Committee assignment is a personal matter, not, except indirectly, a product of constituency characteristics, and there is no particular notion of representation of the total public on any individual committee. Yet for all practical purposes a committee may be the decisive force over an entire domain of policy. The notorious seniority system and the vagaries of career routes also mean that power is exercised in random ways unrelated to any aspect of public choice.

Similarly, the institutionalization of the Presidency makes it difficult to see any straightforward public choice in the exercise of executive power. The White House staff and generally the Executive Office of the President are composed of people whose selection partakes perhaps even less of public choice than overtly civil service positions. At least the rules for the selection of the latter have some public and democratic character. But it would be a useless exercise in sophistry to try to indicate where the popularly chosen, legitimate, representative Presidency ends, and the massive bureaucratic, nonrepresentative Administrative branch begins. The argument here is not merely that other branches are not as clearly representative as commonly thought. Rather, it is that direct popular choice is not the only test of representativeness and indeed may not be the determining one.

If we accept that fundamental argument, the rest follows easily. In social composition the federal bureaucracy ranges more widely than any small popularly elected group could. From this, it is urged we must look at results, and what is done:

> Responsible behavior in the sense of sensitivity to long-range and broad consideration, the totality of interests affected, and the utilization of expert knowledge by procedures that ensure a systematic collection and analysis of relevant facts, is more characteristic of the executive than of Congress. Despite the exceptions, and there are many, this kind of responsible behavior is more expected, more politically feasible, and more frequently practiced in the administrative branch. The bureaucracy headed by the presidency is both compelled and encouraged to respond to, and even to assist in the development of broad publics. . . , [ellipses and punctuation, *sic*] but broad publics seldom emanate from the organization and geographic concentration necessary for effectiveness in the congressional committee process [Long 1962: 68].

On the whole, the argument that "representativeness" is primarily a product remains novel to us. It seems to minimize the difference between democratic and nondemocratic systems by deprecating elections. . . .

How Bureaucracies Can (and Should) Be Representative

We must conclude . . . that bureaucracies are inherently unrepresentative and cannot be microcosmic reproductions of total society. Once that truth is established, we must reevaluate our reasons for pursuing this topic. Why consider the impossible dream in scholarly work. . . ?

The first and shorter answer is to note that the bureaucracy is still at least potentially more representative than other arms of government and that in at least some senses it does in fact manage to be just that—more representative than other units. The second and more complex answer is that for a variety of reasons it is important for bureaucracies to approximate representatives even if they never fully achieve it.

The first answer has, to be sure, some of the aura of "tu quoque" or "you're another." The bureaucracy can be called representative simply because it is more broadly based than other clearly nonrepresentative structures. Nevertheless, this inclusiveness—if generally true—constitutes a sociological fact of importance.

The second answer rests in part on the first. It stresses the functional desirability of just that state of affairs. The virtues of bureaucratic representativeness are similar to the claims made for legislative representativeness with respect to its *consideration* of policy. We would include several advantages that are superficially the same as for legislatures: the comprehensive presentation of formulations of view (political representation) and of types of evidence (functional representativeness). It also involves bringing multiple perspectives into the process of consideration and decision. The many minds brought to bear may not guarantee the best decision but they clearly guard against the worst—the ignorant or the blind leap into action.

With respect to acceptance of decisions, bureaucracies have certain inherent advantages. Diffusion of a policy, explanations of the reasons, and general exhortation are usually best advanced by a broad-based group with access to many strata. Again, a profusion of skills adds to the simple political and geographic advantages the technical possibilities for mustering support. Further, legitimacy can be said to inhere in such a multifaceted structure. . . .

Conclusions

We may summarize: variety begets variety. The very size and diversity of the bureaucracy encourage further diversity. This is not to deny that selectivity and artificial restraint have characterized administrative units. But such discriminatory selection has almost uniformly reflected similar, almost invariably harsher, political disabilities. Because of its size and visibility, government service can be a good index of the degree to which a society is open to talent rather than a vehicle of restricted group power.

And in its greater potential for representativeness the bureaucracy has an unusual opportunity and responsibility for societal integration and community-building. The emphasis on Weberian claims for political neutrality, and subsequent reiteration by the epigone, has been on sterility, gray anonymity, and functional specificity. The perfect bureaucrat, it has been reiterated, is like the traffic light which performs only its functions—no more and no less—without regard to personalities or influence. Any departure from this automatism, "the machine model" in [James] March and [Herbert] Simon's terms, is treated as a departure from perfection. The less creative he is, the less he exhibits initiative, the more he is faceless, the fewer excess skills the bureaucrat brings, the greater he would be deserving in the eyes of these writers.

The essence of the argument of this chapter is the suggestion that the human potentialities brought by bureaucrats to their jobs are inevitable and advantageous. Far from being solely liabilities they may have advantages that far outweigh the alleged—and exaggerated—benefits of neutrality. What is really sought is not cold-fish indifference but responsiveness to political direction, an acknowledgement of democratic political supremacy. But surely the principles supposedly involved in Leninist democratic centralism would suffice, that is, freedom to advocate until a decision is reached but solid and enthusiastic acceptance and support thereafter. The qualities of judgment, information, and fervor that bureaucrats do bring as they aid decision-makers are in fact resources of immense social advantage, not merely weaknesses men are heir to. In particular, the bureaucrats' affinity for the population has great potential advantage for social stability and increased bureaucratic responsiveness. We may ask the paradoxical question, "Neutrality for whom?" And we may replace it with a more realistic and purposive program of a representative, effective, and responsible bureaucracy. . . .

The methods by which representativeness can be sought are, of course, as varied as the societal and historical settings with which one is concerned. Fundamental to the question are the modes of recruitment. As we have seen, recruitment can be made a method of expansion or constriction of representation virtually at will. Ascription—that is, limiting choice to socially or extraneously defined characteristics rather than those functional to the position—can be utilized as a regime prefers. In a caste system where, say, a Brahmin or a Mandarin alone may qualify, it is of course contractive of the range of representation. A quota system on the other hand may enhance representativeness as well as restrict it. American society has generally rejected quotas as a desirable policy, perhaps because it is a snake pit full of dangerous creatures, but other societies have found such arrangements feasible and at least in the short run highly functional. More (or less) representative recruitment may involve expansion in size, simple replacement over time, or enforced replacement at a pace determined by the regime. Total or extremely large-scale turnover is of course a rather good index of a social revolution. Another course might be adoption of a new policy or intensification of an old one as in, for example, the 195[3] creation of the Department of Health, Education, and Welfare with parallel growth in federal governmental involvement in support of education.

In general, recruitment seems close to a necessary (though it is clearly not a sufficient) condition for representativeness. "Virtual representation," by which the decision-makers emphatically project views of others, or semi-official cooptative consulting devices, do not seem to be effective over any prolonged period (for example, over a generation), and they decay with a rapid half-life.

Admission into standard decision units may be enhanced or diminished by shifts in the pattern of units involved in key decisions or the processes by which decisions are made. We may witness a form of this reality if the emerging black majorities in core urban areas succeed in electing black mayors, but political and economic realities diminish the importance and latitude of big-city mayors. On the other hand, a process of consulting for views may become a form of veto, thus expanding the power of the consulted party with only a very subtle change in decision processes. But real shifts in power will ultimately be reflected in institutional patterns.

The insistence on participation has two aspects. First is the simple affirmation that all groups have a right, an access, to position and influence. For this aspect—symbolic and legitimizing—I have suggested the term "representational" participation. But as David Truman has pointed out, access to decision-making is a good index to ultimate influence and is valued in its own right [Truman 1952]. The second type therefore is the active, "functional," robust participation of groups in concrete decisions. This can occur through consultative mechanisms, of course, but it is surer and steadier when the desired diversity is a living reality. The argument for *representational* participation, in short, is that it leads to *functional* effectiveness. Frederick Mosher makes much the same point by referring to "passive" or sociological representation and "active" representation, where an interest is vigorously pursued [Mosher 1968, 11–14].

While some forms of interest representation have had paralyzing, polarizing, and dysfunctional effects, the basic activity seems essential to the operation of any society. Those who have attempted to analyze society in terms of group activity and group pressure have found the tool as sharp (and as dull) in less developed as well as more developed societies.

Finally we must note the "ratchet effect" involved in governmental recognition or withdrawal of power for a group. There is a significant social "multiplier effect" in what is politically done both because such actions tend to be highly visible and because they tend to be enveloped in the invisible rays of legitimacy. What government does is what fixes social policy. The treatment of its constituent individuals and constituent groups in political form is a tip-off and a harbinger of social action in other guises.

It is a "chicken or the egg" question as to whether in this process government precedes or creates smaller social units, or whether the smaller groups are in some genuine sense building blocks of the larger society. In either event, it is clear that the touchstone of power and legitimacy is recognition by the agency that is involved in rationing "the authoritative allocation of values." A group with power will be recognized governmentally and vice versa. There will be a tendency for actual power and its visibility to seek a common level.

With respect to public bureaucracies, societies have immense powers to effect change with spillover into the broader society. The English gentry decided to expand social participation to encompass a newly emergent urban-based middle class. They restructured not only the civil service but also its ancillary training schools, and even the broad field of public and private education. Girding for battle in contrast, the Junker and Japanese elites entrenched themselves in such structures. The results of such policies are clearly seen throughout the history of these countries. Options are thus easily available to decision-makers—within the highly latitudinarian bounds of functional necessity—to construct a purist, self-serving, or a deliberately even neurotically, responsive bureaucratic structure. Tables of organization are not fashioned in heaven; neither are their dimensions immutable.

At first glance "representative bureaucracy" appears to be an oxymoron, inherently contradictory like "cold heat" or, *pace* Mr. Chief Justice Warren, "deliberate speed." Bureaucracies handle matters, perform functions, and are meant to do and be, not represent or mean or symbolize. The functional necessities of such structures presumably dominate their human aspects. The "political" branches seem the places for such participatory relationships.

But our second look has indicated that societal tensions, rates of participation, and exclusions are, in fact, part and parcel of bureaucratic relationships. Furthermore, we have touched on the evidence indicating that bureaucratic effectiveness at the societal level—the degree of governmental penetration in social interaction—is also related to participation in the bureaucracy. Homogenized bureaucracies run the risk of getting better and better at performing tasks which other people regard as of increasingly less importance. When new winds sweep through such structures, they not only infuse fresh thoughts. By their momentum they also have the potential of spreading the effectiveness and purpose of the structure, so that its external reach is extended. In such a process, representativeness is a two-way conduit.

The bureaucracy then emerges as a good, even superior, index of societal cohesion and diffusion. It looms as a more stable and reliable measure of social power than elite studies of legislative bodies or of small inner-circle groups typically examined; further, the requirements for participation turn out to be less rather than more restrictive than legislative or strictly executive roles. Youth, left-handers, atomic physicists, and even classicists are more commonly found in the dusty halls of executive office buildings than in the debating halls of lawmakers. Since bureaucracies are both more stable and better defined than other forms of broad participation, they constitute a more practical index than even voter turnout or more nebulous—though probably more significant—forms of political behavior.

References

Davidson, Roger. 1967. "Congress and the Executive: The Race for Representation," Alfred DeGrazia, ed., *Congress: The First Branch of Government*. New York: Anchor.

Long, Norton. 1962. *The Polity*. Chicago, IL: Rand McNally.

Mosher, Frederick. 1968. *Democracy and the Public Service*. New York: Oxford University Press.

Truman, David. 1952. *The Governmental Process*. New York: Knopf.

Discussion Questions

1. Having read the material in this chapter, answer the question posed in its subtitle, why does the social background of government bureaucrats matter?

2. Weber contends that bureaucracy will be most efficient when bureaucrats behave as impersonal cogs. Krislov counters that it will work better if they can bring their personal outlooks, values, and worldviews to the job. Maybe both are right with regard to certain functions or types of organizations. In dealing with public administrators, including police, in which types of functions or positions would you rather have Weber's cogs? Krislov's more representative bureaucrats? Which type of administrator—Weber's or Krislov's—would you rather be? Why?

3. Kingsley emphasizes that a good deal of the discrimination against women was based on general social views, traditional gender roles, and assumptions about innate characteristics. Can you identify such extralegal attitudes and beliefs that promote or accept discrimination against women and members of minority groups in specific jobs and levels of the public service today?

4. Mosher argues that federal administrators in Washington who hail from Ohio are not bound to represent Ohioans. Suppose a contingent from Ohio are African American. Should they represent African Americans? Why or why not? Consider the same question with regard to other social characteristics, such as ethnicity, gender, religion, parents' occupational background, or whether the administrators grew up in a particular region of the country or in a union household. Can you reach any conclusions about when passive representatives are most likely to want to be active representatives as well?

Chapter 2

Public Personnel Policy and Social Representation

How Do Policies for Recruitment, Selection, Promotion, Pay, and Retention Affect Representative Bureaucracy?

Ensuring equal access to public sector jobs is a relatively recent phenomenon in the United States. In fact, women and racial minorities faced great discrimination well into the twentieth century in their attempts to secure employment with the federal service (Aron 1987; Rosenbloom 1977; Shafritz et al. 1992). Since then, many scholars have devoted their energies to exploring the degree to which women and racial minorities have become integrated into our public bureaucracies. As chapter 1 discussed, the theory of representative bureaucracy suggests that a bureaucracy that is broadly representative of the nation as a whole is expected to produce policy outputs that reflect the political will of the populace. Thus, the first piece of the representative bureaucracy puzzle involves assessing whether or not our public bureaucracies reflect the social and demographic composition of the larger population. This chapter focuses on this question, drawing on excerpts from a number of empirical studies that assess just how representative public bureaucracies are and have historically been in the United States.

Achieving a broadly representative bureaucracy has not always been considered an important goal for personnel policy in the United States (Rosenbloom 1977). In fact, tension exists between those camps who prize neutral competence and merit principles as guiding values for public personnel administration and those who uphold equal employment opportunity and representation of diverse social groups as the most essential values. As early scholars pointed out, women and minorities were generally able to secure government positions within the bureaucracy, but did so most predominantly at the very lowest levels (Meier 1975; Nachmias and Rosenbloom 1973; Rosenbloom 1977). Because policy-making positions are more prevalent in the upper reaches of the bureaucracy, proponents of representative bureaucracy have pushed for laws and administrative remedies to ensure that public bureaucracies adopt equal employment opportunity policies. These policies focus on recruitment, selection, promotion, pay, and retention to increase underrepresented groups' access to and success in public sector positions.

A number of laws and administrative remedies exist within the United States to make the federal workforce more reflective of the nation's diversity, to bring into the fold those groups who had previously been discriminated against and underrepresented. The chapter's first piece provides an historical foundation of the legal issues surrounding the nature and extent of equal employment opportunity and passive representation in the public sector. As Katherine C. Naff (2001) makes clear, equal employment opportunity policy is more complex than it may seem at first blush. Her essay traces the history of equal employment opportunity in the United States from the mid-1900s to the present, clearly identifying and describing the multitude of executive orders, laws, court decisions, and administrative regulations that have bearing on employment practices in the public sector today. As she concludes, "just how one determines the extent to which the bureaucracy is representative, however, is an issue that has never been fully resolved."

How can we tell if a bureaucracy is indeed representative? Scholars have been attempting to answer this question for well over thirty years and in doing so, have developed and utilized a variety of different indices, ratios, and scores. The excerpts we include here contain a fairly comprehensive sample of these measures: the measure of variation (Nachmias and Rosenbloom 1973), the representation and stratification ratios (Sigelman 1976), and affirmative action effort scores (Eisinger 1982).

The second reprint is an early example of an attempt to measure the representativeness of the public sector. Nachmias and Rosenbloom (1973) provide an early empirical assessment of passive representation within the federal bureaucracy. More specifically, they assess racial integration across the federal bureaucracy, determining the extent to which different racial groups are employed within different agencies and across different grade levels. To do so, they introduce the measure of variation: a "sensitive measure which enables one to compare the degree of social integration in different organizations and organizational levels." Because this measure can be used to measure racial integration across agencies and grade levels, it is useful for gauging the success of equal employment efforts. Their measure of variation is still widely used today.

After scholars provided the initial descriptive analyses of the extent to which different demographic groups are employed in public sector positions, they then turned their attention toward understanding why some groups are better represented than others. They address some of the following questions: are women and minorities concentrated within certain agencies or department types? Are women and minorities represented at all levels and within all job categories of the civil service? What might explain the existing variation? The remaining excerpts in this chapter make clear that plenty of variation exists when it comes to passive representation among government bureaucracies. Such research is important for it helps us to assess how successful EEO programs have been, pointing out which factors help or hinder women's and minorities' access to public sector positions.

The last two pieces in the chapter probe the determinants of passive representation for women and minorities within the public sector. Lee Sigelman (1976) focuses on female representation at the state and local level and Peter K. Eisinger (1982) focuses on black representation at the municipal level. Sigelman examines the quantity and quality of female employment in state and local governments, probing the "socioeconomic and political conditions associated with more and better jobs for women in state and local government." Finding variation in women's access to public sector jobs across the fifty states, he tests hypotheses about the conditions likely to facilitate greater female representation in state and local bureaucracies. Among other findings, his data support the hypothesis that women and racial minorities essentially compete against one another for these positions. As such, he warns policy makers and administrators to be on the lookout for such a possibility.

Turning to the determinants of African American representation in municipal bureaucracies, Eisinger uses affirmative action effort scores to compare the percentage of blacks in a city population with the percentage of blacks holding city public sector positions. Like Sigelman, he takes into account a variety of socioeconomic and political factors for explaining variation in black municipal employment. Contrary to Sigelman, though, he finds that the size of the local black population and the local political influence of blacks are important determinants of black access to public sector positions. Taken together, these two excerpts illustrate either that the factors which facilitate minority representation do not always facilitate female representation, or that what works in state government does not always hold true at other levels of government.

Although the numbers of studies on passive representation published in the past thirty years are far too numerous to reprint here, it is our hope that the excerpts contained herein provide a basic understanding of the status of research in this area. We conclude this chapter with a list of questions to prompt discussion and further inquiry.

References

Aron, Cindy Sondik. 1987. *Ladies and Gentleman of the Civil Service*. New York: Oxford University Press.

Eisinger, Peter K. 1982. "Black Employment in Municipal Jobs: The Impact of Black Political Power." *American Political Science Review* 76: 380–392.

Meier, Kenneth John. 1975. "Representative Bureaucracy: An Empirical Analysis." *American Political Science Review* 69(2): 526–542.

Nachmias, David, and David H. Rosenbloom. 1973. "Measuring Bureaucratic Representation and Integration." *Public Administration Review* 33(6): 590–597.

Naff, Katherine C. 2001. *To Look Like America: Dismantling Barriers for Women and Minorities in the Federal Civil Service*. Boulder, CO: Westview Press.

Rosenbloom, David H. 1977. *Federal Equal Employment Opportunity*. New York: Praeger.

Shafritz, Jay M., Norma M. Riccucci, David H. Rosenbloom, and Albert C. Hyde. 1992. *Personnel Management in Government: Politics and Processes*. 4th ed. New York: Marcel Dekker.

Sigelman, Lee. 1976. "The Curious Case of Women in State and Local Government." *Social Science Quarterly* 56 (March): 591–604.

To Look Like America

Katherine C. Naff

Achieving a Representative Workforce

A retrospective view of the government's policies with respect to equal employment opportunity and affirmative action shows a gradual transition from merely ending discrimination in government employment to taking proactive steps to increase the representation of women and people of color in the civil service. Much of the early activity in this area took place within the executive branch through the issuance of executive orders. More recently, the courts have become involved in ruling on the constitutionality of affirmative action programs.

From Nondiscrimination to Affirmative Action

Discrimination against federal employees on the basis of race, creed, or color has been prohibited since the passage of the Ramspeck Act in 1940, which prohibited discrimination based on race with respect to hiring, promotions, transfers, salaries, or in other personnel actions. According to Rosenbloom (1977), the law was significant in that it served as a "catalyst" to further actions taken by the executive branch. For example, the following year, President Franklin Roosevelt issued Executive Order 8802 that, in addition to reinforcing the government's policy of nondiscrimination in government or in defense industries, established the Fair Employment Practice Committee (FEPC) to investigate complaints of discrimination. However, the FEPC had no enforcement powers. Five years later, Congress dissolved the FEPC in an amendment to an appropriations bill (Rosenbloom 1977).

Over the next two decades, responsibility for overseeing employment opportunity (EEO) policies was shifted several times as committees to do so were created and disbanded. In 1964, Congress finally passed a major piece of legislation outlawing discrimination, the Civil Rights Act. The act also established the Equal Employment Opportunity Commission (EEOC) with responsibility for preventing discrimination in private sector employment. A 1965 executive order, E.O. 11246, gave the Office of Federal Contract Compliance Programs (OFCCP) within the Department of Labor authority to monitor and sanction the EEO practices of companies contracting with the federal government. The same executive order transferred responsibility for federal EEO to the Civil Service Commission (CSC), where it remained until 1979. The CSC had been the federal government's central personnel agency since the merit system was established in 1883.

By the late 1960s, it had become clear that a policy of nondiscrimination alone was not sufficient to ensure adequate representation of women and people of color, particularly in upper-level jobs (Rosenbloom 1977). The CSC drafted, for President Nixon's signature, a new executive order (11478) that was slightly stronger, emphasizing recruitment in addition to nondiscrimination. That executive order stated:

> It is the policy of the Government of the United States to provide equal opportunity in Federal employment for all persons, to prohibit discrimination in employment because of race, color, religion, sex, or national origin, and to promote the full realization of equal employment opportunity through a continuing affirmative program in each executive department and agency.

The executive order further required agencies to "maintain an affirmative program of equal employment opportunity." Agencies were to expand recruitment efforts to reach all sources of job candidates, provide training to enhance employees' skills and managers' understanding of the policy outlined in the executive order, and work to improve community conditions that affect employability. In 1971, the CSC took another step. Under pressure from the Commission on Civil Rights, the CSC issued a memo directing agencies to set goals and timetables "where minority employment is not what should be reasonably expected" (quoted in Rosenbloom 1975, 107).

An executive order, while binding on federal agencies, does not have the force of a statute because a subsequent president can revoke the order. The federal government's affirmative employment program was given a statutory basis when the Civil Rights Act of 1964 was extended to federal employment in 1972. The act also provided statutory authority for the CSC's oversight of EEO in the federal sector for the first time and required that agencies maintain affirmative action programs to ensure enforcement of EEO (U.S. Equal Employment Opportunity Commission 1983).

Several years later, in the Civil Service Reform Act (CSRA) of 1978, Congress took additional steps toward endorsing the importance of a representative bureaucracy. The preamble to the law (Pub. L. 95–454) called for a federal workforce "reflective of the nation's diversity." The act abolished the CSC and created in its place the Office of Personnel Management (OPM) and the Merit Systems Protection Board (MSPB). The OPM was given responsibility for establishing a Federal Equal Opportunity Recruitment Program (FEORP). The FEORP program required federal agencies to conduct affirmative recruitment activities aimed at correcting grade levels (5 U.S.C. § 7201). The CSRA further mandated that performance evaluation criteria for members of the then-newly established Senior Executive Service (SES) include their success in meeting affirmative action goals and achievement of EEO requirements (5 U.S.C. § 4313). At the same time, Reorganization Plan No. 1 of 1978 transferred responsibility for the federal government's EEO and affirmative action programs to the EEOC. Thus, although not explicitly mandating a specific affirmative action program, Congress nevertheless signaled its intent that full representation was a goal the government should strive to achieve, rather than simply to ensure nondiscrimination.

Thus, over four decades, employment policies in the federal government gradually shifted from prohibiting discrimination in federal employment to ensuring the full representation of women and people of color at all grade levels. This goal, espoused by the CSC as early as 1971, was endorsed by Congress and codified with the passage of the CSRA in 1978. From time to time members of Congress have introduced bills to derail this objective. For example, in 1995, Representative Charles Canady criticized the Civil Service Reform Act as "[causing] the federal government itself to seek proportionality for its own sake in the federal workforce" (Canady 1995, 2), and introduced a bill (HR 2128) to prohibit the consideration of race or sex in federal hiring and promotion decisions. To date, no such legislation has succeeded. Some argue that such legislation is no longer necessary, because of a 1995 decision of the Supreme Court.

The Role of the Courts

Not surprisingly, given the volatility of the issue, the legitimacy of the goal of achieving a representative bureaucracy has received mixed signals from the courts. In fact, very narrow majorities have handed down some of the most important decisions. The U.S. Supreme Court has clearly gone on record as upholding the imposition of race-conscious affirmative action plans to remedy past discrimination where such discrimination clearly has taken place. An example is *United States v. Paradise* (480 U.S. 150 [1987]), in which the Court upheld a one-black-for-one-white promotion requirement for Alabama state troopers as a result of finding that the Department of Public Safety engaged in a long-standing practice of excluding blacks from employment. Justice Brennan wrote in his opinion . . . [announcing the Court's judgment], "it is now well established that government bodies . . . may constitutionally employ classifications essential to remedy unlawful treatment of racial or ethnic groups subject to discrimination" (480 U.S. at 166). Only three other justices, however, joined that opinion.

The Court has also upheld, albeit narrowly, the use of *voluntary* affirmative action plans designed to increase the representation of women or people of color without a finding of past discrimination. For example, in *Steelworkers v. Weber* (443 U.S. 193 [1979]), the Court held that an employer seeking to adopt a voluntary affirmative action plan need not point to its own discriminatory practice, but could rather defend it on the basis of the existence of a "conspicuous imbalance in traditionally segregated job categories" (443 U.S. at 209). This reasoning was applied a decade later to a public sector jurisdiction in *Johnson v. Santa Clara County* (480 U.S. 616 [1987]), in which a six-justice majority upheld the county agency's decision to consider gender as one factor in evaluating candidates for promotion into a male-dominated job classification. However, in this decision Justice Brennan made it clear that such a voluntary plan was permissible only under certain conditions: (1) There is evidence of a manifest imbalance in traditionally segregated job categories; (2) the plan does not "unnecessarily trammel the rights of male employees or create an absolute bar to their advancement" by establishing a rigid quota system or earmarking of positions; and (3) the plan is temporary, intending only "to attain a balanced work force, not to maintain one" (480 U.S. at 616).

Nevertheless, the decision is significant because it upheld proactive affirmative action in the public sector. Indeed, Justice Stevens noted in his concurring opinion that it is perfectly legitimate for an employer, private or public, to implement an affirmative action program for any number of "forward looking reasons," including "improving services to Black constituencies, averting racial tension over allocation of jobs in a community, or increasing the diversity of a work force, to name a few examples" (Justice Stevens quoting from Sullivan, 100 *Harvard L. Rev.* 78, 96 at 480 U.S. at 647).

For purposes of this discussion of representative bureaucracy, it is also important to note that, until recently, the Court applied a more lenient standard to the federal government's race-conscious policies than to those undertaken by state or local jurisdictions. In *Metro Broadcasting v. Federal Communications Commission* (110 S. Ct. 2997 [1990]), the Court ruled that benign race-conscious measures mandated by Congress to serve governmental objectives—such as diversity—are constitutionally permissible, even if the measures are not designed to compensate victims of past discrimination.

In contrast, the Court invalidated a minority set-aside program employed by the city of Richmond, Virginia. In writing for the Court, Justice O'Connor stressed that state and local governments do not have the power Congress does to decide when such remedies are appropriate (*Richmond v. J.A. Croson*

Company, 488 U.S. 489 [1989]). Where Congress finds that minority owner-ship policies are needed to promote diversity, and that such diversity is an important governmental objective, reasoned Justice O'Connor, such policies are constitutional. However, a local subdivision that wishes to enact such an affirmative action policy must "show that it had essentially become a 'pas-sive participant' in a system of racial exclusion practices by elements of the local construction industry" (488 U.S. at 492).

More recently, however, the Supreme Court has taken a more conserva-tive approach to affirmative action programs, applying a standard of "strict scrutiny" to any race-conscious policies regardless of whether they are pro-mulgated at the federal, state, or local level. In the most recent decision—*Adarand v. Pena* 115 S. Ct. 2097 (1995)—a five-to-four majority of the Court ruled that any racial classification must serve a compelling governmental interest and be narrowly tailored to serve that interest. While explicitly over-turning Metro Broadcasting, the Court, however, left *Johnson* unscathed. Moreover, Justice O'Connor, writing for the Court, noted that there remain circumstances under which governmental intervention may be required to ensure equal opportunities: "Finally, we wish to dispel the notion that strict scrutiny is 'strict in theory but fatal in fact.' . . . The unhappy persistence of both the practice and the lingering effects of racial discrimination against minority groups in this country is an unfortunate reality, and government is not disqualified from acting in response to it" (62 *Law Week* 4533).

Although its interpretation of the ambiguous decision is not the only possible one, the Justice Department (in the Clinton administration) has stated that the benefit to a federal agency of having a diverse workforce could meet the stan-dard under *Adarand* requiring race-conscious programs to promote compelling governmental interests. Justice Department guidance to federal agencies explains:

> Some members of the Court and several lower courts, however, have sug-gested that, under appropriate circumstances, an agency's operational need for a diverse workforce could justify the use of racial considerations. This operational need may reflect an agency's interest in seeking internal diversity in order to bring a wider variety of perspectives to bear on the range of issues with which an agency deals. It also may reflect an interest in promoting com-munity trust and confidence in the agency . . . It would, therefore, not neces-sarily be inconsistent with Adarand for race and ethnicity to be taken into account in employment decisions in order to ensure that decision makers will be exposed to the greatest possible diversity of perspectives. (Schmidt 1996)

Nevertheless, the *Adarand* decision turned up the heat on all affirmative action programs, especially federal ones. It is not surprising that in a 1997 speech, then-acting director of the Justice Department's Office of Civil Rights Isabelle Katz Pinzler urged federal agencies to "really scrutinize each of [their] affirmative action policies and practices to make absolutely sure each is in conformity with the law" (Katz Pinzler 1997, 5).

Executive orders and statutes have, therefore, required agencies to work to increase opportunities for women and people of color for many years. These requirements have been based on an understanding that it is important, for many reasons, for the government to mirror the demographic composition of the citizenry. Recently, the courts have stipulated that affirmative action programs designed to achieve this objective must meet a high standard of strict scrutiny if they are to pass constitutional muster.

Considerable progress has been made in recruiting people of color and women into the government; they now make up [31 and 42] percent of the federal civilian workforce, respectively (U.S. Equal Employment Opportunity Commission 1997a). According to some definitions of "full representation," these numbers suggest that the federal government is close to being a representative bureaucracy (U.S. Merit Systems Protection Board 1996). Just how one determines the extent to which the bureaucracy is representative, however, is an issue that has never been fully resolved.

References

Canady, Charles T. 1995. *Opening Statement for the Hearing on H.R. 2128 before the Subcommittee on the Constitution, Judiciary Committee, U.S. House of Representatives*. 104th Cong., 1st Sess., December 7.

Katz Pinzler, Isabelle. 1997. "The Future of Equal Opportunity Policy in the Public Sector." Address to the Brookings Institution Seminar on Federal Civil Service and Labor Management Reform, Washington, DC. May 14.

Rosenbloom, David H. 1975. "Implementing Equal Employment Opportunity Goals and Timetables in the Federal Service." *Midwest Review of Public Administration* 9(2/3): 107–119.

Rosenbloom, David H. 1977. *Federal Equal Employment Opportunity: Politics and Public Personnel Administration*. New York: Praeger.

Schmidt, John R. 1996. "Post-*Adarand* Guidance on Affirmative Action in Federal Employment." Washington, DC: U.S. Department of Justice. February 29.

U.S. Equal Employment Opportunity Commission. 1997a. *Annual Report on the Employment of Minorities, Women and People with Disabilities in the Federal Government*. Washington, DC: U.S. Equal Employment Opportunity Commission.

U.S. Equal Employment Opportunity Commission. 1983. "Instructions for Preparing Mulit-Year Affirmative Action Plans for Minorities and Women, FY82–FY86." EEO–MD–707. Washington, DC: Equal Employment Opportunity Commission.

U.S. Merit Systems Protection Board. 1996. *Fair and Equitable Treatment: A Progress Report on Minority Employment in the Federal Government*. Washington, DC: U.S. Merit Systems Protection Board.

Measuring Bureaucratic Representation and Integration

David Nachmias and
David H. Rosenbloom

The concept of representative bureaucracy has now occupied an important place in the literature of public administration and political science for some three decades. It has been used as an explanatory tool in discussions concerning political and economic development and the historical and/or contemporary development of national civil services, including those of the United States (Van Riper 1958), Great Britain (Kingsley 1944), India (Subramaniam, 1967), the U.S.S.R. (Fainsod, 1963), and ancient China (Menzel 1963). The concept has also occupied an important place in studies concerning civil rights and equal employment opportunity (Krislov 1967). Moreover, in recent years the creation of a "representative bureaucracy" has become a major objective of federal personnel policy (Rosenbloom 1970, 1973). Despite its widespread use—or perhaps because of it—however, the concept of representative bureaucracy is unclear at several points. The purpose of this article is to overcome some of this ambiguity by suggesting a new way of measuring integration (in the sense of socially, ethnically, and/or racially mixed) in bureaucracies and other forms of organizations. This measure complements existing techniques used to assess bureaucratic representativeness and makes it possible to deal with facets of the concept that previously defied empirical research. . . .

. . . The link between passive and active representation, and a better understanding of what the latter entails, are, of course, crucial to expanding the utility of the concept of representative bureaucracy. Developing more sophisticated approaches concerning the more limited aspect of passive representation would nevertheless be useful at this time, especially in view of the increasing use of "affirmative action" techniques for the hiring and promotion of members of minority groups in public personnel systems.

Assessing Bureaucratic Representativeness

Perhaps the most common approach of determining the degree of bureaucratic representativeness, in the passive sense, has been to compare the proportion of all members of a political community who fall into a specific social category, such as race, ethnicity, class, or religion, to the proportion of all civil servants who also fall into the same category. . . . The implication of this approach is, of course, the normative assumption that a group *ought* to have the same proportional representation in the civil service as it has in the society as a whole. Indeed, as Subramaniam (1967) has pointed out, under a literal reading of this approach representative bureaucracy ". . .would mean a civil service in which *every* economic class, caste, region or religion in a country is represented in exact proportion to its numbers in the population" (p.1010).

Given the above assumption, a somewhat more sophisticated approach would be to follow Subramaniam (1967) in dividing a group's proportion in the civil service by its proportion in the whole society. This provides a single summary figure where 1.0 symbolizes "perfect" proportional representation, more than 1.0 designates a degree of "over-representation" of a specific group, and less than 1.0 indicates "under-representation." . . . The obvious utility of this approach is that it facilitates comparison, both with regard to different time periods and different nations. Thus Subramaniam (1967) was able to make a useful comparison between over-representation of the middle class in the United States and Indian national civil services, finding that in the former it was on the order of 1.35, whereas in the latter it approached 10.

Even the more sophisticated version of the above approach of assessing bureaucratic representativeness has serious limitations, however. First, the index is based on a normative assumption which ignores a number of relevant factors, including the geographical distribution of both social groups and government offices, the distribution of social groups in the *working age* population, and differentiated images with regard to the desirability of working in public bureaucracies and in connection with obtaining the educational and occupational prerequisites required to do so. Secondly, and perhaps more importantly, although the approach does give us an idea of how well various *groups* are passively represented in a bureaucracy, *it does not indicate how well integrated the bureaucracy itself is.* In other words, the proportional approach does not provide much useful information concerning the degree to which the work force of an organization is socially mixed [i.e., diverse]. Such information is, however, of crucial importance from the perspectives of civil rights, equality, and equal employment opportunity programs . . . . Obviously, while one can say something about the representation of various groups within these agencies, one cannot say much concerning the different degrees of integration found within the agencies as whole units. Furthermore, one can say virtually nothing about the latter that would be useful in further empirical analysis. What is needed is a supplementary measure which would provide useful information concerning the degree of integration within the organizational unit as a whole (e.g., the agency, office, bureau, national bureaucracy). Such a measure is introduced in the next section.

Measuring Integration

The greater the number of differences among a group of elements, the more mixed is the group as a whole, and therefore the more variation there is to be found within it. Likewise, the smaller the number of differences, the less mixed is the group and the less variation there is within it. For example, there can be no racial differences in an all caucasian group; but, in a racially mixed group, there will always be a smaller or larger number of racial differences among individuals. The amount of differences will depend on the composition of a given group. Thus, one could base a measure of variation on the total number of differences in the specified social characteristics of a group. Such a measure depends on the total number of differences and on a meaningful transformation of this total into an index.

In order to find the total number of differences in a group, the differences between each social characteristic and every other social characteristic are counted and summed. For example, in a group of eight whites and six blacks, each of the eight whites will differ in race from each of the six blacks, thereby making a total of 48 racial differences. In a group of eight whites and three blacks, each of the eight whites differs from each of the three blacks, producing 24 differences. In a group of f whites and no blacks, the obvious result of no differences is obtained by multiplying f by zero. The procedure for determining the total number of actual differences can be expressed in the following equation:

$$\text{Total Observed Differences} = \sum_{i\,j} f_i f_j, \; i{\neq}j$$

where f = the number of ith social characteristics

For example, in a group of seven whites, five blacks, and three Orientals, there would be: $(7{\times}5) + (7{\times}3) + (5{\times}3) = 71$ differences.

The total of observed differences is meaningful only in relation to some well-defined criterion. The number of observed differences may be related to different criteria for different purposes. Relating the observed differences to the maximum number of possible differences, within the same unit, has the effect of controlling for the number of specified social characteristics in that unit. The maximum number of differences occurs when all the frequencies of individual attributes in the group are equal. Thus, the expected maximum can be computed by equalizing the frequencies and then finding the number of differences that would be observed if all frequencies were equal. In symbols:

$$\text{Maximum Possible Differences} = \frac{n(n-1)}{2}\left(\frac{f}{n}\right)^2$$

where n = the number of social characteristics
      f = total frequency

In the previous example of eight whites and six blacks, the maximum number of racial differences in a group of 14 is 7 (whites) x 7 (blacks) = 49. The relative amount of variation may be measured by the ratio between the observed number of differences and the expected maximum, i.e.,

$$\text{Measure of Variation} = \frac{\text{Total Observed Differences}}{\text{Maximum Possible Differences}}$$

Symbolically, the measure of variation can be expressed in the following equation:

$$MV = \frac{\sum f_i f_j}{\frac{n(n-1)}{2}(\frac{f}{n})^2} \qquad i \neq j$$

For nine whites and three blacks the measure of variation is:

$$MV = \frac{27}{36} = .75$$

Among the 15 members of the three racial groups mentioned above, the mean number of members is five. Multiplying each "5" by every other "5" and summing these products, we find the maximum number of differences to be 75. The observed differences, as already calculated, equal 71. Hence,

$$MV = \frac{71}{75} = .94$$

The measure of variation will always vary between zero and one. If the numerator is zero, the measure will likewise be zero and will indicate the complete absence of variation. In the event of an equal division of observed frequencies of attributes, the numerator and denominator will be identical, and the measure will be 1.00, reflecting maximum integration. Intermediate degrees of integration will take on intermediate values. In closing this section it might be appropriate to mention that the reader can find other attempts to deal with integration in a statistical way in Blalock (1960), Clelland (1966), Roseboom (1966), Martin and Gray (1971), and especially Muller (1970), upon which the measure introduced here leans.

Application

The measure of variation has several important applications with regard to the concept of representative bureaucracy. It is a sensitive measure which enables one to compare the degree of social integration in different organizations and organizational levels. In Table [2.1], which is presented for illustrative purposes, selected federal agencies are ranked according to the degree of integration in their General Schedule workforces. The table contains information that clearly indicates the utility of the measure. Although the Equal Employment Opportunity Commission, which has a very large minority group member component, is the most integrated of the agencies, as might be expected, the Government Printing Office, which has had something of a "ghetto-agency" image, is, in fact, also highly integrated, at least in terms of its General Schedule work force. Similarly, despite its traditional "WASP" image, the General Schedule component of the State Department is relatively well integrated. Agencies responsible for broad social programs, such as Labor, HEW, and HUD, turn out to be well integrated, as expected, perhaps, but so do agencies such as the Civil Service Commission and the Veterans Administration which have not enjoyed favorable images with regard to civil rights and equal employment opportunity in the past (Rosenbloom 1970, pp. 51–52; Krislov 1967, pp. 125–126, 130–131). On the other hand, the Department of Transportation, which has made significant efforts to hire and promote minority group employees to the supergrades, has an overall low level of integration. It is interesting to note further that if an agency were proportionally representative of the social composition of the society as a whole, its measure of variation would be about .30. Thus, more than half of the agencies in Table [2.1] are more integrated, in terms of their social composition, than is the society at large. This suggests that the social composition of agencies may be an important factor with regard to the link between passive and active representation and, therefore, to policy making procedures and outputs as well. While these findings are interesting in themselves, it should be emphasized that the great benefit of using the measure of variation to approach questions of this nature is that it

Table 2.1

The Social Integration of the General Schedule Work Forces of Selected Federal Agencies, 1970

Agency	Percentage					Total	Measure of variation
	Black	Spanish surnamed	American-Indian	Oriental	Other		
EEOC	49.9	9.5	.8	.9	38.9	748	.71
Government Printing Office	53.6	.4	.2	.3	45.6	1,548	.63
State	31.5	2.2	.3	.9	65.1	5,810	.60
Labor	25.7	1.7	.4	.5	71.7	10,535	.52
GSA	24.1	1.6	.2	1.0	73.2	18,931	.51
HEW	21.3	1.5	2.4	.7	74.1	94,502	.51
CSC	23.0	2.3	.2	.7	73.8	5,216	.50
VA	22.0	1.8	.2	1.0	75.1	115,997	.48
HUD	18.6	1.5	.3	.7	78.9	14,721	.43
Interior	4.0	1.7	12.7	.8	80.9	50,725	.41
Post Office	17.9	.6	.1	.6	80.7	2,775	.40
Small Business Administration	11.6	5.4	.4	.5	82.0	4,272	.39
Commerce	14.5	.6	.1	.8	84.0	29,115	.34
Treasury	12.3	1.5	.1	.7	85.4	82,318	.32
GAO	13.6	.6	.1	.4	85.3	4,598	.32
Justice	9.6	2.4	.1	.4	87.5	36,947	.28
Army	8.7	2.2	.2	1.0	87.9	237,914	.27
Defense (Entire)	7.8	2.4	.2	1.0	88.7	600,044	.26
Navy	8.0	1.3	.2	1.3	89.3	158,986	.25
Air Force	4.6	4.3	.3	.7	90.1	151,217	.23
Agriculture	5.5	1.3	.3	.5	92.3	81,437	.18
Transportation	5.4	1.1	.3	.5	92.8	58,690	.17
NASA	2.7	.6	.1	.6	96.0	27,278	.10

Source: U.S. Civil Service Commission, *Minority Group Employment in the Federal Government*, November 30, 1970.

provides a single summary figure, which can, in turn, be used in further analysis.

Another useful application of the measure of variation is to employ it in ascertaining the degree of integration found in specific personnel grades or grade groupings. This has been done, again for illustrative purposes, in Table [2.2], which shows the degree of integration in each of the 18 General Schedule grades. Not surprisingly for those familiar with the federal personnel system and equal employment opportunity in general, the table indicates that the degree of social integration in General Schedule grades is highest in the lower

Table 2.2

Racial and Ethnic Integration in General Schedule Grades in the Federal Service, 1970

Grade	Measure of variation
All grades	.32
1	.71
2	.63
3	.57
4	.50
5	.44
6	.38
7	.31
8	.29
9	.23
10	.14
11	.16
12	.12
13	.10
14	.09
15	.08
16	.06
17	.07
18	.05

grades and lowest in the higher grades. The nature of this inverse relationship is such that there are only two grades (11 and 17) which are more integrated than the next lowest grade. Grades 1–6 are more integrated and grades 7–18 less integrated than is the General Schedule work force as a whole. For the practitioner, this would probably suggest that in the future equal employment opportunity efforts should be concentrated on grades 7 and above, precisely where past EEO programs have been weakest (Rosenbloom 1970, 1973).

A third application of the measure of variation demonstrates that its utility is not confined to the realm of description. We have found that: (1) there is considerable variance in the degree of integration in the General Schedule work forces of federal agencies; and (2) the degree of integration in General Schedule grades is inversely associated with grade level. These findings raise the question of whether the different degrees of social integration in agencies is related to the distribution of *positions* within agency General Schedule grade structures. In other words, can one talk in terms of a relative positional influence within agencies which affects social integration? For example, given the inverse relationship between social integration and grade level, we would expect an agency that has three-fourths of all its employees in the lower half of the General Schedule to be considerably more integrated than one in which three-fourths of all employees were in grades GS 10–18.

In order to assess the relationship between the distribution of positions within the General Schedule grade structures of agencies and the degree of integration in these agencies, we first used the measure of variation to ascertain the degree of inequality between the number of positions in the General Schedule grade groupings of 1–9 and 10–18 within individual agencies. The results of this procedure are presented in Table [2.3]. Subsequently, the measure of variation thus obtained was correlated with agency integration levels (as presented in Table [2.1]). As can be readily seen in Table [2.3], there is not very much variation in the distribution of positions between the upper and lower grades. Nor is there a significant relationship between this distribution and levels of social integration in agencies ($r = -14$). Thus, *in general*, whether an agency is well integrated or not does not appear to be related to the distribution of positions within its General Schedule grade structure. On the other hand, using the measure of variation in this way does enable the researcher to identify those agencies, such as the Government Printing Office and the Veterans Administration, which do have a relatively heavy concentration of positions in one part of their grade structures. Such an identification is useful in itself, and if coupled with further analysis, might help make it possible to adopt general equal employment opportunity procedures to the particular needs of such agencies.

Conclusion

The measure of variation discussed in this essay is a useful analytic tool which can be employed in studying several facets of bureaucratic representation. It should be used in conjunction with other tools, such as Subramaniam's "representational ratio," in order to provide a more complete and meaningful picture of the extent to which the work forces or memberships or organizations are socially integrated. Using the two measures to supplement each other makes it possible to learn something about both the position of individual groups in organizations and the social composition of the organizations themselves. The measure of variation, however, is not limited to descriptive use alone and for that reason it can have significant applications in the further exploration of the concept of representative bureaucracy.

As noted earlier, one of the major problems confronting anyone who attempts to deal with the concept of representative bureaucracy lies in discerning the relationship between passive and active representation. Mosher (1968) identified several variables that are likely to affect this relationship. Among them were: the length of time in the organization, the nature and strength of the organization's socialization process, the nature of the position, the length and content of preparatory education, and the strength of associations be-

Table 2.3

Distribution of Position in Agencies by Grades Group

Agency	Grades GS 1–9	Grades 10–18	Measure of variation
State	3,691	2,119	.93
Treasury	51,345	30,973	.93
Defense (entire)	397,978	202,066	.89
Army	161,250	76,664	.87
Navy	102,754	56,232	.91
Air Force	103,141	48,076	.87
Justice	23,162	13,785	.94
Post Office	1,154	1,621	.97
Interior	30,153	20,572	.96
Agriculture	53,396	28,041	.90
Commerce	16,202	12,913	.98
Labor	4,928	5,607	.99
HEW	67,571	26,931	.82
HUD	6,993	7,728	.99
DOT	20,829	37,861	.97
CSC	3,271	1,945	.93
EEOC	384	364	.99
GAO	2,197	2,401	.99
GSA	13,371	5,560	.83
GPO	1,331	217	.48
NASA	7,978	19,300	.82
Small Business Administration	2,161	2,111	.99
VA	92,516	23,481	.65

yond the agency (p. 13). It is reasonable to assume that an organization's social composition and the degree to which it is integrated also tends to determine the link between passive and active representation. Whether civil servants conceive of themselves as being representatives of the social groups in which they have their origins, or think that representation of such groups should be a part of their role, is likely to be partially dependent on the extent to which members of their groups and members of other, and perhaps competing, groups are found within an organization. In the absence of research on this question, we cannot know precisely how different levels of integration would affect the relationship between passive and active representation. . . . Perhaps under empirical analysis it would be possible to find a critical point at which the translation from purely passive representation to active representation as well becomes particularly commonplace and strong. The measure of variation, by providing a single summary figure measuring the degree of integration of the composition of work forces, is an appropriate tool for attacking these questions.

. . . The measure of variation also has considerable importance from the

point of view of equal employment opportunity, as is suggested by the foregoing applications. It could, for example, be a useful aid in studying such
phenomena as racial and ethnic "tipping," i.e., the tendency of bureaucracies
and agencies to become rapidly less integrated and more dominated, in terms
of social composition, by members of minority groups after their proportion
reaches a certain point. For instance, Krislov (1967) has observed that it has
been the experience of the Patent Office that ". . . after the percentage of
Negro employees goes over 50, white workers withdraw more and more from
the employment by requesting a transfer or leaving the agency" (p. 132).
But, is this generally true in other agencies as well? Is the "tipping" point
related to agency size and location? Would there be a similar tendency if the
percentage of blacks were 25, that of Spanish-surnamed employees were 25,
and that of Indians were 5? Using the measure of variation in investigating
such questions might not only increase our knowledge regarding their answers, but might also make it possible to find the point or points at which
stable integration could be maximized in practice.

In sum, the measure introduced in this essay is an analytic tool of considerable promise for future research in the general area of representative bureaucracy. It enables the research to complement existing measures in an
effort to gain a better understanding of the nature of the social composition
of organizational units, subunits, and levels. It could be used as an aid in
investigating several major questions pertaining to the concept of representative bureaucracy, including those involving the crucial link between passive and active representation. The measure also has widespread utility with
regard to equal employment opportunity, including the identification of EEO
problem areas and advances, and the investigation of racial and/or ethnic
tipping. In short, the measure could be of considerable descriptive and analytic use to both those interested in theoretical and practical research concerning the social composition of organizations.

References

Blalock, H.M. 1960. *Social Statistics*. New York: McGraw Hill.
Clelland, R.C., et al. 1966. *Basic Statistics With Business Application*. New York:
Wiley.
Fainsod, Merle. 1963. "Bureaucracy and Modernization: The Russian and Soviet Case."
In J. La Palombara (ed.), *Bureaucracy and Political Development*. Princeton, NJ:
Princeton University Press.
Kingsley, J. Donald. 1944. *Representative Bureaucracy*. Yellow Springs, OH: Antioch
Press.
Krislov, Samuel. 1967. *The Negro in Federal Employment*. Minneapolis: University
of Minnesota Press.

Martin, J.D., and L. Gray. 1971. "Measurement of Relative Variation: Sociological Examples." *American Sociological Review* 36 (June): 496–502.

Menzel, Johanna, ed. 1963. *The Chinese Civil Service.* Boston: D.C. Heath.

Mosher, Frederick C. 1968. *Democracy and the Public Service.* New York: Oxford University Press.

Muller, John H., et al. 1970. *Statistical Reasoning in Sociology.* New York: Houghton Mifflin.

Roseboom, W.W. 1966. *Foundations of the Theory of Prediction.* Homewood, IL: Dorsey.

Rosenbloom, D. H. 1970. *The Civil Service Commission's Role in the Federal Equal Employment Opportunity Program, 1965–1970.* Washington, DC: U.S. Civil Service Commission.

Rosenbloom, D.H. 1973. "The Civil Service Commission's Decision to Authorize the Use of Goals and Timetables in the Federal Equal Employment Opportunity Program." *Western Political Quarterly* 26(2): 236–251.

Subramaniam, V. 1967. "Representative Bureaucracy: A Reassessment." *American Political Science Review* 61(4): 1010–1019.

Van Riper, Paul P. 1958. *History of the United States Civil Service.* Evanston, IL: Row Peterson.

The Curious Case of Women in State and Local Government

Lee Sigelman

In recent years, increasing attention has been devoted to the occupational status of American women, so that a good deal is known about female employment patterns and their determinants (Oppenheimer 1970; Kreps 1971). But research on the occupational standing of women has almost invariably concentrated on the private sector—a curious omission in light of the oft-perceived obligation for the government work force to reflect the composition of the population along salient lines of social cleavage (sex, race, etc.). "Representative bureaucracy" has been defended on several grounds: enhancing administrative responsiveness in an era of increasing bureaucratic domination of the policy-making process; redressing the unrepresentativeness of other branches of government, particularly the legislative; providing underprivileged groups with an avenue of social mobility; setting a good example for private sector employers; and legitimizing government in the eyes of affected groups (Krislov 1971).

Most available information about female public employment focuses on the federal level. . . . Far less is known about the employment of women in state and local governments, which constitute the largest group of employers in the nation for which no comprehensive information is available on the composition of the work force (U.S. Commission on Civil Rights 1969). A 1963 survey of major department and agency chiefs in state government indicated that only 2 percent of the 933 executives responding were women (Wright and McAnaw 1965). By the early 1970s, a follow-up study suggested little change in the sexual composition of this top decision-making elite, which had increased only to 3.1 percent female (Botner 1974). At the local level, virtually the only available data pertain to city managers. Only 57 of the 5,336 members of the International City Management Association are women. Furthermore, of 2,534 American municipalities, only 15—none larger than 13,000—had female city managers in 1972 (Rubin 1973; Mohr 1973). Except for some scattered reports on female employment in specific locales

From Lee Sigelman, "The Curious Case of Women in State and Local Government," *Social Science Quarterly*, March 1976, pp. 591–604. Copyright © 1976 by Southwestern Social Science Association. Reprinted with permission.

(New York Commission on Human Rights 1971) and some impressionistic accounts of the subject (Eyde 1973; Lambight 1970), these few studies apparently constitute the sum and substance of published material on the employment of women in state and local government. . . .

. . . [W]hat can be said about female employment in state and local government? Are women employed in proportion to their share of the working-age population? Have they made significant breakthroughs into executive-managerial and professional-technical positions, or are they largely restricted to lower-level posts? What socioeconomic and political conditions are associated with more and better jobs for women in state and local government?

The Quantity and Quality of Female Employment

The Quantity Dimension. In order to answer these questions, we devised summary measures of the quantity and quality of female employment in state and local government. The quantity measure, called a *representation ratio*, indexes the extent to which the sexual composition of state and local bureaucracy accurately represents the sexual composition of a state's working-age (18–65) population. Using data taken from the BIPP [Bureau of Intergovernmental Personnel Program] surveys and the 1970 census, we computed each state's female representation ratio according to the following formula:

$$\text{Female Representation} = \frac{\text{Female Percent of Government Employees}}{\text{Female Percent of Working-Age Population}}$$

This ratio equals 1.00 when the female proportion of state and local employees exactly matches the female proportion of a state's working-age population. A lower representation ratio designates numerical underrepresentation of women, and a higher ratio signifies overrepresentation (Grabosky and Rosenbloom 1975).

Examining the female representation ratios in Table [2.4], one is immediately struck by the fact that in *every* state, without exception, women have gained public employment at least in proportion to, and in some cases well beyond, their share of the working-age population. Moreover, there is remarkably little fluctuation among states, as indicated by the low level of dispersion around the mean representation ratio of 1.27. State representation ratios range only from a low of 1.04 in Idaho to a high of 1.51 in Hawaii, and the coefficient of variability is an extremely low 0.09. In terms of the sheer quantity of employment in state and local government bureaucracies, then, we are presented with a relatively invariant situation of female overrepresentation.

Table 2.4

Female Representation and Stratification Ratios, by State

State	Rep. Ratio	Strat. Ratio	State	Rep. Ratio	Strat. Ratio
Alabama	1.35	0.64	Montana	1.26	0.52
Alaska	1.43	0.57	Nebraska	1.24	0.49
Arizona	1.17	0.49	Nevada	1.22	0.59
Arkansas	1.26	0.66	New Hampshire	1.25	0.52
California	1.42	0.71	New Jersey	1.31	0.59
Colorado	1.33	0.68	New Mexico	1.25	0.69
Connecticut	1.30	0.57	New York	1.23	0.77
Delaware	1.21	0.58	North Carolina	1.38	0.64
Florida	1.39	0.65	North Dakota	1.27	0.47
Georgia	1.42	0.75	Ohio	1.19	0.82
Hawaii	1.51	0.74	Oklahoma	1.29	0.66
Idaho	1.04	0.38	Oregon	1.08	0.37
Illinois	1.30	0.61	Pennsylvania	1.09	0.57
Indiana	1.26	0.67	Rhode Island	1.17	0.45
Iowa	1.24	0.45	South Carolina	1.43	0.67
Kansas	1.41	0.63	South Dakota	1.27	0.46
Kentucky	1.32	0.71	Tennessee	1.36	0.79
Louisiana	1.39	0.73	Texas	1.18	0.58
Maine	1.08	0.37	Utah	1.10	0.44
Maryland	1.34	0.75	Vermont	1.19	0.50
Massachusetts	1.24	0.67	Virginia	1.46	0.65
Michigan	1.26	0.63	Washington	1.17	0.60
Minnesota	1.25	0.45	West Virginia	1.24	0.63
Mississippi	1.32	0.59	Wisconsin	1.12	0.37
Missouri	1.35	0.66	Wyoming	1.23	0.39

The Quality Dimension. But even a high total percentage of female employees may mean little if women are largely relegated to lower-level (less prestigious, less powerful, less remunerative) positions and are effectively restricted from the high decision-making echelon. Our measure of the quality of female employment, called a *stratification ratio*, indexes the extent to which women are distributed evenly throughout the various employment levels rather than being concentrated in lower-level positions. We separated state and local positions into two categories—higher-level (executive-managerial and professional-technical) and lower-level (clerical-office and custodial-service)—and computed each state's female stratification ratio according to the following formula:

$$\text{Female Stratification} = \frac{\text{Female Percent of Higher-Level Posts}}{\text{Female Percent of Lower-Level Posts}}$$

Parallel to the representation ratio, the stratification ratio equals 1.00 when the female percentages of the two employment levels are exactly equivalent.

Table [2.4] reveals that women are disproportionately found in lower-level positions in *every* state, without exception. The mean stratification ratio, 0.59, indicates that women are underrepresented by a factor of roughly 40 percent in higher-level posts in the typical state. Even the state with the most even sexual distribution, Ohio (0.82), falls substantially short of the female break-even point of 1.00.

Although the sheer quantity of female employment in state and local government is substantially greater than the quality of their employment, there is one key similarity between the representation and stratification ratios presented in Table [2.4]. We commented above on the low state-to-state variability of female representation ratios. The range of stratification ratios is also quite restricted, running only from 0.37 in Wisconsin to 0.82 in Ohio—a lack of dispersion reflected in the coefficient of variability of only 0.20. In stark contrast to representation, however, we find in the case of female stratification a relatively invariant pattern of female subordination.

The Overall Pattern. What can be said about the overall pattern of female employment in state and local government? These governments have made a good deal more progress in attracting sheer numbers of women than in advancing women to all employment levels. Not a single state has a female representation ratio as *low* as 1.00, but not a single state has a female stratification ratio as *high* as 1.00.

Although there is no necessary relationship between quantity and quality in female employment, in fact in states where women are successful on one dimension, they tend to be more successful on the other dimension as well; the correlation between female representation and female stratification is an impressive .639. Although these dimensions of employment can vary independently, and although states tend to perform much better on the first dimension than on the second, the simple fact is that where women have penetrated state and local government in large numbers, they have also been more successful at gaining higher-level positions.

Conditions Facilitating Female Employment

Both women and racial minorities fare best in private sector employment in locales which are more "modern" and "progressive" by socioeconomic and political standards—typically in settings where the populace is better educated, where governments are marked by greater vitality and innovativeness, and where there are fewer cultural restraints barring the progress of minorities and women. . . . (Sherman 1973; Cooney 1975; Winegarden 1972; Dye 1971).

. . . In order to examine the possibility that the same conditions undergird female employment in state and local government as well, we correlated the female representation and stratification ratios with several characteristics of the American states:

1. Median education, as determined by the 1970 census. We should expect female representation and stratification ratios to be higher in states with better educated, and presumably more enlightened, populations.
2. Region, a dummy variable, with the 11 states of the Confederacy comprising the South (0) and the remaining 39 states comprising the non-South. Both female employment ratios are expected to be higher outside the South.
3. Political culture, a continuum running from "moralistic" through "individualistic" to "traditionalistic," as described by Elazar [1966] and operationalized by Sharkansky [1969]. Female representation and stratification should be highest in the more progressive, moralistic states and lowest in the less advanced, traditionalistic states.
4. Inter-party competition, as determined by Ranney [1971]. Party competition is usually understood as a mark of political vitality and as a spur to popular political involvement. We would expect party competition to be positively related to female representation and stratification.
5. The status of the Equal Rights Amendment, either 1 (passed) or 0 (not passed). Passage of the ERA ought to indicate effective political organization of the women's movement and/or relatively widespread acceptance of a broader social and political role for women. In either case, passage should be associated with greater quantity and quality of female public employment.
6. Innovativeness, as measured by Walker's [1969] index of policy innovation, a summary of the speed with which states have adopted 88 different policy measures. Women ought to have made more employment progress in states which are innovative in a variety of contexts.

Table [2.5] presents the Pearsonian correlations between female representation and stratification and these six characteristics, and reveals that female public employment is indeed related to these characteristics—and in some cases, substantially so—*but in precisely the opposite of the predicted direction.* That is, women actually do worse in the more modern, progressive states. Contrary to prediction, female representation and stratification ratios are inversely related to median education, are higher in the South than elsewhere, are higher in the more traditional political cultures, are higher in states which lack a tradition of inter-party competition, are higher in states which have *not* passed the

Table 2.5

The Determinants of Female Public Employment

Correlate	Representation	Stratification
Median education	−.327	−.378
Region	−.436	−.343
Political culture	.339	.528
Party competition	−.494	−.405
E.R.A. status	−.300	−.183
Innovation	−.143	.086

Equal Rights Amendment, and are higher in less innovative states; although the coefficient linking stratification and innovativeness is actually in the predicted direction, the magnitude of the correlation (.086) is hardly impressive.

These are curious findings, indeed. How could our expectations, which initially seemed so reasonable, have proved to be so wrong? We must consider the possibility that they are spurious—that some third factor affects these relationships in such a manner that their "true" nature is obscured. In striving to account for the unexpected findings presented in Table [2.5], we considered four possibilities: the attractiveness of public employment, professionalism in the public service, the impact of political reform, and female-minority competition.

The Attractiveness of Public Employment. According to this thesis, the pro-male bias of job competition is especially pronounced in more traditional areas, where popular attitudes are less supportive of female employment. Moreover, it is precisely in these areas that public employment is least attractive economically. The compensation of public servants is apt to be low, both absolutely and compared to private sector salaries (Legler 1974), so men gravitate to private sector jobs, leaving more of the less attractive public sector jobs to be filled by women. Where public employment is more attractive, more men would be found in state and local government. The vital variable explaining female employment, according to this interpretation, is economic; if this is true, controlling for the economic attractiveness of public employment should wipe out the strong inverse correlations reported in Table [2.5].

Professionalism in the Public Sector. A second interpretation is built upon the generalization that the sexual composition of an occupation indicates the degree to which that occupation is professionalized. In Western nations, the most highly professionalized occupations have historically been almost the exclusive province of men, while certain less highly professionalized occupations have attracted more women (Vollmer and Mills 1966). Extrapolating this generalization, it may well be that the prime determinant of female employment patterns is the level of bureaucratic professionalism in state and local government. Moreover, there is ample reason for expecting that bureaucracies are more highly professionalized in less traditional settings [Sigelman 1976]. In sum, women do best in more traditional settings because of the low professionalism of the public service there; if this is true, controlling for the level of bureaucratic professionalism should cause the negative correlations of Table [2.5] to disappear.

The Impact of Political Reform. A related but distinct reading of the female employment situation keys on the impact of political reforms. According to this interpretation, the patronage-based personnel systems often found in more traditional states encourage nepotism and recruitment through political ties. Revolt against this sort of political chicanery, of course, has led to the adoption in many settings of comprehensive merit systems. What concerns us here is that such reforms can work to the profound disadvantage of minority groups, as students of "good government" movements in city politics are acutely aware (Karnig 1975). Patronage systems, according to this argument, encourage job-holding among groups whose qualifications may be marginal and whose alternate avenues of social mobility may be effectively closed. If this logic can be applied to women as well as to racial and ethnic minorities, then it would seem that women fare better in more traditional settings because of the unreformed character of the public personnel system there.

Female-Minority Competition. The assumption underlying the fourth interpretation is that, in today's quota-conscious, affirmative action-oriented market, the relevant labor force dynamic is less female-male competition than it is female-minority group member competition (Rosenbloom 1973). If women are in direct competitions with minorities for public employment, then we would expect women to fare best where minorities fare worst. And here is the crucial link—for minorities fare worst in the more traditional areas, particularly in the South. Unwilling or unable to recruit minority bureaucrats, recruiters in the South and other traditional areas rely more heavily on women to staff government positions. Administrators in the more racially progressive settings may be more attuned to the demands of minorities, and hence focus their recruiting efforts there—to the disadvantage of women. If this were true, the correlations in Table [2.5] are artifacts of the racial composition of state and local bureaucracy, and should diminish when the racial factor is controlled.

Testing the Interpretations. . . . . Far from wiping out the inverse relationships, controlling for public service attractiveness has no effect whatsoever. Further statistical analysis, not presented here, reveals that this explanation fails because the hypothesized link between job attractiveness and the female employment measures is very weak. There is, then, simply no basis for accepting the first interpretation of our curious findings.

Nor does the second interpretation, which focuses on professionalism in the public service, fare much better. . . . [T]he relationships remain remarkably constant irrespective of which control variable is introduced. Here again, the weak link is the relationship between female employment and the control variables. Rather than being negatively related to female representation and stratification, as predicted, the four professionalism indicators are in fact positively linked. In this context, it can hardly be considered surprising that controlling for professionalism fails to modify our earlier findings. . . .

. . . [W]e see that our earlier findings cannot be attributed to the political reform factor, for controlling for the effects of merit system coverage does not diminish the traditionalism-female public employment relationships. Neither the quantity nor the quality of female employment is closely related to merit system coverage ($r = -.169$ and $-.033$, respectively), so the key premise upon which the political reform explanation was constructed is simply incorrect.

Finally, let us turn to the fourth interpretation, dealing with job competition between women and minorities. We know from previous research that minorities are most poorly represented in state and local government in the more traditional areas—so the first link on the explanatory chain is secure. Moreover, the employment prospects of minority group members and women are, as predicted, inversely related. In fact, the inverse relationship between minority and female stratification is quite substantial ($= -.505$). Minority and female representation are also inversely related, though the magnitude of this correlation is lower ($r = -.279$). In short, where the quantity and quality of minority public employment are high, the quantity and quality of female public employment tend to be low. Thus, of the four interpretations, the fourth is by far the most accurate . . . In some cases (as with the Equal Rights Amendment and Walker's innovation index), the relationship between traditionalism and female employment vanishes altogether when the effects of minority employment are controlled. In other cases (median education and region), a relationship remains, albeit a greatly attenuated one. In the remaining instances (political culture and party competition), substantial relationships remain, at least for female stratification. Minority-female competition is thus not a total explanation, but clearly it is a factor which helps us to account for the curious pattern of findings uncovered in Table [2.5].

Conclusion

What does this study suggest about female employment in state and local governments? In the first place, we have discovered an important difference between the quantity and the quality of female public employment. In every state, women are represented in government service at least in proportion to their share of the working-age population. But in no state have women escaped being disproportionately relegated to lower-level jobs. Interestingly, a very similar pattern was unearthed in our previous study of minority groups in state and local government—a correspondence which leads us to propose that attempts to broaden the employment base of the public sector tend to work from the bottom up. Whereas it is relatively easy to attract sheer numbers of employees from previously neglected groups, higher-level staffing presents a far more difficult problem.

Although state and local governments perform far better on the quantity than the quality dimension, we discovered that where women are represented in larger numbers, they have also been more successful at gaining higher-level positions. To the extent that state representation and stratification ratios are interrelated, we can conclude that there is something of a unidimensional aspect to female public employment that is distinctly missing from minority public employment.

Our most provocative findings concern the conditions which facilitate female public employment. In complete contrast to our expectations, we found that the quantity and quality of female public employment are actually higher in more traditional settings. In attempting to account for this finding, we tested four interpretations, but only one—the female-minority competition interpretation—was supported by our data. According to this interpretation, women do well in the more traditional areas precisely because minorities do so poorly there; the more progressive states, on the other hand, seem more responsive to demands for minority representation—a responsiveness which seems to work to the disadvantage of women. The policy implications of this interpretation are unsettling—for it would seem that there is something of a zero-sum game quality between the employment prospects of women and minorities. Clearly, policy-makers and personnel administrators must guard against playing off the interest of one group against those of the other.

But even the female-minority competition interpretation cannot fully account for the unexpected pattern of findings summarized in Table [2.5]. Why, beyond the female-minority competition factor, do women fare better in the more traditional areas? In attempting to answer this question, future researchers will have the benefit of a far more comprehensive data base than that employed here, because in the wake of recent legislation, states and localities have had to begin keeping far more comprehensive records on the characteristics of their personnel. The availability of such data should also allow future researchers to chart the dynamics of female employment, gauging the progress of women over time and comparing that progress to minority employment trends.

References

Botner, Stanley B. 1974. "Personal and Career Characteristics of State Government Administrators." *State Government* 47 (Winter): 54–58.

Cooney, Rosemary S. 1975. "Female Professional Work Opportunities: A Cross-National Study." *Demography* 12 (February): 107–120.

Dye, Thomas R. 1971. *The Politics of Equality*. Indianapolis: Bobbs-Merrill.

Elazar, Daniel. 1966. *American Federalism: A View from the States*. New York: Crowell.

Eyde, Lorraine D. 1973. "The Status of Women in State and Local Government." *Public Personnel Management* 2 (May/June): 205–211.

Grabosky, Peter N., and David H. Rosenbloom. 1975. "Racial and Ethnic Integration in the Federal Service." *Social Science Quarterly* 56 (June): 71–84.

Karnig, Albert K. 1975. " 'Private-Regarding' Policy, Civil Rights Groups, and the Mediating Impact of Municipal Reforms." *American Journal of Political Science* 19 (February): 91–106.

Kreps, Juanita. 1971. *Sex in the Market Place*. Baltimore: Johns Hopkins University Press.

Krislov, Samuel. 1974. *Representative Bureaucracy*. Englewood Cliffs: Prentice-Hall.

Lambight, W. Henry. 1970. "The Next Step Manpower Policy." *Public Personnel Review* 31 (January): 27–30.

Legler, John B. 1974. "Trends in State and Local Government Employment in the Southeast." *Georgia Government Review* 6 (Spring): 1–5.

Mohr, Judith. 1973. "Why Not More Women City Managers?" *Public Management* 55 (February): 3–5.

New York Commission on Human Rights. 1971. The Employment of Minorities, Women and the Handicapped in City Government: A Report of a 1971 Survey.

Oppenheimer, Valerie. 1970. *The Female Labor Force in the United States*. Berkeley: University of California Press.

Ranney, Austin. 1971. "Parties in State Politics." In Herbert Jacob and Kenneth Vines, eds., *Politics in the American States*. 2d ed. Boston: Little, Brown, pp. 82–121.

Rosenbloom, David H. 1973. "A Note on Interminority Group Competition for Federal Positions." *Public Personnel Management* 2 (January/February).

Rubin, Claire. 1973. "Where Are the Women in Management?" *Public Management* 55 (February): 8–9.

Sharkansky, Ira. 1969. "The Utility of Elazar's Political Culture: A Research Note." *Polity* 2 (Fall): 66–83.

Sherman, Lucille O. 1973. "Women in the Labor Force: Relationships Among Occupational Attachments, Family Statuses, and Poverty." Unpublished Ph.D. dissertation, University of Georgia.

Sigelman, Lee. 1976. "The Quality of Administration: An Exploration in the American States." *Administration and Society* 8 (May): 107–144.

U.S. Commission on Civil Rights. 1969. *For ALL the People . . . By ALL the People*. Washington, DC: U.S. Government Printing Office.

Vollmer, Howard M., and Donald L. Mills, eds. 1966. *Professionalization*. Englewood Cliffs: Prentice Hall.

Walker, Jack. W. 1969. "The Diffusion of Innovations Among the American States." *American Political Science Review* 63(3): 880–899.

Winegarden, C.R. 1972. "Barriers to Black Employment in White-Collar Jobs: A Quantitative Approach." *Review of Black Political Economy* 2 (Spring): 13–24.

Wright, Deil S., and Richard L. McAnaw. 1965. "American State Executives: Their Backgrounds and Careers." *State Government* 38 (Summer): 146–153.

Black Employment in Municipal Jobs:
The Impact of Black Political Power

Peter K. Eisinger

The task of monitoring the accession of blacks to elected office in the United States has occupied substantial scholarly energies over the past decade (see, for example, Campbell and Feagin 1975; Cole 1976; and Karnig 1976). Much of this work has accomplished what are essentially census functions, documenting the numerical revolution in black representation, its regional incidence, and the distribution of black officeholders across types of jurisdictions and offices. Some of these studies have also explored the political structural and socioeconomic conditions under which blacks are likely to be elected, particularly to offices in urban government (e.g., Bullock 1975; Jones 1978). There are still few explorations of the impact of black officials, however, and those that do exist are comparatively rudimentary. After more than a dozen years of sustained black electoral achievements in urban politics, it is appropriate to begin more systematic inquiry regarding the extent to which electoral political success has produced substantive benefits for blacks. . . .

. . . There is, of course, a long tradition of studies of urban machines whose very raison d'être in many cases was the ethnic quest for the substantive rewards of politics. Indeed, a number of scholars have shown that the rise of the Irish in certain places at least led to the disproportionate capture by that group of jobs in the public sector (Clark 1975; Erie 1978). One problem with our understanding of the Irish phenomenon, however, is that there has been little systematic comparative effort to related Irish employment gains to variations in Irish political power. Furthermore, since the benefits, if any, that have accrued to other groups that practiced a politics of ethnicity have not been studied systematically, it is possible to interpret Irish achievements, if we continue to insist upon a political explanation, as a product of their special political genius in an age before the rationalization of municipal personnel systems through civil service reform. Whether or not other groups—blacks in the present

From Peter K. Eisinger, "Black Employment in Municipal Jobs: The Impact of Black Political Power," *American Political Science Review*, 1982, pp. 380–383, 385–389, 391–392. Copyright © 1982 by The American Political Science Association. Reprinted with permission from Cambridge University Press.

case—can expect similar gains as a result of their political successes in the contemporary period is an open question.

Black Employment in Local Government

One divisible benefit whose distribution may be influenced from city hall is employment in the local public sector. Although today the hiring of municipal employees is governed almost entirely by civil service rules, affirmative-action doctrines provide a means by which some degree of racial advantage may be introduced into the most rationalized personnel systems. Studying the extent to which blacks have penetrated the municipal service has a number of virtues that bear on an examination of the possibilities of a black ethnic politics.

To begin with, public employment achievements themselves have important implications for the economic well-being of the black community. The local public sector, Proposition 13 fever notwithstanding, is still a modest growth industry. Work in public-sector employment is not only more secure than comparable private-sector work, but in many job categories, it is generally better paid. Blacks also have better access to high-paying managerial and professional employment in the civil service than in the private sector (Erie 1978).

Significant racial representation in public employment may also enhance minority power, as Kranz points out (1976, p. 94), particularly in bureaucratic policymaking, information gathering, agenda setting, and implementation. Minority gains at the managerial level also have implications for recruitment and promotion policies within agencies which may, even in a civil service system, be advantageous to minority workers.

Black public employment not only possesses the virtue of significance as a goal to be sought in politics, but, for our purposes, it is also an easily measurable, divisible, and relatively unambiguous prize. The percentage of blacks in the total municipal work force of any given city as well as the percentage of blacks in selected occupational categories in the local public sector, offer several dependent variables amenable to varieties of regression analysis. Affirmative-action data for individual cities make it possible to establish comparisons across cities as units of analysis in which black electoral strength varies. In contrast, a number of important studies to date of the impact of black political power are case studies focusing on a single city or on a limited number of cities controlled by blacks (Keech 1968; Levine 1974; Cole 1976; Jones 1978; Eisinger 1983). Although these authors are able to identify a variety of apparent consequences of black power, they have not always been able to distinguish with precision those consequences that occurred as a direct function of black power or to measure those impacts, nor have they sorted out in any systematic way alternative or contributing explanations for black gains . . . .

. . . Two studies suggest what is for present purposes a crucial link between the local political system and the rational bureaucratic world of civil-service hiring. Thompson's investigation (1978) of city personnel administrators,. most of whom are appointed by municipal chief executives, found that those who are sympathetic to minorities are more likely than others to launch efforts to recruit blacks. Furthermore, they are willing to endorse modifications in hiring and recruitment standards and practices to facilitate minority hiring. The study does not supply data on the results of these actions. Eisinger's examination (1980) of politics in Detroit and Atlanta under black mayors argues for the importance of mayoral leadership in achieving affirmative action gains in the civil service. In those cities the political system appears to work its way into the administration of personnel practices in several specific ways. The black mayors appointed black personnel administrators, ordered special recruitment efforts within the minority community, pushed for a reassessment of selection procedures which led to a de-emphasis of written examinations, and appointed a number of black department heads, who have the final responsibility for choosing names from the civil-service examination lists. In Atlanta the black mayor appointed the first city affirmative-action officer, whose post had been created but unfilled under the preceding white mayor. Levels of minority employment in those cities rose sharply, suggesting that even in a world of universalistic selection procedures, personnel practices are apparently subject to local politics.

Data and Hypotheses

Under the Equal Employment Opportunity Act of 1972, Title VII of the Civil Rights Act of 1964, which prohibited discrimination in private employment, was extended to state and local governments (Hill 1977). The law requires local government units to file annual affirmative-action reports on the race and sex of all full-time employees, except those in education, by function and occupational category. The data on which the following analysis is based are drawn from those EEO-4 reports filed by individual cities with the U.S. Equal Employment Opportunity Commission.

Since the law prohibits the EEOC from releasing these data except in aggregate form, information had to be gathered from cities themselves. Affirmative action officers or personnel departments in a sample of cities with populations over 50,000 were asked to supply the percentage of blacks in the total municipal work force and in each of the two top civil service occupa-

Table 2.6

Black Municipal Employment Levels, U.S. Municipalities, and Sample of Forty-three Cities

	U.S., 1974[a] %	U.S., 1978[a] %	43 Cities, 1973[b] %	43 Cities, 1978 %
Total black full-time civil service municipal work force[c]	19.0	20.2	26.5 (106.5)	32.9 (119.5)
Black city civil service administrators and officials	6.3	7.7	9.3 (35.9)	14.8 (47.5)
Black city civil service professionals	12.6	13.4	11.2 (43.6)	18.2 (61.0)

Sources:
[a]U.S. Equal Employment Opportunity Commission, *Minorities and Women in State and Local Governments, 1974* (1977) *and Minorities and Women in State and Local Government, 1978* (1980). Data are based on all 1,120 municipalities employing 100 or more full-time workers.
[b]Figures in parentheses are affirmative action effort scores. They are mean ratios of percent black in particular work force categories to percent black in the city population (1970).
[c]Does not include school personnel or CETA workers.

tional categories (administrators and professionals) for 1973 and 1978. Of the 131 cities sampled, 85 (65 percent) finally responded. Thirty-six of the responding cities, however, have extremely small (less than 10 percent) or nonexistent black populations, and an additional six cities could supply only partial data. The final analysis, then, is based on complete data from forty-three cities with more than 10 percent black population in 1970. The median 1970 population of the forty-three cities was 361,000; on the average 28 percent of their inhabitants were black.

Black employment levels in the forty-three cities are somewhat higher than the national averages compiled by the EEOC, as data in Table [2.6] show. Figures also indicate growth in the percentage of blacks in municipal employment both in the nationally aggregated totals from 1974 to 1978 and among the forty-three cities between 1973 and 1978.

Among the sample cities, blacks are over-represented in the total work force according to the affirmative action effort scores but underrepresented in the highest or prestige occupational categories. Effort scores are ratios of percent black in the total work force or in individual occupational categories to the percent black in the city population. Disproportionate hiring of black workers in unskilled, clerical, and menial city jobs accounts for the over-representation. Effort is calculated on the basis of percent black in 1970.

Since we cannot assume a constant rate of increase in the black population during the 1970s across cities, we must be less than confident about the validity of the absolute magnitudes of the 1978 scores and of the true dimensions of the change in effort between 1973 and 1978. In this study, the change in effort over time is not analyzed, pending availability of 1980 census data. Nevertheless, effort scores do suggest the relative magnitude of black underrepresentation is different occupational categories within cities, and I have used the 1978 effort scores in a limited way as the best basis of intercity comparison of proportional hiring available . . . .

. . . To explore the impact of black electoral power on variations in levels of black representation in the local public work force, we may focus on several hypotheses regarding the receptivity of the personnel system to minority hiring.

Hypothesis No. 1. Black municipal employment levels are a function of the presence of black office holders. In other words, as blacks gain political authority, their presence in public sector jobs rises. Welch and Karnig (1979, p. 106) caution that the power of mayors to implement policy goals is greatly constrained by a variety of forces beyond their control, but several case studies of cities with black mayors indicate that the racial composition of the public work force did change under the black chief executives (Levine 1974, p. 79; Eisinger 1980).

It is also possible that as blacks achieve substantial representation on city councils, legislative pressures can be brought to bear on the operations of the personnel system. Thus we would expect that the presence of a black mayor and/or strong (proportional) representation of blacks on the city council will be associated with high levels of black employment.

Hypothesis No. 2. Black municipal employment levels are a function of the size of the black population in the city. A substantial black population may simply offer such a large labor pool that public employers will naturally draw more or less proportionally upon it for workers. The history of job discrimination in America, however, should make us suspicious of the power of such natural processes. Black achievements in every area have seldom come as a matter of random happenstance but have instead been the products of agitation, pressure, and authority. Before the great local electoral mobilization of blacks in the 1970s, a large black population alone was certainly no guarantee of significant black penetration of the municipal work force, particularly in job categories valued especially by whites.

A modification of the large labor pool argument is that the city as an employer is faced with a growing lack of white interest in municipal jobs and therefore has little choice but to hire blacks where they constitute a substantial portion of the available work force. Although we have no data on levels of white interest in central-city jobs, we may infer declining interest from patterns of white migration to the suburbs. Such population shifts are associated with suburban job growth (U.S. Dept. of HUD, 1980, pp. 1–17); they have also accounted disproportionately for black population gains in the central cities during the 1970s (*New York Times*, April 16, 1981).

A large black population indicates not only a big labor pool, however, but also a voting bloc of major proportions. Local government employment opportunities for blacks, then, may be a function of the size of this bloc. Although we have no way of measuring comparative levels of black electoral turnout or bloc voting tendencies across a large number of cities, we can tap black electoral mobilization. Mobilization is measured here as the percentage change in the number of all local blacks elected to public office between 1973 and 1977, including not only city but also state and national officials. It is certainly not unreasonable to view mobilization levels as closely related to the character of black voting behavior, and given case study evidence on the impact of black voting (Keech 1968), it is plausible to hypothesize a link between electoral behavior and employment gains.

Hypothesis No. 3. Black municipal employment levels are a function of characteristics of the black labor pool. The characteristic most relevant to assessing the employability of a particular labor pool is its education level. Hall and Saltzstein (1977) found in their study of twenty-six Texas cities that the level of education among Hispanics (but not among blacks) explained some small part of the variance in the percentage of Hispanic professionals in the city work force. We would not expect educational level to be associated with black presence in the total work force, since most cities have de-emphasized written examinations for unskilled and semiskilled jobs since the Supreme Court decision of *Griggs v. Duke* (1971). But it is plausible to suppose that as more blacks in the labor pool have college degrees, as a group they will be more competitive for administrative and professional occupations.

Hypothesis No. 4. Black municipal employment levels will vary depending on whether the local public sector is expanding or contracting. Given the low seniority levels among black public-sector employees as a group, public sector contraction is said to have a greater impact on black employment than on white. In New York City, for example, a 13 percent reduction in the city work force in the mid-1970s translated into a loss by 40 percent of the city's black male workers (Pascal 1979). Personnel cuts in Detroit in the recession of the late 1970s also hit black workers particularly hard (*New York Times*, September 7, 1980).

By the same logic it may be argued that in a period of expanding public employment, blacks will tend to catch up as city governments strive to meet affirmative action goals or to deflect black pressures or both by distributing generous shares of plentiful public jobs.

Testing the Hypotheses

An examination of the simple correlations between the black employment variables and the measures selected to test the four hypotheses shows that the most important independent variable is the percentage of blacks in the city population (Table [2.7]). As we have observed, there are at least three possible explanations for such a finding, and they are not simple to sort out. One explanation is that since there are more blacks in the available labor pool, they will more or less naturally find their way into the hiring process in proportions consistent with their presence in the population. A second possibility is that cities in which blacks constitute a large part of the population are cities that have been abandoned by large numbers of whites seeking employment elsewhere, thus leaving municipal employment to blacks. A third explanation is that a large black population represents such a potentially formidable voting bloc that blacks are able to compete successfully with white job seekers in the public sector. Black employment, in other words, is responsive to black political influence.

Let us test these three explanations. Table [2.8] presents a series of partial correlations in which the percentage of blacks in the population is controlled. There is some support for the natural hiring process explanation, particularly as it relates to low prestige (semiskilled and unskilled) city jobs. We may infer this simply because the two major political variables, black mayor and black mobilization, are related somewhat more strongly to the percentage of blacks in administrative and professional positions than to the percentage of blacks in the total work force. This finding suggests that political energies are focused on jobs that count, leaving mainly labor-market factors, such as the racially skewed distribution in the population of formal job qualifications (measured, say, by comparative racial school dropout rates; see Hill 1978, p. 30), to influence staffing of low-prestige jobs. The partial correlation analysis, then, supports the proposition that both political and natural hiring processes may be at work, depending on the category of jobs in question.

We could be more confident that natural processes offer a major explanation, however, if we were to find a positive relationship between black employment and the presence of a municipal residency requirement for public jobs, controlling for percentage of blacks. In such cases cities would be obliged to draw only on the local labor pool; suburban job aspirants, mostly whites, would be eliminated from the competition for central-city civil service jobs (whether they wanted such jobs or not). Among the forty-three cities, 23 (53 percent) have enforced residency requirements, but as Table [2.8] shows, the relationships between black employment levels and the existence of a resi-

Table 2.7

Black Employment Levels, Racial Variables, and the Public Sector: A Simple Correlation Matrix (Pearson r)

Independent variables	Black total work force (1978) %	Affirmative action effort[a]	Change 1973–78, black employment %	Black administrators (1978) %	Affirmative action effort	Change 1973–78, black administrator %	Black professionals (1978) %	Affirmative action effort	Change 1973–78, black professionals %
Percentage black (1970)[b]	.87*	—	.11	.76*	—	-.19	.81*	—	.12
Black mayor (1977)[c]	.58*	.03	.02	.68*	.47*	-.01	.64*	.28**	-.09
City council representation ratio (1977)[c]	-.11	-.21	.03	-.02	.09	.16	-.05	-.03	.21
Black mobilization score (1973–1977)[c]	.16	.10	.25*	.01	-.09	.07	.05	.03	-.08
Growth of public sector (1973–78)[d]	.22***	-.20***	.01	.12	.16	.14	.15	.14	.40**
Percentage blacks with college degree (1970)[b]	.02	.48*	-.00	-.02	.18	.27**	-.03	.15	-.08
Residency requirement[e]	.05	-.34*	.09	.11	-.20	-.25*	.19	-.02	-.23*
City population (1970)[b]	-.08	-.16	.01	.03	.05	-.00	-.02	-.10	-.07

*$p < .001$.
**$p < .05$.
***$p < .10$.

[a] *Source:* No coefficient is provided for the relationship between percent black and effort, since effort is calculated on the basis of the former.

[b] *Source:* U.S. Census, 1970.

[c] *Source:* Calculated on the basis of data in Joint Center for Political Studies, *The National Roster of Black Elected Officials* (JCPS, 1973 and 1977 editions, Washington, DC).

[d] *Source:* Calculated from data in U.S. Department of Commerce, Bureau of the Census, *City Employment in 1973* and *City Employment in 1978* (Washington, DC).

[e] *Source:* Telephone survey of city clerks.

Table 2.8

Partial Correlations Between Black Employment Variables and Selected Independent Variables, Controlling for Black Population

Independent variables	Black total work force %	Black administrators %	Black professionals %	Change, 1973–78 employment %	Change black administrators %	Change black professionals %
Residency law	.35**	-.09	-.02	.13	-.28***	-.28***
Black mayor	.18	.37**	.30**	-.03	.14	-.16
Black mobilization score	-.01	.21	.16	.28**	.13	-.13
Population growth, 1970–80[a]	.12	.14	-.06	-.04	.43**	.17
Percent growth in metropolitan white-collar manufacturing jobs 1972–77[b]	-.06	-.02	-.05	.03	-.20	-.17

**p < .05.
***p < .10.

[a] U.S. Bureau of the Census, preliminary 1980 census reports.
[b] U.S. Department of Commerce, Bureau of the Census, 1977 *Census of Manufactures* (October 1980, Washington, DC).

dency requirement are negative. Blacks are more likely to find municipal employment in cities where the possibility exists for competition with the largely white suburban labor force, which suggests that the workings of "natural" hiring processes do not constitute a sufficient explanation. It is not simply the greater availability of black workers in cities with residency laws that accounts for patterns of black employment.

Even though the possibility for substantial white competition for municipal jobs exists in cities where blacks have achieved significant penetration of the public sector, it may be the case that whites are simply not interested in city jobs. We have no data to determine individual-level preferences among white job seekers, but we have several aggregate-level variables, that are suggestive of preferences. For example, white workers' lack of interest in municipal jobs may perhaps be inferred from white flight from the central city, much of which, presumably, is responsive to suburban job growth. In this case we should find that as whites vacate the city (producing an overall population decline), black municipal employment levels should rise. But the partial correlations in Table [2.8] show just the opposite; black employment is in most cases positively related to city population growth during the 1970s.

Perhaps in those cities where blacks have achieved significant penetration of the city work force, whites have chosen to pursue more attractive job possibilities in the private sector, leaving the public sector to blacks. If this were the case, we should find that black employment and growth of white-collar manufacturing jobs in the metropolitan private sector should vary positively; that is, as prestigious opportunities in the private sector expand, competitive pressure for public jobs should lessen, enabling blacks to win more city jobs. But the relationships, though generally quite weak, are negative. Competition for city jobs should be sharper where there is less growth or no growth in the private sector, but in city employment, blacks nevertheless do relatively better in some small measure under those conditions.

The evaporation of white interest, as far as we may hope to infer it from these aggregate data, does not provide a convincing explanation of the strong relationship between black population and black unemployment; nor is the natural hiring process explanation entirely satisfactory, although it certainly appears to be a contributory factor. There is, however, a third explanation, namely a political one. Case studies that extend as far back in time as Keech's examination of black voting in Tuskegee and Durham (1968, pp. 76–8; see also Campbell and Feagin 1975; Jones 1978) suggest that politicians, both white and black, are under pressure to distribute goods such as public jobs to blacks where blacks constitute a significant or potentially significant voting bloc.

As we see in Tables [2.7] and [2.8], the black mobilization score, our surrogate for black voting energy and success, is generally related in the predicted direction to black employment. This finding offers modest support for a political explanation.

A political explanation of black municipal employment levels need not rely entirely on the presumed influence of black voting blocs, however. A central assumption in the practice of ethnic politics is that a particular group will be in a more powerful position to have its demands met if it has a coethnic in a position of authority than if it must supplicate an officialdom controlled by other groups. There are, indeed, positive relationships in Tables [2.7] and [2.8] between levels of black public employment and the presence of a black mayor, but black proportional representation on city councils appears to be of little consequence.

The likelihood that a city will have a black mayor is, not surprisingly, strongly related to the percentage of blacks in the city's population ($r = .58$), which suggests that we may face a problem of multicollinearity. Although I shall deal again with this potential problem below, it is important to note that the variable, *black mayor*, has a certain logical integrity quite separate from *black population*. It has already been argued that local chief executives can be important in the personnel process in an authoritative way if they wish. In addition they exercise a certain moral authority from the vantage point of city hall. It would appear that black mayor and percentage of blacks in the city population are sufficiently distinct theoretically to permit, for example, their simultaneous inclusion in a multiple regression.

That seats on the city council offer black representatives little opportunity for influence over personnel policies (Table [2.7]) suggests the degree to which employment policy is an executive rather than a legislative function. More generally, the absence of impact of black council representation on measurable policy confirms the similar findings of Welch and Karnig (1979, pp. 111, 115).

Table [2.7] also shows that the black power variables are more strongly positively related to absolute levels of black city employment than to the effort scores; that is to say, blacks are more likely to approach or exceed proportional representation where they represent a smaller part of the population. Part of the explanation for this pattern may lie in the simple arithmetic of public-sector expansion and job turnover. Although a substantial number of positions in city employment have been made available to blacks in the last decade, the number of job openings may simply not have been great enough to permit blacks to catch up to their proportional share in cities where they constitute a large proportion of the population.

The variable measuring the level of black education represents an attempt to test Hypothesis Number 3, that black employment levels are a function of the characteristics of the black labor pool. The percentage of blacks with college educations was chosen over mean level of black education to explore in particular the relationship between the size of an educated labor pool and the achievement of occupations requiring advanced schooling. My assumption is that the greater the proportion of people holding a college degree, the more competitive the group will be in the quest for prestige city jobs. The percentage of blacks with a college education ranged from 2.2 in Newark to 9.3 in Hampton. Table [2.7] shows, however, that there is no relationship between education and absolute black employment levels in any job category. Variations in black employment are not apparently a function of variations in the quality of the labor pool.

Finally, let us examine the support for the expanding pie notion, namely that blacks will tend to do better in public employment where the city work force is expanding. The data in Table [2.7] show consistent support for this hypothesis. Growth during the 1970s seems particularly to have multiplied black professional opportunities. Of course, this general finding does not necessarily contradict or displace the previous arguments concerning the influence of black voting power and the impact of black political authority. The exercise of authority in this case—that is, the capacity to influence the distribution of public jobs—depends on the ability either to produce those jobs or to take advantage of jobs already available. . . Black power is necessary in some modest measure to convert opportunities into black gains . . . .

Conclusion

In an essay written near the beginning of the serious mobilization of black urban electoral efforts, Frances Fox Piven (1973) was greatly pessimistic about the capacity of blacks to penetrate the local public job sector. Blacks, she wrote, "come at a time when public employment has been pre-empted by older groups and is held fast through civil service provisions and collective bargaining contracts. Most public jobs are no longer allocated in exchange for political allegiance, but through a 'merit' system based on formal qualifications" (p. 380). As we have seen in the foregoing analysis, however, black municipal employment increased in the 1970s, and part of the explanation appears to lie in the growth of black influence over city hiring practices.

The basic conclusions of this analysis may be summarized as follows.

1. An expanding public sector appears at some very modest level to be a facilitating condition of black employment, but it is not a sufficient explanation.
2. As they have been measured here, educational characteristics of the

black population have virtually no independent effects on black employment levels in the prestige occupations.

3. The percentage of blacks in the population emerges as the most important predictor of black employment. A partial correlation analysis showed that a political explanation of this relationship—that a large black population represents a large black voting bloc—is somewhat more satisfactory to entertain than arguments relating to the concentration of blacks in the labor market or the lack of white interest in city jobs.

4. The presence of a black mayor has a modest incremental effect on levels of black employment and on affirmative action effort, enabling us ultimately to conclude that a small but discernible portion of black employment is a product of black political authority. This is particularly the case in the area of hiring of civil service administrative officials and professionals. We may speculate that the penetration by blacks of these job categories in all likelihood will not only enhance black influence in bureaucratic policymaking but will also contribute to the formation of a black bureaucratic middle class. Both possibilities warrant future investigation.

It is apparent from our examination of black public employment at the local level that the contemporary practice of a politics of ethnicity—the allocation of divisible goods to a particular group as a consequence of political influence or control—is an apparent, although perhaps limited, possibility in modern American cities. Future research must be alert to other ways in which such patterns of practice may be emerging, particularly in the areas of municipal contracting with minority-owned firms and affirmative action employment in private-sector businesses competing for public-sector contracts.

The conclusions suggest that municipal government in America, despite its fiscal troubles and its economy of dependency, is not a merely symbolic prize for minority groups to capture. It is often assumed that city government is powerless to affect the economic well-being of minority urban dwellers because local resources are neither expanding nor wholly controlled by city hall. But affirmative action in city employment is redistributive of existing resources, and to some modest degree those redistributive processes appear to be subject to the pressures of local black political influence.

References

Bullock, C.S. 1975. "The Election of Blacks in the South: Predictions and Consequences." *American Journal of Political Science* 19: 727–739.

Campbell, D., and Feagin, J.R. 1975. "Black Politics in the South: A Descriptive Analysis." *Journal of Politics* 27: 129–159.

Clark, T. 1975. "The Irish Ethic and the Spirit of Patronage." *Ethnicity* 2: 305–359.

Cole, L. 1976. "Electing Blacks to Municipal Office." *Urban Affairs Quarterly* 10: 17–39.

Eisinger, P. 1980. *The Politics of Displacement: Racial and Ethnic Transition in Three American Cities*. New York: Academic.

Eisinger, P. 1983. "Black Mayors and the Politics of Racial Economic Advancement." In W.C. McReady (ed.), *Culture, Ethnicity, and Identity*. New York: Academic Press.

Erie, S. 1978. "Politics, the Public Sector, and Irish Social Mobility: San Francisco, 1870–1900." *Western Political Quarterly* 31: 274–289.

Hall, G., and Saltzstein, A. 1977. "Equal Employment Opportunity for Minorities in Municipal Government." *Social Science Quarterly* 57: 864–872.

Hill, H. 1977. "The Equal Employment Opportunity Acts of 1964 and 1972: A Critical Analysis of the Legislative History and Administration of the Law." *Industrial Relations Law Journal* 2: 1–96.

Hill, R. 1978. *The Illusion of Black Progress*. Washington, DC: National Urban League.

Joint Center for Political Studies. 1979. *Roster of Black Elected Officials*. Washington, DC: JCPS.

Jones, M. 1978. "Black Political Empowerment in Atlanta." *The Annals* 439: 90–117.

Karnig, A.K. 1976. "Black Representation on City Councils." *Urban Affairs Quarterly* 12: 223–242.

Keech, W. 1968. *The Impact of Negro Voting*. Chicago: Rand McNally.

Kranz, H. 1976. *The Participatory Bureaucracy*. Lexington, MA: Lexington Books.

Levine, C. 1974. *Racial Conflict and the American Mayor*. Lexington, MA: Lexington Books.

Pascal, A. 1979. "The Effects of Local Fiscal Contraction on Public Employment and the Advancement of Minorities." Paper presented at a conference sponsored by the Lincoln Institute of Land Policy, June 19–20, 1979, Cambridge, MA.

Piven, F.F. 1973. "Militant Civil Servants in New York City." In W. Burnham (ed.), *Politics/America*. New York: Van Norstrand, Reinhold.

Thompson, F. J. 1978. "Civil Servants and the Deprived: Sociopolitical and Occupational Explanations of Attitudes Toward Minority Hiring." *American Journal of Political Science* 22: 325–347.

U.S. Department of Housing and Urban Development 1980. *The President's National Urban Policy Report*. Washington, DC: Government Printing Office.

Welch, S., and Karnig, A. 1979. "The Impact of Black Elected Officials on Urban Expenditures and Intergovernmental Revenues." In D. Marshall (ed.), *Urban Policy Making*. Beverly Hills, CA: Sage.

Discussion Questions

1. How might recent decisions handed down by the Supreme Court (as discussed in the excerpt by Naff) affect the passive representation of various social groups within the bureaucracy?
2. What factors affect the degree to which minorities and women have

access to public sector positions? Do you think these factors are more, less, or equally as important as equal employment opportunity programs?

3. What do you think prompted Charles Canady (R-FL) to introduce legislation prohibiting the use of race or sex in federal hiring decisions? If passed, what effects, if any, do you think such legislation would have on the overall demographic composition of the federal workforce?

4. How would you characterize the relationship between merit systems and passive representation in the United States? Is there an inherent tension between the two concepts? Can we adopt personnel practices that embrace both values?

Chapter 3

Social Representation and Public Administrators' Worldviews

What is the Linkage Between Social Background and Civil Servants' Policy Preferences?

The last chapter examined the passive, or demographic, representativeness of government bureaucracies, but not all scholars concur that the existence of passive representation within a bureaucracy or organization will necessarily lead to active representation therein. A bureaucracy that looks like the population it serves may or may not effectively translate the policy wishes of the population into public policy. A fundamental issue is whether or not the values, opinions, and attitudes of the general public are adequately shared and reflected by members of the public service. Thus, this chapter entertains arguments and evidence surrounding the relationship between bureaucratic and public attitudes.

We begin the chapter with an excerpt of a piece by Seymour M. Lipset (1952), one of the first scholars to suggest that the social values of bureaucrats do indeed affect governmental decision making. Lipset questions the presumed neutrality of civil servants, taking political scientists to task for their failure to consider the ways in which social background and attitudes of government bureaucrats affect implementation of government policy. If individual bureaucrats bring their own attitudes to work, as Lipset suggests they do, we cannot assume that bureaucracy is a neutral body simply enforcing the dictates of its political superiors. Studying government bureaucracy in Saskatchewan, Canada, Lipset claims "civil servants have been known to reduce the significance of reforms directed against their own group" (p. 268). Rather, they bring their own self-interest, prejudices, and values to the table and work against policy directives that are contrary to their liking. As he argues, "the behavior of an individual or group in a given situation cannot be considered as if the individual or group members had no other life outside the given situation" (p. 272). Thus, Lipset encourages political scientists to pay greater attention to individual bureaucrats and the ways in which they are able to shape government action, especially taking into account their own values and perspectives. Although he is not usually cited in the literature on representative bureaucracy, his argument is nonetheless relevant to current scholarship.

But can we assume that bureaucrats' values and perspectives are always relevant to their work? What do we know about these values and perspectives and from where they originate? The second excerpt in the chapter, written by Kenneth J. Meier and Lloyd G. Nigro (1976), attempts to answer this question. Meier and Nigro flesh out and critique the prevailing model of the theory of representative bureaucracy. As they explain, the model consists of a series of "four variables linked in a developmental sequence"—social origins, socialization experiences, attitudes, and behavior. The model presumes that administrators' social origins affect their socialization experiences, which in turn affect their attitudes, which ultimately affects how they make administrative decisions. For example, if upper-class citizens have different life experiences from middle- and lower-class citizens, if racial groups have different experiences from one another, if women and men have divergent life experiences, these experiences lead to the development of different attitudes, which then come into play when policies and decisions are made by the respective administrators.

However, Meier and Nigro argue that the theory has "serious deficiencies," noting that empirical verification is necessary for examining the presumed linkages between the four variables. From there, they flesh out one of the most enduring debates in the representative bureaucracy literature: whether social origins or agency socialization experiences do more to shape individual bureaucrats' attitudes. Do social origins affect the decisions made by bureaucrats? Or do agency affiliation and socialization exert greater influence on the attitudes of bureaucrats? Meier and Nigro juxtapose social origins against agency affiliation to see which variable is a better predictor of federal civil servants' attitudes. In the end, they conclude that "although both origins and agency affiliation have an impact on attitudes, agency affiliation is a more likely predictor than origins" (p. 467). As such, they suggest the theory be revised.

The remaining articles find evidence to the contrary, however. Comparing public administrators with members of the general public, Rosenbloom and Featherstonhaugh (1977) question whether or not attitudes rooted in social origins disappear after years of government employment. Their research suggests that attitudes among blacks in the general public are reproduced among blacks in public sector positions, and Dolan (2002) uncovers a similar pattern for gender. Even after controlling for seniority (used as a proxy for agency socialization), they find that "black public servants are more likely than whites to be able to articulate values and perspectives which are most closely associated with blacks as a social group" (p. 881). As such, the logical corollary is that agency socialization does not obliterate attitudes that are rooted in experiences associated with race. In short, "bureaucratic employment does not erase the consequences of race" (p. 879).

While most of the excerpts discussed thus far examine federal bureaucrats, Hale and Branch (1992) focus their attention on state administrators. They begin by assuming gender affects one's life experiences, that women and men have "different views of the world based upon their role in it and how it affects them" (p. 190). Thus, they accept as a given that social origins do indeed affect socialization experiences. From there, they proceed to assess whether or not gendered life experiences translate to gendered attitudes about representative bureaucracy and workforce reforms. They find that executive men and women do differ from one another in their attitudes about a variety of workplace issues that have special salience for women. To explain such a finding, they argue that women and men experience the workplace differently and that such experiences color their policy relevant attitudes. Again, the finding runs counter to the expectation that bureaucratic culture will minimize differences between the sexes.

As the excerpts included here suggest, the relationship between social origins and political attitudes is still not entirely clear. The pieces included in this chapter provide a sample of the representative bureaucracy scholarship surrounding bureaucratic attitudes. As detailed here, some of the earliest scholarly works seem to provide evidence that socialization experiences within public sector organizations are more powerful predictors of administrators' attitudes while more recent studies suggest that social origins really do continue to shape attitudes, even accounting for years of work within a particular organization. The discussion questions at the end of the chapter are designed to elicit further discussion and analysis of these competing findings.

References

Dolan, Julie. 2002. "Representative Bureaucracy in the Federal Executive: Gender and Spending Priorities." *Journal of Public Administration Research and Theory* 12(3): 353–375.

Hale, Mary M., and M. Frances Branch. 1992. "Policy Preferences on Workplace Reform." In *Women and Men of the States,* ed. Mary E. Guy. Armonk, NY: M.E. Sharpe, pp. 189–204.

Lipset, Seymour M. 1950. *Agrarian Socialism.* Berkeley, CA: University of California Press.

Meier, Kenneth J., and Lloyd Nigro. 1976. "Representative Bureaucracy and Policy Preferences: A Study in the Attitudes of Federal Executives." *Public Administration Review* 36 (July/August): 458–469.

Rosenbloom, David H., and Jeannette G. Featherstonhaugh. 1977. "Passive and Active Representation in the Federal Service: A Comparison of Blacks and Whites." *Social Science Quarterly* 58 (March): 873–882.

Bureaucracy and Social Change

Seymour Martin Lipset

Civil servants, of course, do not operate in a social vacuum. Their opinions about relative "right" and "wrong" are determined, like those of all persons, by pressures existing in their social milieu. A department official is interested not only in whether a minister's proposals can be put into practice, but with the effect of such policies on the traditional practices of the department and on its long-term relations with other groups. A reform which may be socially desirable, but which disrupts the continuity of practices and interpersonal relations within the department, will often be resisted by a top-ranking civil servant. He is obligated to protect those beneath him in the administrative hierarchy from the consequences of a change in policy.

Second, and equally important, the opinion of government officials on the feasibility of any proposal is necessarily colored by their political outlook and by the climate of opinion in their social group. Many top-ranking civil servants in Saskatchewan are members of the upper social class of Regina. Most of their social contacts are with people who believe that they will be adversely affected by many C.C.F. [Cooperative Commonwealth Federation] policies. Government officials who belong to professional or economic groups whose position or privileges are threatened by government policies tend to accept the opinion of their own group that reforms which adversely affect the group are wrong and will not work. Cabinet ministers who desire to make social reforms may therefore be dependent for advice on permanent civil servants who, in part, are members of the special-interest group which the ministers oppose. In Saskatchewan, as in other places, civil servants have been known to reduce the significance of reforms directed against their own group. They could hardly have been expected to draw up effective safeguards against "evils" the very existence of which they denied. . . .

. . . In recent years many have become concerned with the problem of bureaucracy in a large-scale society. The sheer size and complexity of social organizations, whether private or public, have created the need for a new

From Seymour Martin Lipset, "Bureaucracy and Social Change," *Agrarian Socialism* (Berkeley, CA: University of California Press, 1950), pp. 267–268, 271–263, 275. Copyright © 1971 by The Regents of the University of California. Reprinted with permission from University of California Press.

"class" of administrators or bureaucrats to operate them efficiently. This new administrative group, necessarily, has been given a large amount of discretionary power. Once entrenched in corporations, trade-unions, political parties, and governments, the administrators develop "vested interests" of their own which may conflict with the interests of those who placed them in office. It seems to be universally true in social organization that men in power seek to maintain and extend their power, status, and privileges. Modern democratic society, therefore, faces the dilemma of making extensive grants of power without at the same time abdicating the right of the democratic constituency to change the policies and the personnel of the bureaucracy.

The justified concern with the dangers of oligarchic or bureaucratic domination has, however, led many persons to ignore the fact that it does make a difference to society which set of bureaucrats controls its destiny. There are bureaucracies and bureaucracies. To suggest, as many social scientists have done, that trade-unions, cooperatives, corporations, political parties, and states must develop a bureaucratic social structure in order to operate efficiently still leaves a large area of indeterminate social action for a bureaucratically organized society. Bureaucrats are human beings, not automatons. The desire to maintain a given bureaucratic organization is only one of the complex series of factors determining their actions. In a given situation, each group acts somewhat differently, according to its background. The reactions of the Russian "socialist" bureaucrats to problems of power were very different from those of the English socialist bureaucrats. A deterministic theory of bureaucratic behavior, such as that advanced by Robert Michels or James Burnham, neglects the implications of an alternative pattern of bureaucratic response.

The focus on a single theory of bureaucracy has been encouraged by a lack of a sociological approach among political scientists. For the most part they have not raised questions about the social origins and values of government administrators and the relationship of such factors to government policy. It is possible that the political scientists' blindness to the sources of civil-service "biases" may be related to their own identification with the government administrator, and their disinclination to accept the fact that the behavior of their own group is determined by person "prejudice-creating" factors. Political scientists accepted the values of an unbiased civil servant who makes his decisions after analyzing the facts, presents the data to his minister, carries out the policy of the government in power, and then reverses his policy when a new government comes into office. Political history has been analyzed mainly in terms of struggles among interest groups and political parties. The civil service, like the political scientists, was simply a passive, neutral factor.

In recent years, however, political scientists have become aware of the fact that the government bureaucracy does play a significant role in determining policy. They still, however, leave the bureaucrat in a social vacuum. They now recognize that he plays an active role, but the determinants of that role are analyzed purely on the bureaucratic level. The bureaucrat's actions are analyzed on the basis of the goals of the civil service—self-preservation and efficiency. These interests may be defined in terms of prestige and privilege, preservation of patterns of organization or relationships within a department, or maintenance of department traditions and policies. There is little recognition that the behavior of government bureaucrats varies with the nongovernmental social background and interest of those controlling the bureaucratic structure. Members of a civil service are also members of other nongovernmental social groups and classes. Social pressures from many different group affiliations and loyalties determine individual behavior in most situations. The behavior of an individual or group in a given situation cannot be considered as if the individual or group members had no other life outside the given situation one is analyzing.

The direct relationship between class affiliations of members of a bureaucracy and the policies of the government has been demonstrated in the English civil service. J. Donald Kingsley [1944] has shown that as England changed from an aristocratically controlled nation to a capitalist state its civil service changed correspondingly. The aristocrats who once dominated the British civil service gradually gave way to members of the middle class.

The experiences in Saskatchewan also indicate the relationship between the background and the actions of the civil service. Trained in the tradition of a laissez-faire government and belonging to conservative social groups, the civil service contributes significantly to the social inertia which blunts the changes a new radical government can make. Delay in initiating reforms means that the new government becomes absorbed in the process of operating the old institutions. The longer a new government delays in making changes, the more responsible it becomes for the old practices and the harder it is to make the changes it originally desired to institute. The problem has not been crucial in Saskatchewan because of the small size of the government and its fairly limited powers. On a larger scale, however, as in Great Britain today, dependence on a conservative bureaucracy may prove to be significant in the success or failure of the Labor Government.

The suggestion that shake-ups in the civil service on the expert policy-making level may be necessary at times for the adequate functioning of democratic government has rarely been considered by North American political scientists. On this continent, the problem of the civil service has traditionally been that of patronage appointment with its resultant inefficiency and malpractice. European social theorists, on the contrary, have been concerned with the implications for social change of a permanent governmental bureaucracy with its own vested interests and social values.

The necessity to face up to the problem of bureaucratic resistance to change becomes urgent only when a "radical" party comes to office. The theory of civil-service neutrality breaks down when the total goals of the state change. A change from the Liberal to the Conservative Party or from the Democratic to the Republican Party does not usually require a civil servant to make any major adjustments. The functions of the department and of the government as a whole remain fairly constant.

The socialist state, however, which has as its goal a reintegration of societal values, giving priority of government services to groups that had been neglected and securing a large measure of government control, may fail in its objectives if it leaves administrative power in the hands of men whose social background and previous training prevent a sympathetic appreciation of the objectives of the new government. . . .

. . . There is no simple solution to the dilemma of keeping government administration efficient as well as responsive to the will of the electorate. The increase in the power, functions, and sheer size of modern government necessitates the search for some means of controlling the bureaucracy. It is utopian to think that the electorate's dismissal of the inexpert politician, who formally heads the bureaucracy, will by itself change the course of bureaucratic activities. As Max Weber [1947] stated: "The question is always who controls the existing bureaucratic machinery. And such control is possible only in a very limited degree to persons who are not technical specialists. Generally speaking, the trained permanent official is more likely to get his way in the long run than his nominal supervisor, the Cabinet Minister, who is not a specialist."

Government today is a large-scale administrative job requiring experts to operate it. Unless the electorate is given the opportunity to change the key experts as well as the politicians, elections will lose much of their significance. This problem will become more and more significant as efforts are made to increase the economic and social welfare role of the state.

References

Kingsley, J. Donald. 1944 *Representative Bureaucracy.* Yellow Springs, OH: Antioch Press.
Weber, Max. 1947. *The Theory of Social and Economic Organization,* trans. by Talcott Parsons and A.M. Henderson. New York: Oxford University Press.

Representative Bureaucracy and Policy Preferences: A Study in the Attitudes of Federal Executives

Kenneth John Meier and Lloyd G. Nigro

Public administrators are considered key actors in allocating resources among competing political forces. Administrative decisions, as Appleby so often observed, are political decisions, and controlling administrative power is a critical issue in a democratic polity (Appleby 1949). Among the many strategies of control suggested is representative bureaucracy (Bendix 1949; Kingsley 1944; Krislov 1974; Larson 1973; Levitan 1946; Long 1952; McGregor 1974; Meier 1975; Mosher 1968; Subramaniam 1967; Van Riper 1958; Warner et al. 1963).

The fundamental axiom/proposition underlying the concept of representative bureaucracy is: *if the attitudes of administrators are similar to the attitudes held by the general public, the decisions administrators make will in general be responsive to the desires of the public.* Advocates of a "representative bureaucracy" emphasize the apparent weaknesses of *external* political controls on administrative action and argue that *internal* controls on behavior are necessary to keep public bureaucracy responsive to the people. The basic element of internal control is a congruence of attitudes between administrators and the public at large that promotes responsive decisions and policies.

Implicit in the attitude congruence argument is the premise of many decision theorists that if two people rationally seek to maximize a given set of values (attitudes) under identical conditions with the same information, they will arrive at the same decision (Downs 1967; Hitch 1965; Schultze 1968; Simon 1957). Therefore, if civil servants hold attitudes identical to the public's, their actions should be within the public's zone of acceptance. This, of course, does not mean that administrative decisions and public opinion will always coincide, because administrators have access to information and expertise not available to the bulk of the citizenry. The theory of representative bureaucracy, thus, begins with the following definition of responsiveness: If administrators and the public share value orientations, then the administrators will advocate and pursue [the same] courses of action the public would if it were able to congregate and had the administrators' expertise and information.

The theory of representative bureaucracy does not stop with the similarity of attitudes or values proposition. In fact, no attempt at explicating or investigating representative bureaucracy has relied solely on the attitudes argument. Tracing back the process of attitude formation, proponents contend that attitudes are determined by the individual's social environment. Different social classes and ethnic groups, the reasoning goes, have different child raising practices, experiences, and socialization patterns (Hodges 1964). Attitudes, therefore, should vary as a function of demographic origins. The test of a bureaucracy's representativeness, then, is whether or not the demographics of its membership resemble those of the general population.

At this point, tracing out the key elements of the "theory" of representative bureaucracy is useful. Four variables are included—social origins, socialization experiences, attitudes, and behavior. They are linked in a developmental sequence. The theory contains three theorems. First, differences in social origins are a major factor in differences in socialization experiences. Second, socialization experiences have a strong influence on political attitudes. Third, attitudes are strongly related to actual behavior. These three theorems underlie the "theory" of representative bureaucracy. . . .

. . . Two often made "factual" claims are connected with the above theorems. The first is that bureaucrats and the population do have similar social origins. The second and far more important assertion is that the two groups hold similar attitudes; this assertion is derived through a confirmation of the first "factual" claim and the specified theoretical linkages. These two empirical generalizations and the three theorems form the core of the theory of representative bureaucracy.

A Critical Analysis of the Theory

Since the goal of a "representative bureaucracy" is a current policy issue, the validity of its theoretical justification is of more than academic concern. Adequate prescription requires that the theory be logically sound as well as empirically supportable. The "theory" of representative bureaucracy as it stands has six serious deficiencies.

A definition of representation is needed: The proponents of representative bureaucracy—as a group—lack a sound or even a consensual definition of representation. Kingsley's (1944) definition, for example, differs significantly from Mosher's (1968); the disagreement centers on who should be represented by the bureaucracy (Kingsley 1944; Mosher 1968). Kingsley believes that bureaucracy should represent the dominant forces in society, while Mosher contends that the entire society should be represented. Using Mosher's definition, Kingsley's "representative" bureaucracy would be highly un-representative. Further, most scholars use a *passive* rather than *active* model of representation, the position is not unanimous. Rather than measuring representation directly in terms of attitudes or behavior, the key variables to be represented become social origins. But even Mosher (1968) admits we know little about the relationships between an individual's background and current attitudes and behavior. In short, instead of attempting to measure representativeness *directly*, analysts have traditionally relied on secondary variables (social origins) as indicators of attitudes and behavior—a questionable procedure.

The assumption traditional controls are ineffective: A second limitation is found in the assumption that traditional controls over administrative power (executive hierarchy, legislative oversight, judicial review, etc.) are largely ineffective. This assumption merits scrutiny because representative bureaucracy is presented as a method of democratic control when external political mechanisms are inadequate. The political functions of a representative bureaucracy are theoretically tied to the inefficacy of external controls. The actual effectiveness of external political controls, however, is an empirical question almost totally ignored by theorists of representative bureaucracy. In other words, the entire framework needs specification of the conditions conducive to the successful operation of traditional controls. The conditions under which representative bureaucracy is a feasible alternative also need to be set forth.

The social origins and socialization experiences linkage: A third problem relates to the argument that social origins determine socialization experiences. First, little is known about the socialization experiences of different social groups, and, second, the linkage is unimportant for empirical purposes. Recent studies have argued that people from widely varying social backgrounds can experience similar childhoods (socializing experiences); ample room exists to question the deterministic model of the relationship between origins and socialization (Barber 1970). Also, if social origins determine socialization and if socialization determines attitude orientations, then the correlations between attitudes and social origins should be high. The whole proposition, therefore, can be operationally restated to assert that social origins are good predictors of attitudes.

Social origins and political attitudes: The causal linkage between social origins and political attitudes postulated by the "theory" is highly debatable; some theoretical reasons exist to suggest that the linkage need not be strong. The reasons may be summarized as follows:

1. Socialization is a learning process; and, as such, cannot be expected to terminate abruptly when the person enters the civil service. Socialization is a continuous process. It is "developmental in nature, that is, it occurs in a regular progression from infancy to old age" (Brim 1966). The role, therefore, an agency provides for an individual may be as important an influence as childhood training. Studies by Janowitz (1960), Kaufman (1960), and Baldwin (1968) indicate that organizations are powerful socializers.
2. Civil servants, especially high level administrators, differ significantly from a randomly selected group with the same social origins. They are unusually upward mobile. Clearly if socialization continues throughout the life cycle, the different experiences resulting from upward mobility should distinguish this group (Barber 1970).

The assertion that socioeconomic origins determine the attitudes and values of highly mobile, adult bureaucrats, is obviously in need of revision.

Attitudes and behavior: The idea that attitudes influence/determine behavior, on the surface, appears unlikely to evoke criticism since much of social psychology is based on this assumption. Many psychologists, however, dispute this assumption. The relationship between attitudes and behaviors is a critical issue to the theory of representative bureaucracy because if attitudes are unrelated to behavior, then the entire conceptual structure of representative bureaucracy collapses.

Allan Wicker, reviewing 33 studies of attitude-behavior relationships, concludes that, "Taken as a whole, these studies suggest it is considerably more likely that attitudes will be unrelated or only slightly related to overt behaviors than that attitudes will be closely related to actions. . . Only rarely can as much as 10 per cent of the variance in overt behavior be accounted for by attitudinal data" (1969). Wicker's warning must be heeded, but his conclusion is too harsh for three reasons. First, the recognized problems of measurement error and low reliability found in many common attitude measures attenuate relationships with behavior (Converse 1964). Second, political scientists using multiple indicators have often found strong correlations between attitudes and behavior, usually vote choices (Campbell et al. 1960; Kovenock et al. 1970; Patterson et al. 1974). These studies indicate that under certain conditions political attitudes are highly correlated with political behavior. Finally, for most of the studies cited by Wicker, adequate explanations for the low correlations are available (Kiesler et al. 1969).

Failure to deal with bureaucratic differentiation: A final logical weakness is the contention that the entire bureaucratic apparatus must or should be representative of the population as a whole. Given the stated central purpose of representation, i.e., responsiveness, this is a misconception because *the* bureaucracy does not make decisions or policies. The individual agencies, bureaus, and their controlling administrative elites dominate the process. Given the structure of American politics—especially agency-interest group relationships—the responsiveness of bureau elites is the crucial question. The representativeness of these elites becomes a central issue. The existing theoretical framework should be revised to reflect knowledge about the sociopolitics of public organizations. . . .

Data and Methods

Data: The data for this article are from an original survey of the federal supergrades (GS 16 to GS 18) conducted during July 1974. A ten percent random sample was drawn from lists provided by the U.S. Civil Service Commission. The survey was conducted by mail, and 469 or approximately 56 per cent of the respondents returned questionnaires. The returns were determined to be representative of the entire higher civil service with regard to agency, location, age, length of service and several other known population parameters provided by the Civil Service Commission. The questionnaire replicated Warner's, as used in *The American Federal Executive*. Warner's questionnaire was supplemented with approximately 50 attitude questions taken from national sample surveys. . . .

Attitudes: A basic problem in selecting the elite and mass attitudes to be compared is resolving a conflict between two criteria that may be mutually exclusive. On the one hand, the attitude should be relevant to elite behavior, that is, predictably related to specific administrative actions. On the other hand, the attitudes must also be comprehensible to the mass publics, be a part of the political process with which they have some familiarity. These two criteria are at opposite poles of a continuum. The more relevant an attitude is to elite behavior, the more specific it is to the behavior and the less it can be comprehended by mass publics. The more comprehensible the attitude to the mass public, the more general it is, and the less relevant it is to specific actions taken by administrators.

Any selection of attitudinal indicators must then be a compromise between two somewhat mutually exclusive criteria. The attitude items selected for comparison were the NORC national priorities questions where the respondent indicates whether he favors increased, decreased, or the same level of spending in a policy area. The items are fairly close to a rigid Fishbein (1967) definition of attitudes requiring an evaluative response. As such they would be good indicators of behavior if additional belief statements could be added linking the attitudes to actions. In addition, they are likely to be salient to mass publics since many political campaigns are structured to emphasize or de-emphasize a policy area (Pennock 1952). . . .

An Operationalization of Representative Bureaucracy . . .

. . . Model I operationalizes the theory of representative bureaucracy's contention that demographic origins are the major determinants of the higher civil servant's attitudes. The 11 demographic origin variables are related to the 12 attitudes by multiple regression as shown in Model I (see Figure [3.1]). The curved lines indicating unspecified relationships between the exogenous variables have been omitted. Since we were not concerned with the interrelationships among the origins' variables, the model was estimated with a single equation for each attitude. Path analysis was used to determine the total and direct impact of each variable (Goldberger 1970).

Table [3.1] shows the total impact the demographic variables have on each of the policy attitudes. Total impact is the influence one variable has on another directly and also through all other variables included in the model. Table [3.2] shows the direct impact (path coefficients) the demographic variables have on each of the attitudes. The direct impact of each demographic origin variable on the attitude is its *unmediated* influence. Since the criterion for selecting significant relationships was the significance scores of the regression coefficients, the magnitude of the path coefficients is only a rough indicator of the relationship's significance.

Demographic variables fare poorly as predictors of the attitudes of the higher civil servants. The multiple correlation coefficients range from .14 for defense spending to .32 for welfare spending, the overall average being .21. These low correlations indicate that on the average the demographic variables account for 5 per cent of the variance in attitudes. As for individual relationships with the attitude variables, Table [3.1] reveals that all the correlations between demographic origins and attitudes are small. Thirty-four of the 132 correlations are significant, but the largest simple correlation, between age and minority spending, is only −.16.

The direct impact of each of the origin variables on attitudes is more informative because the direct impacts control for all other origin variables. Table [3.2] indicates that of the 132 possible relationships between

Figure 3.1 **Demographic Origins (D), Agency Affiliation (A), and Attitudes (V)**

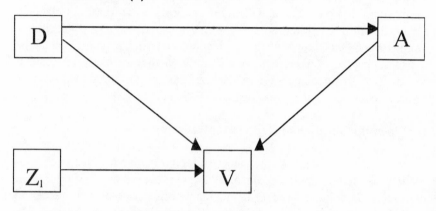

Predictions:

Representative bureaucracy	Agency socialization
$r_{DV} > 0$	$r_{AV} > 0$
$r_{DV \cdot A} > 0$	$r_{AV \cdot D} > 0$
$r_{AV \cdot D} = 0$	$r_{AV \cdot D} > r_{DV \cdot A}$

demographics and attitudes, in only 29 cases did an origin variable have a significant impact. Since the significant relationships are substantively important for the theory of representative bureaucracy because they indicate which characteristics must be represented, they merit discussion. The most important trait is race; it has a significant (but statistically unimpressive) direct impact on eight attitudes, these being environment, space, health, drugs, education, welfare, minorities, and agriculture. Education and age are the second most important. Each has a significant direct impact on five attitudes. Age is related to environment, health, crime, foreign aid, and minorities. Education is related to environment, urban problems, foreign aid, welfare, and minorities. Initial occupation (health, urban problems, and crime) and northeastern origins (crime, defense, and foreign aid) have three significant direct impacts. Western origins impact on attitudes toward environment and crime, while southern origins impact in the drug area and midwestern origins are related to attitudes concerning crime. Finally, sex has a direct impact on attitude toward foreign aid.

The results of the analysis based on Model I are clearly contrary to the predictions of the theory of representative bureaucracy. In fact, knowing the origins of the supergrades tells us little about their attitudes and correspondingly less about their policy-making behavior.

Table 3.1

Total Impact of Demographics on Policy Attitudes—Correlations

Demographic	Environment	Space	Health	Urban	Crime	Drugs	Education	Defense	Foreign Aid	Welfare	Minorities	Agriculture
Urbanism	.03	-.01	.02	.07	-.09*	-.04	-.01	-.03	.02	.08*	.01	-.05
Occupation father	.03	-.05	-.07	.05	-.04	-.01	-.03	.04	-.04	-.01	.00	.01
First occupation	-.01	-.05	.06	.09*	.08*	.03	.03	-.04	.06	.05	-.02	.00
Education	.09	-.06	-.02	.10*	-.01	-.04	.02	-.05	.11*	.15*	.10*	-.07
Age	-.12*	-.05	-.12*	-.03	.12*	.03	-.04	.02	-.14*	-.08	-.16*	.02
Sex	.01	.02	-.05	-.03	-.05	-.03	.02	.03	.10*	.02	.01	-.01
Race	.12*	-.07	.08*	.02	.07	.11*	.15*	-.06	.05	.14*	.13*	.10*
Northeast	.06	-.04	.07	.09*	-.12*	-.11*	.03	-.07	.08*	.08*	.06	-.08*
South	-.04	.03	.01	-.04	.12*	.13	.04	.03	-.03	-.15*	-.02	.05
Midwest	-.05	.06	-.02	.00	-.01	-.03	.00	.03	.03	.11*	-.03	-.01
West	.09*	-.03	-.10*	-.07	-.05	.06	-.08*	-.03	-.07	-.04	.00	.06
R =	.23	.15	.22	.18	.25	.19	.20	.14	.24	.32	.24	.15

*Significant at .05 level.

Table 3.2

Direct Impact of Demographics on Policy Attitudes of the Higher Civil Service—Path Coefficients

Demographic	Environ- ment	Space	Health	Urban	Crime	Drugs	Educa- tion	Defense	Foreign Aid	Welfare	Minorities	Agriculture
Urbanism	.00	.00	-.01	.04	-.05	.00	-.03	-.02	-.01	.05	-.02	-.04
Occupation father	.03	-.04	-.07	.03	-.04	.00	-.03	.05	-.06	-.03	.01	.04
First occupation	-.02	-.03	.08*	.07*	.09*	.04	.02	-.03	.06	.03	-.03	.00
Education	.08*	-.06	-.03	.08*	.00	-.03	.02	-.06	.09*	.15*	.10*	-.07
Age	-.11*	-.05	-.13*	-.02	.10*	.01	-.03	.01	-.11*	-.05	-.15*	.01
Sex	-.01	.03	-.05	-.04	-.05	-.02	.03	.04	.09*	.01	.00	.00
Race	.12*	-.08*	.09*	.04	.06	.08*	.17*	-.06	.07	.19*	.16*	.08*
Northeast	.15	.06	.12	.06	-.29*	-.03	.05	-.15*	.16*	.10	.10	-.07
South	.05	.11	-.05	-.02	-.11	.13*	.03	-.06	.07	-.11	.01	-.01
Midwest	.08	.13	.08	.02	-.24*	.03	.03	-.09	.14	.14	.04	-.03
West	.14*	.04	-.05	-.05	-.21*	.07	-.09	-.09	.00	-.02	.02	.02

*Significant at .05 level.

The Agency Socialization Alternative

Model I demonstrated the relatively minor influence social origins have on the political attitudes of the supergrades. Given the low explanatory power of Model I, some room clearly exists for incorporating alternative hypotheses into an explanation of the attitudes held by these civil servants. One alternative explanation with a substantial base in sociological theory and research is that organizations are potent socializers of their members. If this is the case, agency affiliation is likely to be a powerful predictor of attitudes. . . .

. . . The traditional theory of representative bureaucracy and the agency socialization model reach different conclusions regarding the major influences on the administrator's attitudes. The theory of representative bureaucracy, relying on social origins, predicts that the correlation between social origins and attitudes is greater than zero. In the previous section, we found that this was indeed the situation. The theory also predicts that origins and attitudes will be positively related when agency affiliation is controlled, and that the correlation between agency affiliation and attitudes is spurious when social origins are controlled. The assertion that agency-attitude correlations are spurious is derivable from the theory's argument that origins are *the* cause of attitudes. Even if one is unwilling to interpret representative bureaucracy in such narrow terms, the theory would still predict that origins would be *more* important than current affiliation in predicting attitudes and, hence, behavior.

Table [3.3] presents the respective influences of agency affiliation and demographic origins on political attitudes. The results are fairly clear and consistent. Social origins have a greater impact on attitudes about improving the conditions of minority groups. On the issue of welfare outlays, the agency and origin factors have approximately the same impact. Since "welfare" and minority programs have relatively low popularity with the American public, and minorities are a group with no large established agency to advocate and transact around their interests, the stronger impact of demographic origins is not surprising.

In all other attitude areas, however, agency affiliation outweighs social origins. On space exploration and foreign aid the differences are striking. Significant differences are also to be found in the areas of environmental protection, health care, urban problems, crime control, drug abuse, education, military allocations, and agriculture.

Model II, therefore, does not demonstrate that either demographic representation or agency socialization is not useful in the study of civil servant's attitudes and, by implication, their behavior. Instead, the analysis suggests

Table 3.3

**Multiple Partial Correlations Between Attitudes and Agency/
Demographics Controlling for Demographics/Agency**

Policy area	Demographics	Agency
Environment	.19	.34
Space	.15	.48
Health care	.20	.26
Urban problems	.15	.23
Crime control	.25	.32
Drug abuse	.18	.30
Education	.15	.24
Defense	.11	.30
Foreign Aid	.25	.46
Welfare	.31	.31
Minorities	.24	.20
Agriculture	.17	.25

that although both origins and agency affiliation have an impact on attitudes, agency affiliation is a more likely predictor than origins. On most issues, knowing the administrator's current affiliation is far more important than a knowledge of his demographic origins. Apparently, agency socialization tends to overcome any tendency for the supergrades to hold attitudes rooted in their social origins.

Conclusion

The "theory of representative bureaucracy" is inadequate as a normative theory of political control and as an empirical description of reality. Its theoretical linkages are critically weakened by unsupported empirical assertions, untenable assumptions, vague definitions, and poorly defined units of analysis. Further problems are raised by the discovery that the supergrades are an unrepresentative demographic group holding quite representative attitudes; social origins say little about policy preferences in this case. It is obvious that the entire theory of representative bureaucracy is in great need of major revision, and that more systematic and viable explanations of political control and policy preferences are required. . . .

. . . A bureau or an entire administration can point to increased numbers of minorities at high levels and imply that policies are, therefore, more responsive. However, our analysis suggests the contrary; simple demographic representation cannot be taken as an accurate indicator of responsive policies. The policies themselves must be examined.

References

Appleby, Paul H. 1949. *Policy and Administration*. University, Ala.: University of Alabama Press.

Baldwin, Sidney. 1968, *Politics and Poverty*. Chapel Hill: University of North Carolina Press.

Barber, James A., Jr. 1970. *Social Mobility and Voting Behavior*. Chicago: Rand McNally.

Bendix, Reinhard. 1949. *Higher Civil Servants in American Society*. Boulder: University of Colorado Press.

Brim, Orville G. 1966. "Socialization Through the Life Cycle." In Orville G. Brim and Stanton Wheeler (eds.), *Socialization After Childhood*. New York: Wiley, p. 17.

Campbell, Angus, Philip E. Converse, Warren Miller, and Donald Stokes. 1960. *The American Voter*. New York: Wiley.

Converse, Philip E. 1964. 'The Nature of Belief Systems in Mass Politics." In David Apter (ed.), *Ideology and Discontent*. New York: the Free Press, pp. 206–261.

Downs, Anthony. 1967. *Inside Bureaucracy*. Boston: Little-Brown.

Fishbein, Martin. 1967. *Readings in Attitude Theory and Measurement*. New York: Wiley.

Goldeberger, Arthur S. 1970. "On Boudon's Methods of Linear Causal Analysis." *American Sociological Review* 35: 97–101.

Hitch, Charles. 1965. *Decisionmaking for Defense*. Berkeley: University of California Press.

Hodges, Harold M. 1964. *Social Stratification*. Cambridge, Mass.: Schenkman.

Janowitz, Morris. 1960 *The Professional Soldier*. New York: Free Press Glencoe.

Kaufman, Herbert. 1960. *The Forest Ranger*. Baltimore: Johns Hopkins Press.

Kiesler, Charles A., Barry E. Collins, and Norman Miller. 1960. *Attitude Change*. New York: Wiley.

Kingsley, J. Donald. 1944. *Representative Bureaucracy*. Yellow Springs, OH: Antioch Press.

Kovenock, David E., Philip L. Beardsley, and James Prothro. 1970. "Status, Party Ideology, Issues and Candidate Choice. "International Political Science Association, Munich, Germany.

Krislov, Samuel. 1974. *Representative Bureaucracy*. Englewood Cliffs, N.J.: Prentice-Hall.

Larson, Arthur D. 1973. "Representative Bureaucracy and Administrative Responsibility." *Midwest Review of Public Administration* 7 (April): 79–90.

Levitan, Daniel M. 1946. "The Responsibility of Administrative Officials in a Democratic Society." *Political Science Quarterly* 61 (December): 562–598.

Long, Norton E. 1952. "Bureaucracy and Constitutionalism." *American Political Science Review* 46 (September): 808–818.

McGregor, Eugene B. 1974. "Social Equity and the Public Service." *Public Administration Review* 34 (January/February): 18–28.

Meier, Kenneth J. 1975. "Representative Bureaucracy: An Empirical Analysis." *American Political Science Review* 69 (June): 526–543.

Mosher, Frederick C. 1968. *Democracy and the Public Service*. New York: Oxford University Press.

Patterson, Thomas E., Robert D. McClure, and Kenneth J. Meier. 1974. "Issue Voting and Voter Rationality." Paper presented at the American Political Science Association meetings, Chicago, Illinois.

Schultze, Charles L. 1968. *The Political and Economics of Public Spending*. Washington, DC: The Brookings Institution.

Simon, Herbert A. 1975. *Administrative Behavior*, 2d ed. New York: The Free Press.

Subramaniam, V. 1967. "Representative Bureaucracy: A Reassessment." *American Political Science Review* 61 (December): 1010–1019.

Van Riper, Paul P. 1958. *History of the United States Civil Service*. New York: Harper and Row.

Warner, W. Lloyd, Paul P. Van Riper, Norman H. Martin, and Orivis F. Collins. 1963. *The American Federal Executive*. New Haven: Yale University Press.

Wicher, Allan W. 1969. "Attitudes Versus Actions." *Journal of Social Issues* 15 (Autumn): 41–78.

Passive and Active Representation in the Federal Service: A Comparison of Blacks and Whites

David H. Rosenbloom and Jeannette G. Featherstonhaugh

For about three decades, representative bureaucracy has been a concept of considerable importance as an explanatory tool in discussions of the United States federal service. However, the concept remains somewhat ambiguous and underdeveloped. Its origins, meanings, and applicability have yet to be explored fully. This study seeks to develop the concept of representative bureaucracy further by analyzing empirically the extent to which differences associated with racial background carry over into a bureaucratic setting. The importance of such an enterprise is heightened at the present time by the fact that the creation of a socially representative bureaucracy has recently become an objective of federal personnel administration (Rosenbloom, 1973, 1975). . . .

Policy Framework

In his classic essay on public administration in the United States, "The Study of Administration," Woodrow Wilson (1941: 501) wrote, "The ideal for us is a civil service cultured and self-sufficient enough to act with sense and vigor, and yet so intimately connected with the popular thought, by means of elections and constant public counsel, as to find arbitrariness or class spirit quite out of the question." While few have disagreed with the objective of developing a personnel and organizational system which would at once assure efficiency and political responsiveness to the population at large, in practice, efforts to maximize these values have presented a dilemma. For the most part, reforms of the public service have tended to increase efficiency at the expense of responsiveness, or responsiveness at the expense of efficiency.

From David H. Rosenbloom and Jeannette G. Featherstonhaugh, "Passive and Active Representation in the Federal Service: A Comparison of Blacks and Whites," *Social Science Quarterly*, March 1977, pp. 873, 874–883. Copyright © 1977 by Southwestern Social Science Association. Reprinted with permission.

Thus, the four major kinds of public service reform have been less than fully satisfactory. The spoils system tended to maximize political responsiveness to electoral majorities and political authorities, but public administration was corrupt and inefficient. Merit oriented reform, on the other hand, has increased efficiency, but provides no guarantee of responsiveness. Indeed, so vulnerable were the American civil service reformers on this point that they often argued that responsiveness was of only secondary importance because public bureaucracies had almost no legitimate political role. Subsequent attempts to assure greater efficiency in conjunction with the scientific management approach have similarly failed to address themselves adequately to the question of responsiveness. Nor have efforts to reorganize public bureaucracies in order to make them more responsive to political authorities generally been effective.

The most recent approach has emphasized the inclusion in the bureaucracy of all those major social groups, such as blacks, Chicanos, and women, who have heretofore not participated in it to the same extent as other citizens. The vehicle for achieving this goal is "affirmative action." Its basic rationale is the assumption that the inclusion of members of various social groups in a civil service facilitates greater bureaucratic responsiveness. Equally basic is the corollary belief that once there is a sufficient concentration of minority personnel in the federal service, the groups from which they come will be more adequately represented within the political system.

Analysis

The existence and nature of a link between passive and active representation has been contested in the literature of the social sciences (Lipset 1952; Dresang 1974; Meier 1975; Meier and Nigro 1976). Clearly, it is a question of major analytic, political, and policy importance. On the one hand, it has sometimes been assumed that as social group identification becomes more salient to an individual bureaucrat, the more likely that person will be to represent actively his or her group. In contrast to this general approach, several have argued that the nature of bureaucratic recruitment and socialization upon one's behavior are such that they are likely to remove the impact of one's social roots and outlook in a bureaucratic setting. In order to learn more about these matters, we developed a secondary analysis of data generated by Jennings and associates (1969) in their 1967 study of the attitudes of federal employees toward political participation. Although these data are a decade old, they were gathered at a time when racial cleavages and consciousness were highly visible and pronounced, and thus are well suited to an analysis of the matters under investigation. Our analysis indicates that, at least in the federal service during the peak of the Civil Rights Movement, important differences among the outlooks of civil servants could be attributed to race. Moreover, a comparison of federal employees with other citizens at the time indicates that some of the effects of social group membership on attitudes toward political participation were not erased by bureaucratic employment.

Table [3.4] presents a comparison between the activity and attitudes of black and white federal employees on several dimensions of political participation. It indicates, that, on the whole, black federal servants were more activity-oriented, although they appear to have felt less efficacious. Thus, black bureaucrats were more likely than whites to have strong party identification, to try to change a local or national law, to contribute to a political campaign, if asked, and to display a campaign button or bumper sticker. On the other hand, black employees were somewhat less likely to vote, and more likely to feel that they had no control over government and that public officials do not really care what they think.

At this point it should be stressed that the data strongly suggest that these differences were not due to the effects of rank or occupation. Black employees were (and remain) heavily concentrated in the lower levels of the federal bureaucracy. However, whether confined to the ranks in which blacks were most concentrated or inclusive of all levels, the results of the comparison between black and white federal employees' attitudes and political involvement are not substantially different. Moreover, controls on socioeconomic status indicated that differences between black and white federal employees could not be attributed to this factor.

For the sake of comparison, the table also presents the political activity and attitudes of the general population, by race. The data for the latter were generated by the S.R.C. [Social Research Consortium] *1966 Election Study*. It is evident that, overall, there is a considerable divergence between the outlooks of federal employees and other citizens. Consequently, it appears that recruitment mechanisms and bureaucratic socialization may serve to differentiate federal employees from the rest of the population, and that, at least with reference to political activity and attitudes, federal servants do not faithfully reflect the outlooks of the citizenry at large. However, the table can be seen in another light as well. If one compares the positions of black and white federal employees relative to their social groups in the society as a whole, a considerable congruence emerges. Thus, black employees tend to be in a position vis-à-vis white employees similar to that of black citizens vis-à-vis white citizens. This finding suggests that, notwithstanding the apparent effects of recruitment and socialization, bureaucratic employment does

Table 3.4

Political Activity and Attitudes of Federal Employees and the General Population Compared, by Race

	Positive responses					
	Federal servants			General population		
	Percent white	Percent black	Significance level	Percent white	Percent black	Significance level
Follows public affairs	88 (733)	85 (127)	.457	67 (1,136)	54 (134)	.004
Cares about congressional elections	31 (753)	39 (123)	.106	62 (1,097)	54 (120)	.121
Voted in 1964	92 (712)	93 (118)	.202	—	—	—
Always votes in presidential elections	62 (739)	49 (121)	.002	53 (1,100)	36 (129)	.000
Always votes for same party	34 (732)	59 (119)	.000	44 (971)	66 (100)	.000
Strong party identification	27 (764)	42 (127)	.001	—	—	—
Favors campaign contribution deduction	36 (728)	52 (117)	.001	—	—	—
Favors government pay for campaigns	24 (721)	33 (114)	.048	—	—	—
Asked for political opinion	24 (762)	15 (127)	.035	17 (1,136)	13 (134)	.297
Asked to give money to party	14 (765)	7 (127)	.058	20 (1,125)	10 (134)	.008
Would give if asked	36 (505)	56 (100)	.000	21 (800)	38 (99)	.000
Displayed button or sticker	17 (766)	25 (127)	.047	—	—	—
High probability success change local law	10 (623)	19 (95)	.000	48 (901)	41 (107)	.225
High probability success change national law	6 (596)	11 (99)	.071	29 (938)	30 (97)	.893
Would try to change local law	37 (690)	49 (110)	.026	60 (1,011)	57 (112)	.623
Would try to change national law	33 (704)	48 (115)	.003	50 (1,017)	41 (113)	.071
Agree, citizens have no control over government	19 (747)	35 (125)	.000	35 (1,074)	48 (126)	.006
Agree, voting only way to influence government	50 (757)	74 (123)	.000	71 (1,091)	82 (121)	.014
Agree, government too complicated to understand	52 (747)	60 (125)	.103	71 (1,096)	82 (123)	.013
Agree, public officials do not care	15 (738)	27 (116)	.002	36 (1,042)	55 (115)	.000

Table 3.5

Black and White Federal Employees' Responses Compared by Level of Seniority

Item	Percent white	(N)	Percent black	(N)	Significance level	Group
Follow public affairs	88	(376)	85	(73)	.683	<15 yrs.
	88	(389)	85	(54)	.684	>15 yrs.
Vote in presidential elections	87	(356)	77	(69)	.043	<15 yrs.
	93	(382)	85	(52)	.073	>15 yrs.
Always for the same party	35	(353)	65	(68)	.000	<15 yrs.
	32	(378)	51	(51)	.013	>15 yrs.
Voted in 1964	90	(341)	91	(68)	.994	<15 yrs.
	93	(370)	96	(50)	.615	>15 yrs.
Strong party identification	22	(375)	41	(73)	.001	<15 yrs.
	32	(388)	43	(54)	.174	>15 yrs.
High probability of success (local)	09	(312)	21	(58)	.021	<15 yrs.
	10	(310)	16	(37)	.381	>15 yrs.
Would try (local)	39	(334)	46	(66)	.420	<15 yrs.
	36	(355)	55	(44)	.024	>15 yrs.
High probability of success (national)	05	(288)	12	(58)	.052	<15 yrs.
	07	(308)	10	(41)	.717	>15 yrs.
Would try (national)	35	(340)	46	(69)	.009	<15 yrs.
	32	(363)	50	(46)	.021	>15 yrs.
Favor campaign	36	(358)	54	(67)		
Favor campaign	36	(358)	54	(67)	.010	<15 yrs.
Contribution deduction	36	(369)	50	(50)	.079	>15 yrs.
Favor government pay for campaign	24	(353)	27	(68)	.713	<15 yrs.
	25	(367)	44	(46)	.012	>15 yrs.
Would contribute to party	37	(250)	65	(52)	.000	<15 yrs.
	35	(254)	46	(48)	.189	>15 yrs.
Displayed button or sticker	20	(376)	29	(73)	.114	<15 yrs.
	15	(389)	20	(73)	.114	>15 yrs.
Agree, no control over government	20	(336)	33	(72)	.019	<15 yrs.
	19	(380)	38	(53)	.003	>15 yrs.
Agree, voting only way to control	49	(372)	76	(70)	.000	<15 yrs.
	51	(384)	72	(53)	.508	>15 yrs.
Agree, government too complicated	56	(374)	64	(73)	.209	<15 yrs.
	48	(372)	54	(52)	.508	>15 yrs.
Agree, public officials don't care	15	(365)	29	(66)	.013	<15 yrs.
	15	(372)	24	(50)	.127	>15 yrs.

not erase the consequences of race in influencing attitudes toward political participation.

In an effort to learn more about the impact of bureaucratic socialization, we examined the effects of seniority on the attitudes and activity of civil servants. Table [3.5] compares the responses of black employees who had less than 15 years seniority and those who had over 15 years, with the responses of white federal employees of similar seniority. Although there is some shifting of opinion, the gap between the responses of black and white federal employees does not grow smaller with the acquisition of seniority. Hence, to the extent that seniority and socialization are interconnected, the latter does not account for the difference between black federal employees and black citizens. To what, then, can these differences be attributed? Although there are insufficient data to answer conclusively, it is logical to assume with Meier, that they are largely the result of recruitment processes which lead some to seek and obtain employment with the government and others to look elsewhere for careers.

Conclusion

This analysis, although limited in scope, strongly suggests that passive bureaucratic representation can serve as a prerequisite for greater active representation. While it is evident that the attitudes of federal employees toward political participation are different from those of the general population, it is also apparent that racial background continues to influence the outlooks of individuals even after they become public bureaucrats. Thus, there are substantial differences between black and white federal servants with regard to matters of political participation. Moreover, these differences parallel those found within the general population. This suggests that while recruitment processes tend to differentiate public bureaucrats from citizens at large, the "passive representatives" of a group are, nevertheless, more likely to reflect the general outlook of their social community than are other bureaucrats. This finding leads to two additional conclusions. First, insofar as we can generalize from this study, the objective of establishing representative public services can be defended on the grounds that a more socially pluralistic public bureaucracy is also likely to be a more politically representative one. The data presented here indicate that, to the extent that an opportunity arises, black public servants are more likely than whites to be able to articulate values and perspectives which are most closely associated with blacks as a social group. Hence, social representation can generate active representation of the groups from which the "passive representatives" come. Thus, a civil service whose personnel comprise a social microcosm of the society as a whole has greater potential to be more representative and responsive to the citizenry than one which is only partly reflective of the population in its composition.

Second, it is evident that we need to know much more about the nature of the links between passive and active representation, and the circumstances in which the latter is likely to emerge concretely in terms of bureaucratic outputs. Even where "passive representatives" desire to become "active representatives," they may have insufficient opportunities to do so or may be ineffective in their efforts. In addition, the orientation of public bureaucrats in this regard is likely to vary with the extent to which they feel a relatively specific social group consciousness. Hence, it is evident that if representativeness and responsiveness are desired in public bureaucracies, assuring a high level of passive representation is only one step. Considerable attention will have to be paid to determining how the potential advantages of passive representation can be realized. This is likely to take us down a long road toward a better understanding of organizational dynamics in public administration.

References

Dresang, D. 1974. "Ethnic Politics, Representative Bureaucracy and Development Administration: The Zambian Case." *American Political Science Review* 68 (December): 1605–1617.

Jennings, M.K. 1969. *The Federal Civil Service Employees Study* (Ann Arbor: ICPR).

Lipset, S. 1952. "Bureaucracy and Social Change," in R. Merton, A. Gray, B. Hockey, and H. Selvin, eds., *Reader in Bureaucracy* (New York: Free Press).

Meier, K. 1975. "Representative Bureaucracy: An Empirical Analysis." *American Political Science Review* 69 (June): 526–542.

Meier, K., and L. Nigro. 1976. "Representative Bureaucracy and Policy Preferences: A Study in the Attitudes of Federal Executives." *Public Administration Review* 36 (July/August): 458–469.

Rosenbloom, D. 1973. "The Civil Service Commission's Decision to Authorize the Use of Goals and Timetables in the Federal Equal Employment Opportunity Program." *Western Political Quarterly* 26 (June): 236–251.

Rosenbloom, D. 1975. "Implementing Equal Employment Opportunity Goals and Timetables in the Federal Service." *Midwest Review of Public Administration* 9 (April/July): 107–120.

Wilson, W. 1941. "The Study of Administration." *Political Science Quarterly* 56 (December): 481–506.

Policy Preferences on Workplace Reform

Mary M. Hale and M. Frances Branch

Differential Impact of Workplace Policies on Women and Men

Instead of being gender-neutral, many public polices often have a differential impact on women and men. This has much to do with the fact that policies often regulate the lives of women differently than they regulate the lives of men (Muncy 1991). Policies also produce unintended consequences, such that solving the problems of one group creates problems for other groups. Examples include policies dealing with family structure, economic development, employment, housing, civil rights enforcement, crime prevention, and the environment. In these areas, policies designed to remediate or prevent problems for government, business, or society disadvantage one sector to advantage another. Policies that promise to produce a win-win situation usually produce a win-draw-lose situation. Policies attempting to promote workplace reform have the same effect.

In the past three decades, American women and men, particularly women, experienced major changes in family structure, career choices, political influence, and economic development roles. It is commonly known that women and men sometimes view, approach, and address issues differently. Such gender differences are reflected in their different views of the world based upon their role in it and how it affects them. Differences show up in women's and men's biases about economic status, their views on competition, and their political preferences.

In this chapter, gender preferences regarding workplace policies important for human resource management are examined. These policies are of interest because they have the potential for promoting individual opportunities for career growth as well as providing a means for public agencies to capitalize on the abilities of capable employees. They are also important because they shine a spotlight on inequalities in benefits and governing power, and they limit, both directly and indirectly, opportunities for employment and advancement.

Trends in Gender Preferences

In response to the changing labor force, human resources management has become increasingly interested in policies involving economic issues such as those revolving around equal employment opportunity, pay equity, and alternative work options such as flex-time, job sharing, work sharing, child care, and leave options. Reflecting the changing circumstances of the work force, these policies are intended to enable organizations to manage their people, time, and space resources more effectively, and to enhance individual opportunities to pursue career development and enrich work experiences.

Gender and policy preferences are linked because contemporary workplace policies differentially advantage one sex over another. In this particular body of research, three research questions are of interest in determining what gender differences, if any, exist among high-level administrators in state government regarding their preferences for various workplace policies:

1. Is there a difference between female and male administrators' support for policies that advance the reality of representative bureaucracy, affirmative action, and prohibition against discrimination?
2. Is there a difference between female and male administrators' support for policies that advance child care, pay equity, job sharing, and flexible work schedules?
3. Is there a difference between female and male administrators' degree of support for "adaption" (doing things better) or innovation (doing things differently)?

Administrators' Preferences

The surveys of public administrators included several workplace policy items pertaining to equal employment opportunity issues and support for child care, pay equity, job sharing, and flexible work schedules. The administrators were asked to indicate a score of 1 to 5 showing their degree of agreement with certain statements. Responses indicated the following: 1 = strongly disagree; 2 = disagree; 3 = neither agree nor disagree; 4 = agree; and 5 = strongly agree.

Table [3.6] shows how women and men differ in their views about representative bureaucracy. The numbers reported represent the mean responses for women and for men. Significance tests were performed to identify statistically significant differences between the sexes.

Table 3.6

Attitudes Toward Representative Bureaucracy

	Women		Men
Statement 1: Employees in state government should reflect the ethnic/racial makeup of the population.			
Alabama	2.95		2.70
Arizona	4.05	*	3.16
Texas	3.20	*	3.10
Utah	3.91	*	3.22
Wisconsin	3.80	*	3.10
Statement 2: Employees in state government should reflect the gender makeup of the population.			
Alabama	2.87	*	2.13
Arizona	4.02	*	2.98
Texas	3.30	*	2.90
Utah	3.99	*	2.94
Wisconsin	3.80	*	3.00

$*p < 0.05$.

In all cases, women showed more support for a representative bureaucracy than men did. In fact, all comparisons were in the same direction. On only the first question, about a representative bureaucracy in terms of its ethnic/racial composition, did one state, Alabama, fail to reach significance. It is noteworthy that in each state men showed more support for the representation of ethnic/racial groups than they did for gender representation. Women, on the other hand, rated both similarly.

Table [3.7] shows how women and men differ in their attitudes toward affirmative action. Notice that, across the board, women favor affirmative action more than men. And men favor affirmative action more for minorities than they do for women in each state except Alabama. The differences reach statistical significance in all comparisons except in Texas with regard to the question about preferential treatment for minorities. The direction of the difference, though, is consistent with that found in the other states.

The uniformity in responses across the states is remarkable. These policy issues, representative bureaucracy and affirmative action, fall along gender lines. Women favor both to a higher degree than do men. The status quo currently favors white men. Obviously, as a group, they stand to lose the most if these two policies were to be fully implemented and this point is not lost on the respondents. These responses are consistent with those appearing in Table [3.8], which presents responses first to a question that inquired into respondents' perception of the status of white males in the work force, and

Table 3.7

Attitudes Toward Affirmative Action

	Women		Men
Statement 3: Females should receive preference where female and male applicants are of equal ability and females are under-represented on a department's work force.			
Alabama	2.90	*	2.58
Arizona	3.74	*	3.01
Texas	3.40	*	2.90
Utah	3.41	*	2.72
Wisconsin	3.80	*	3.00
Statement 4: Minorities should receive preference where applicants are of equal value and minorities are under-represented on a department's work force.			
Alabama	2.81	*	2.31
Arizona	3.79	*	3.18
Texas	3.30		3.10
Utah	3.65	*	2.85
Wisconsin	3.80	*	3.20

*$p < 0.05$.

second, to a question that asked them for a report of their personal experience. Keep in mind that, from the standpoint of an objective observer, all respondents are those "who have made it." They have reached managerial positions that only a small proportion of employees in state agencies ever reach. Also, keep in mind that perceptions, whether or not they reflect reality, have a substantial impact on policy debates.

The scores reveal that while women tend to disagree mildly that white males are sometimes discriminated against, men tend toward agreeing with the statement. Across all states, this difference reached statistical significance. However, when asked whether they believed they personally had been discriminated against, men disagreed fairly strongly compared with their response to the prior perceptual question. In three states, Arizona, Texas, and Utah, women reported significantly more discrimination than men did.

We believe these results send a loud message about the diminishing likelihood of men speaking for women and advancing women's opportunities for equal opportunities for job advancement. These male administrators, who are in decision-making positions and who far outnumber the women, report that, even in the face of personal experience to the contrary, men are discriminated against in hiring and promotion. Since perceptions, with or without facts at hand, color policy debates, this is an omen with which women must reckon.

Table 3.8

Attitudes Toward Personal Discrimination

	Women		Men

Statement 5: White males are sometimes discriminated against in either hiring or promotion.

	Women		Men
Alabama	2.43	*	3.37
Arizona	2.50	*	3.04
Texas	2.40	*	3.40
Utah	1.88	*	2.68
Wisconsin	3.00	*	3.80

Statement 6: I personally believe that I have been discriminated against in either hiring or promotion.

	Women		Men
Alabama	2.08		2.01
Arizona	2.69	*	1.88
Texas	2.60	*	2.20
Utah	2.71	*	1.87
Wisconsin	2.20		2.40

*$p < 0.05$.

Now we turn to attitudes on workplace reform. The policy areas include child care, pay equity, job sharing, and flexible work schedules; these are issues that are usually framed as "women's issues." Table [3.9] shows the level of support for these reforms among women and men who have made it into administrative ranks most likely without benefit of these.

As Kawar (1989, p. 100) has noted, "these issues have been unsuccessful in receiving legislative consideration at either the state or federal levels. Pay equity and child care have occasionally been placed on the federal agenda but no national policy has evolved." While both women and men demonstrated support for all four policies related to workplace reform, women were substantially more supportive, suggesting that as decision makers, they would make a difference in the outcome of policy debates over these issues if their voices were to be heard.

The importance of child care is generally agreed upon by both women and men, although women support it significantly more than men. Women and men in all states were most supportive of pay equity, although there were significant differences between the sexes in each state surveyed. Perhaps support for this policy is strong because if it were to be enacted, everybody would win. Women would be helped personally by pay equity since their pay would increase, and married men would be helped indirectly by the increased salaries that their wives would bring home. Job sharing was favored more

Table 3.9

Support for Workplace Reform

	Women		Men
Statement 7: I personally support issues related to child care.			
Alabama	3.96	*	3.56
Arizona	4.40	*	3.76
Texas	4.30	*	3.40
Utah	4.43	*	3.77
Wisconsin	3.50	*	3.10
Statement 8: I personally support issues related to pay equity.			
Alabama	4.58	*	4.12
Arizona	4.69	*	4.23
Texas	4.80	*	4.40
Utah	4.76	*	4.41
Wisconsin	3.60	*	3.00
Statement 9: I personally support issues related to job sharing.			
Alabama	3.84		3.56
Arizona	4.25	*	3.56
Texas	4.10	*	3.60
Utah	4.50	*	3.99
Wisconsin	3.90		3.70
Statement 10: I personally support issues related to flexible work schedules.			
Alabama	4.13	*	3.71
Arizona	4.38	*	3.97
Texas	4.30	*	3.40
Utah	4.65	*	4.20
Wisconsin	4.20		4.00

*$p < 0.05$.

strongly by women than by men to the point that a statistically significant difference occurred between the sexes in their degree of support for it in Arizona, Texas, and Utah. Women favored flexible work schedules significantly more than men did in Alabama, Arizona, Texas, and Utah.

In spite of the fact that women tended to favor these reforms significantly more than men did, men nevertheless showed support across the board. Perhaps this is a sign that these reforms are becoming less of a "women's issue" and more of a "family issue" across the states. The consistent and statistically significant differences shown in Tables [3.6] through [3.9] provide evidence that gender patterns exist with regard to support for various policies. We are led to speculate, then, that with more women gaining entrance to decision-making posts in state government, it is more likely that these policies will be seriously discussed and will find their way onto the legislative agenda in the near future.

These gender differences inevitably reflect different views on the best way to bring about change. Since government is the engine that drives change in this nation, we can anticipate that, as the demand for workplace reform increases, the role of government in making it happen will increase. And since the respondents to this survey are already in the engine, it is even more likely that such changes will take place.

There are indications that the policies that will eventually be adopted will represent less "adaption" and more "innovation." The survey data show that there is strong support among women for workplace reforms that would decrease the negative impact that family responsibilities have on their careers. Because of this, there is a likelihood that women will reject slower modes of change and insist upon innovation. The fact that men also favor these policies further heightens this likelihood. And, finally, the fact remains that these issues are already bubbling to the surface and are being discussed. For example, alternative work options have been experimented with in several settings and this interest, coupled with the fact that more and more women are entering the labor force, promises to leave the door open to more innovations. . . .

The Influence of Gender on Policy Preferences

There are two explanations that provide a foundation for understanding how gender affects workplace policy preferences. The first, in which gender is viewed as a dependent variable [*sic*], is socialization. Previous studies have shown that socialization likely explains men's concerns and preferences for individual rights and self-interest and women's concerns for interdependence, responsibility, and compassion (Gilligan 1982; McClelland 1975).

The second explanation, using gender as an intervening variable, has to do with differences in prior work experiences. . . . [F]emale administrators are more likely to have had experience in the helping agencies. Having direct work and life experience dealing with peoples' problems with daily living is likely to allow women to be more sensitive to the needs of people as compared with their male counterparts, who may be more accustomed to dealing with impersonal concerns such as highway construction or tax collection.

This difference in work experience is likely to lead to gender differences in the preferences or priorities for various workplace agenda items. As Kingdon (1984, p. 101) notes, topics sometimes become prominent agenda items "partly because important policy makers have personal experiences that bring the subject to their attention." While strategies that facilitate child care, pay equity, job sharing, and flex-time, are important in addressing and confronting the responsibilities facing both women and men, they will have the most salience for women who fit either of the following categories:

1. women who have historically had to choose between obligating themselves to family responsibilities or work in ways men have not;
2. women whose potential for full-time employment and career advancement has been affected by barriers erected because of their sex.

There are several implications of gender differences regarding policy preferences. The first has to do with the relationship between gender recruitment into educational and employment settings and agenda change. In the agenda-setting state of the policy process, women and men may differ over whether and to what degree a problem should be a concern for government. As Kingdon (1984, p. 160) notes, agenda change occurs either because "incumbents in positions of authority change their priorities and push new agenda items; or the personnel in those positions changes, bringing new priorities onto the agenda by virtue of the turnover." As the number of women and their visible participation in decision-making positions (Kingdon's "visible cluster") increases, the chances of particular subjects being given a higher priority on a governmental agenda are enhanced.

Similarly, women's growing presence in graduate public administration programs that turn out trained female administrators is likely to influence long-term agenda setting. As their careers develop, graduates achieve influential decision-making posts in government and are able to affect policy choices. Agencies that hire and promote women as administrators in significant numbers are likely to recognize different policy agendas and outcomes than those that remain dominated by men. The support for decisions made regarding these policies, including which alternatives and solutions are aired, is affected by who the participants are and which problems are on their minds (Kingdon 1984).

The second implication of gender differences has to do with their potential political importance in the workplace. Over the past thirty years, women have developed powerful social and political voices. Their voices and votes play a critical role in mass opinion, politics, and government. With women's continuing move into administrative positions, it is likely that their "preference power," combined with their knowledge of the policy process and their skills for mentoring and coalition building can be used to advance workplace reform. Their influence can make a difference both in the types of policies proposed and in the outcome of these policies.

The third implication is that organizations with more flexible workplace policies will be better able to facilitate the recruitment and retention of valuable employees. They will also be able to enhance overall morale and thereby increase their vitality. Unlike changes to provide pay equity and child care, which are more adaptive in nature, options such as flex-time and job sharing require organizational innovation. While men appear to support the innovative policies more than the adaptive policies, it is important to realize that the innovations they support are more applicable to men than are the adaptions. . . .

Conclusion

These research findings are offered with three caveats. First, while the number of state agencies with a significant number of women in the upper grade levels is increasing, there are still agencies and departments with no women in these top grades. Until women become, and are recognized as, powerful actors in the policy arena, their ability to influence the allocation process will continue to lag significantly behind that of men. Second, while public administrators are able to influence the policy process by direct involvement (that is, allocate public resources and guide implementation), they may or may not be direct policy makers (in the form of elected officials or political appointees). To understand the full impact of gender preferences on policies, this research should be replicated with other policy makers and political elites in elective, judicial, and appointive offices. Third, it is important to consider the many constraints bounding the policy stream. Participants in the policy process, including administrators, are not free or neutral actors; rather, "their actions are limited by the mood of the mass public and the preferences of specialized publics and elected politicians" (Kingdon 1984, p. 217).

Despite the fact that women still have a long way to go in achieving their rightful place in state government, sufficient progress has been made to allow us to ask whether female administrators make a difference. The support of the majority of administrators reported in this chapter for policy issues of child care, pay equity, job sharing, and flexible work schedules is sufficient to suggest optimism for future workplace reforms. The findings suggest that, among these decision makers, concern about these issues currently exists. Women's greater degree of support is likely to continue for two reasons: the historical view that these are "women's issues" has assisted women's success in building a strong political base, and women show no signs of giving up on promoting their interests. Since women are comprising a growing proportion of the work force, their continued involvement will make a difference on the outcome of these issues.

The link between gender and policy preferences observed in this research shows that gender differences exist and there is the potential to shape workplace policies of the future. Attention to these differences may allow workplace policies to be more inclusive in consideration of both societal segments—women and men—and may indeed be the driving force behind changes in workplace alternatives. The financial and economic impact of the policy areas examined in this research directly affect all members of society. In recognizing the importance of family and personal responsibilities faced by both women and men in the work force, we must attend to finding alternatives. Public work and private lives must inevitably blend to a greater degree than they currently do.

References

Gilligan, C. 1982. *In a Different Voice*. Cambridge, MA: Harvard University.

Kawar, A. 1989. "Women in the Utah Executive Branch of Government." In *Gender, Bureaucracy and Democracy: Careers and Equal Opportunity in the Public Sector*, ed. M.M. Hale and R.M. Kelly. Westport, CT: Greenwood.

Kingdon, J. W. 1984. *Agendas, Alternatives, and Public Policies*. Glenview, IL: Scott, Foresman.

McClelland, D.C. 1975. *Power: The Inner Experience*. New York: Irvington.

Muncy, R. 1991. *Creating a Female Dominion in American Reform*. New York: Oxford University Press.

Discussion Questions

1. Under what conditions is it more or less likely that bureaucrats' attitudes will be translated to actual behavior? Are all attitudes relevant to administrative behavior? Which attitudes would you argue are most relevant to administrative behavior and processes? Which are least relevant?

2. Does attitude congruence between bureaucrats and ordinary people guarantee that bureaucrats will make decisions that reflect the public interest? Why or why not?

3. Why do you think existing studies have reached different conclusions about the relationship between social origins and attitudes? What might explain the different findings?

4. None of the studies excerpted here examine bureaucratic attitudes at more than one point in time. Does this present any problems? If you were going to design a study to assess bureaucrats' attitudes and how they may or may not be affected by organizational socialization, how might you do so?

5. Do life experiences really differ all that much according to social origins? Or is it possible that differences within a social group are more substantial than those between groups?

Chapter 4

Social Background, Life Experience, and Policy Advocacy

Why Do Civil Servants Act on Policy Preferences Derived from Their Social Backgrounds and Life Experiences?

The third piece of the representative bureaucracy puzzle posits that administrators' attitudes ultimately affect their eventual policy decisions. If we presume that individuals from different backgrounds develop different attitudes (as discussed in chapter 3), we then expect that these different attitudes will produce positive policy outcomes for different social groups. This chapter focuses on the link between social origins and policy outputs and on the links between social origins, attitudes, and policy outputs, drawing from a number of empirical studies that explore the connection between bureaucrats' social backgrounds, their attitudes, and the decisions they ultimately make as public administrators.

We begin this chapter with an early theoretical piece written by Frank J. Thompson. Some thirty years after it was originally published, this piece continues to inform and shape debate over which conditions facilitate and which hinder the link between passive and active representation in American bureaucracies. Thompson provides a solid foundation for future research by specifying the conditions under which public administrators are likely to press for policy outcomes that benefit members of their own social group and when they are not likely to do so. As he explains, linkage between passive and active representation "is, at least in part, a function of conditions in the organization's environment, the issue area under consideration, the mobilization of employees into organized groups, and the positional and physical location of minority civil servants within the agency." He also cautions scholars to remember that "an impressive array of influences can debilitate linkage between passive and active representation." Many of the following articles cite his work and specify their models to take into account his arguments (see also Meier [1993] for an updated discussion).

The remaining articles focus on the extent to which the racial or gender composition of a public bureaucracy affects its policy outputs. In choosing pieces for inclusion, we have attempted to provide balanced coverage of three things: the locale in which the bureaucracy is situated (state or federal government), the type of administrator under study (street-level, management, or executive) and the social origin of the administrator (race and/or gender). Until very recently, most empirical research has focused on the link between social origins and policy outputs, entirely bypassing the role of attitudes in the mix. In other words, instead of assessing whether individual administrators' social origins first shape attitudes and then affect policy outputs in predictable ways, the middle step has generally been omitted and administrators' social origins have been directly linked to policy outputs. Examples of such work include Meier and Stewart (1992), reprinted here, and Hindera (1993a, 1993b). The piece by Meier and Stewart (1992) is widely recognized as the very first study in the field of representative bureaucracy to link social origins of bureaucrats to their eventual policy decisions. They focus on African American street-level bureaucrats (teachers) and managers (principals) in state educational bureaucracies to test whether the proportion of black teachers or principals in a school district affects the educational outcomes for black students in that district. In doing so, they conclude that "bureaucrats are able to influence not only public policy outputs but also public policy outcomes in predicted ways."

More recent research examines whether or not attitudes intervene between social origins and policy outputs (Naff 1998; Selden et al. 1998; Selden 1997). Although the work in this area is still preliminary and examines only a few different types of public organizations, some inconsistencies are already apparent. Reprinted here, Selden et al. (1998) probe the relationship among social origins, attitudes about assisting minorities, and eventual policy outputs. In doing so, they find that minority administrators are more likely to feel a special responsibility to advocate minority interests, attitudes that seem consistent with behaving as an active representative for one's own social group. When they turn to these administrators' behavior, however, they find that attitudes are a significant predictor of behavior while race is not. In other words, agreeing that one has a special responsibility to minorities is of greater importance than one's racial background. Katherine C. Naff's work, also reprinted here, reaches different conclusions. Using self-reported measures of policy attitudes and behavior, she finds that Hispanic supervisors in the federal government are more likely than non-Hispanic administrators to make efforts to recruit and hire Hispanic individuals, almost regardless of their own attitudes about the value of having a racially diverse work force. What is most interesting is that she finds, contrary to Selden et al. (1998), that Hispanics do not differ all that much from non-Hispanic whites in their attitudes about the importance of a representative bureaucracy, but nonetheless, they behave in ways that are consistent with representative bureaucracy theory. That is, Hispanics are more likely than non-Hispanic whites to recruit other Hispanics for employment within the federal government, even if they do not agree that having a broadly representative bureaucracy is a worthwhile and important goal. This suggests that Hispanic identity, or social origins, may exert greater influence over behavior than do attitudes.

A couple of final notes: First, some discussion of Frederick Mosher's distinction between active and passive representation appears in the original text of just about every piece we have included in this chapter. For the sake of conserving space, and because we have excerpted Mosher's exact words in chapter 1, we have generally omitted such discussion from the excerpted articles reprinted in this chapter. Second, without a doubt this chapter contains the most statistically sophisticated articles in the bunch. Where possible, we have omitted some of the more complex statistical language and discussion of methodological concerns at the same time being careful to preserve the logic and findings of each original piece (of course readers can consult the originals for all of the methodological details).

References

Hindera, John J. 1993a. "Representative Bureaucracy: Further Evidence of Active Representation in the EEOC District Offices." *Journal of Public Administration Research and Theory* 3 (4): 415–429.

Hindera, John J. 1993b. "Representative Bureaucracy: Imprimis Evidence of Active Representation in the EEOC District Offices." *Social Science Quarterly* 74 (1): 95–108.

Meier, Kenneth J. 1993. "Representative Bureaucracy: A Theoretical and Empirical Exposition." In *Research in Public Administration*, vol. 2, ed. James L. Perry. New Greenwich, CT: JAI Press.

Meier, Kenneth J., and Joseph Stewart, Jr. 1992. "The Impact of Representative Bureaucracies: Educational Systems and Public Policies." *American Review of Public Administration* 22 (September): 157–171.

Naff, Katherine. 1998. "Progress Toward Achieving a Representative Federal Bureaucracy: The Impact of Supervisors and their Beliefs." *Public Personnel Management* 27 (Summer): 135–150.

Selden, Sally Coleman. 1997. *The Promise of Representative Bureaucracy: Diversity and Responsiveness in a Government Agency*. Armonk, NY: M.E. Sharpe.

Seldon, Sally Coleman, Jeffrey Brodney, and J. Edward Kellough. 1998. "Bureaucracy as a Representative Institution: Toward a Reconciliation of Bureaucratic Government and Democratic Theory." *American Journal of Political Science* 42 (July): 719–744.

Minority Groups in Public Bureaucracies: Are Passive and Active Representation Linked?

Frank J. Thompson

The purpose of this essay is to examine the relationship between passive and active representation of minority racial groups within governmental bureaucracies in the United States. At present, there is considerable disagreement over the degree to which greater passive representation of a minority group contributes to its active representation. Rosenbloom (1973, 250), for instance, concludes that in the United States we probably assume too much when we take it for granted that increased hiring of minorities "will have more than marginal impact on active representation." Kranz (1974, 435), however, suggests that once employed, minorities "as a group will more closely mirror the needs and wishes of their group, whether overtly or subconsciously, than non-minorities do." Mosher notes only that the linkage between passive and active representation is complex and enigmatic.

In order to shed some light on this linkage, I have conducted an exhaustive search of the literature. Unfortunately, existing analyses deal only tangentially with race and active representation in bureaucracies; a disproportionate amount of evidence concerns only certain kinds of minorities in certain occupations, and much of the data derives from studies with serious methodological flaws. Still, the available evidence is sufficiently rich to permit informed speculation about the link between passive and active representation.

First, however, a more precise statement of the problem is essential. What, in fact, does it mean to say that civil servants actively represent their racial communities? Supplementing Mosher's initial definition with Hanna Pitkin's (1967, 113–143) concept of representation as "acting for," some clarification is possible. The concept of active, or substantive, representation means more than an administrator sympathizing with his/her racial group; it means

---

From Frank J. Thompson, "Minority Groups in Public Bureaucracies: Are Passive and Action Representation Linked?" *Administration and Society*, August 1976, 202–205; 212–218. Copyright © 1976 by Sage Publications. Reprinted with permission from Sage Publications, Inc.

more than an official having the same values as that group. Instead, it focuses on the actual behavior of officials, on whether they act for or on behalf of their racial communities. Beyond this, precise definition of active representation poses a thorny problem. Is it active representation when administrators do what the majority of their race wants? Or does active representation occur when administrators promote the "real interests" of their group regardless of what group members want? The debate among political philosophers continues; there is no simple solution. For present purposes, I will assume that behavior actively represents a racial community when it increases the wealth, prestige, or other advantages associated with belonging to that race. I intend this definition to be a relatively broad one. In this regard, I am assuming that "other advantages" include less tangible benefits such as having better access to empathetic, respectful treatment from police officers, health professionals, and the like. While there are alternative definitions, the one chosen comes close to common notions of representation. Moreover, at least one study has shown that this definition is conducive to operationalizing the concept.

Utilizing this conception of active representation, the question remains: are minority civil servants more likely to represent the substantive interests of their racial communities than are their white counterparts? Answering this question requires reconciliation of two opposing sets of arguments and data. . . .

The Skeptical Perspective

The literature of organization theory, public administration, and related fields is replete with reasons for doubting that greater passive representation of a racial group will beget greater active representation. One alleged barrier to linkage is work socialization. Such socialization presumably washes out special sympathies civil servants initially felt toward their racial groups. Jobs, after all, shape values. Prolonged exposure to certain organizational culture, a specific set of role expectations, and a particular array of professional associations tends to breed a similar Weltanschauung among employees (Janowitz 1960; Kaufman 1971; Meier and Nigro 1975; Skolnick 1967). This job socialization helps explain why high-level officials from different class origins, different regions of the country, and different backgrounds often have similar policy orientations (Garnham 1975; Meier and Nigro 1975).

Lack of sufficient numbers of minorities in high-level posts is, presumably, a second roadblock. Even if nonwhite officials sympathize more with their racial communities than officials of other origins, they may not be in a position to help.

Third, the possibility of formal organizational sanctions may inhibit substantive representation (Meier 1975, 528, 542). Sanctions may assume overtly punitive forms as with discipline. Even minor gestures of sympathy by public servants toward members of their own race can provoke swift punishment. Thus, a black policeman in Oakland, California, attempted to relate to minority youth by giving the clenched fist salute as he cruised in a patrol car. His partner soon complained, and the police chief later reprimanded the black officer. After a series of other skirmishes with the police hierarchy, the black policeman left the department. Sanctions may also assume more covert forms such as being passed over for promotion. Nonwhite administrators who wish to join the upper echelons posses[s] a strong incentive to behave in ways congenial to those who do the promoting, most of whom are white. In this vein, one student of the racial situation in the military notes: "While increasing minority cultural diversity will be apparent in the armed services, officers and enlisted men who rise to the top ranks now and in future years will tend to be those lifetime careerists who most closely emulate the central professional ideals and values of the service" (Stillman 1974, 227). Thus, if more minorities win top jobs, active representation of the nonwhite community may still not increase much.

Peer pressures, presumably, comprise a fourth barrier to active representation. The pressures placed on members of a primary group to conform are notorious. When people belong to a primary work group which has norms that run counter to their values, even officials sympathetic to their race are unlikely to promote its interests.

A fifth factor which could inhibit representative action is uncertainty. Ignorance may shroud goals, means, or both (see, e.g., Hawley 1974; Lipsky 1972). With respect to goal uncertainty, officials from a racial group may face the quandary of discerning just what the proper racial perspective is with respect to their agency's mission. In attempting to pick up cues from his or her racial community, the administrator may encounter silence or a gaggle of conflicting views. Two observers of black elected officials note, for example, that "the demands and expectations of their black constituents are often amorphous, incoherent, inarticulate, conflicting and contradictory. Black elected administrators are therefore faced with the problem of rendering articulate the inarticulate interests of their constituents" (Nelson and Van Horne 1974, 530). Uncertainty over means can also plague officials. Social engineering in many policy arenas is still primitive. For example, it is one thing to commit oneself to teaching disadvantaged students; it is another to succeed. Where there is a will, there need not be an obvious way, or even any way.

At least ostensibly, then, a strong case can be made that passive representation will fail to foster active representation. . . .

Reconciliation: Some Sources of Linkage

... The appropriate question is less *whether* a link exists than *under what circumstances* it exists. Ideally, it would be useful to construct a model which specifies these circumstances, the degree of active representation which they promote, and the precise causal dynamics involved. Unfortunately, the available evidence cannot sustain such a full-blown model. It is, however, possible to suggest some intervening factors which tend to affect whether passive-active linkage will occur in the case of minorities. As will become apparent in the discussion which follows, linkage is, at least in part, a function of conditions in the organization's environment, the issue area under consideration, the mobilization of employees into organized groups, and the positional and physical location of minority civil servants within the agency.

The Environmental Factor.

1. *Linkage is more likely when institutions and groups in society articulate an ideology of minority pride and press for the advancement of minority interests.* What occurs in bureaucracy cannot be detached from trends and forces in society. During the sixties and on into the seventies, many racial groups in the United States became more aggressive politically and began to develop a new sense of pride in their respective heritages. The slogan "black is beautiful" conjures up much of the spirit.

The growing presence of racial pride has probably increased the link between passive and active representation. For when a racial group lacks pride in its origins, civil servants from that group will more readily feel ashamed of their backgrounds. They will be more driven internally to play down their racial roots and to assimilate. To this end, civil servants may ferret out feelings of sympathy for their racial group and shuck off as many accoutrements of their origin (e.g., speech patterns, styles of dress) as they can. Pride in race can help counteract these tendencies. It can stiffen resistance to white peer groups that seek to impose their frame of values on minority employees. It can make minority civil servants more willing to risk organizational sanctions on behalf of representing their racial community. In fact, racial pride may strengthen the resolve of minority officials to change the organizational definition of what behavior is to be sanctioned. In the case of a police department, for instance, minority officials may convince their peers and superiors that "rapping" with black juveniles while on duty is not a tactic to avoid serious police work or a sign of disloyalty toward the rest of the department. In sum, pride in racial identity may give minority employees the strength to combat the very forces that often retard linkage between passive and active representation.

In a related vein, the presence of politically mobilized minority groups in the society can also mute the impact of those forces which work against linkage. Not only can such groups keep racial perspectives salient, they may at times blow the whistle on specific nonwhite officials who depart from the "appropriate" perspective on an issue. Minority administrators may, therefore, become more inclined to represent their racial group for fear of being denounced (e.g., called Oreo, Red Apple, or worse) or for fear of precipitating movements to remove them from office. Such concerns are likely to be prominent among minorities who are higher administrators, since these officials are more visible targets for minority activists in the community.

Political mobilization by minority groups and the development of an ethos of racial pride may well help explain some of the apparent contradictions in the data presented earlier. Consider the studies by Reiss (1973) and Alex (1969), which suggest that black police officers are just as harsh in dealing with black citizens as white officers. Alex's data derive from interviews conducted in late 1964 and in 1965. Reiss' assistants gathered information during the summer of 1966. Thus, both of the studied groups contained few individuals who had been educated and undergone formative socialization during a time when minority political activism and the ethos of black pride were fully in bloom. In fact, most of the black officers in the study groups probably grew to maturity during the decade of the fifties. Were Alex and Reiss to conduct the same studies today, their results might well reveal that black officers nurture less punitive orientations toward black offenders. This result would be especially likely if their new samples were to include younger black officers who graduated from high school in the late sixties and early seventies.

Issue Area.

2. *Linkage is more likely when minority officials deal with issues which have patent ramifications for the well-being of their race.* Means-ends uncertainty can be a formidable barrier to minority civil servants bent on representing their racial group. But such uncertainty need not invariably be a problem. Much depends on the issue area involved. Certain agencies tend to deal with issues which have fairly clear implications for the minority employee who wishes to help his or her group. Those involved in planning eligibility requirements for public welfare may, for instance, possess a relatively lucid understanding of what policies will foster the interest of their racial community. By contrast, minorities who work for an agency like the Maritime Administration probably see fewer connections between many of their decisions and the benefits received by blacks, Chicanos, or other minorities.

Issues which directly collide with the self-interest of the minority employee are especially likely to trigger a link between active and passive representation (see Downs 1967). Black officers' groups, for example, stress both the elimination of racism in internal personnel processes and in the provision of service to the minority community. To no one's surprise, they usually place greater emphasis on personnel matters. Reducing racial barriers to successful careers in the bureaucracies where they work is, of course, of utmost personal advantage to these civil servants. The fact that their behavior is self-serving should not disguise its substantively representative character, however. Battles won in reducing job discrimination in bureaucracies often set precedents which enlarge employment opportunities for an entire race.

Employee Mobilization.

3. *Linkage is more likely when minority employee associations exist in an agency.* These associations can embed the minority civil servant in a peer group which encourages and reinforces any inclination to help the civil servant's racial community. In this and other ways, such associations serve as socializing agents—making employees more aware of racial perspectives on an issue. Moreover, these groups at times provide protection against those inside the bureaucracy who pose a threat. Racial organizations may offer legal help, publicly denounce those who attack one of their members, or use some other form of reprisal.

Positional and Physical Location.

4. *Linkage is more likely when minorities occupy discretionary jobs, especially if those jobs are in the lower echelons.* Capture of positions where incumbents possess the discretion to shape the delivery of important services is also crucial if the passive representation of a minority group is to contribute to its active representation. As emphasized previously, significant discretion often exists at the bottom of the hierarchy (e.g., among counselors) as well as at the top. In fact, members of the lower ranks who occupy discretionary positions are probably more inclined to represent their racial communities than their superiors. These minority employees have usually been exposed to the homogenizing influences of work socialization for shorter periods than their superiors and, consequently, have had less opportunity to become "organization" men and women. By contrast, minority officials who hold top-level posts will often have had to incorporate the standards of white officials into their value hierarchies in order to rise in the bureaucracies.

5. *Linkage is more likely when members of a minority group work in close proximity to one another.* Proximity can also give birth to a link between passive and active representation. Interaction among members of a minority group increases where agencies are racially homogeneous. This interaction can serve as midwife to distinct racial perspectives on questions of policy. Peer pressure against speaking out for racial interests can shift in just the opposite direction. Civil servants who are aggressive advocates for their racial community may well face fewer organization sanctions in such a context.

Although proximity, on the whole, probably produces greater linkage, it is important to note that under some circumstances a paradox can arise. Suppose minority officials primarily cluster in one agency while white employees prevail in other units. In such a case, it will be easier for those who wield power to use the minority agency for symbolic or showcase purposes and to center important decision-making authority in white units. Thus, minority civil servants, as a result of their intermingling, may try harder to represent their racial group than they would in a more integrated setting. But as a result of their segregation, they may have fewer resources with which to exert influence. Their efforts at active representation may, therefore, abort. Nonetheless, *other things being equal*, it seems plausible that minority employees who interact more frequently with other civil servants of their own race will more readily foster active representation.

In sum, then, there is no sense in denying that an impressive array of influences can debilitate linkage between passive and active representation. Of equal importance, however, is the fact that other circumstances can help counteract these influences. These countervailing factors can be environmental (e.g., a pervasive ethos of racial pride within a social group, vigorous minority groups in the community). They can also be organizational—having to do with the issue area under consideration, the mobilization of minority employees within the agency, and the positional and physical location of these employees. Future research will, it is hoped, specify additional factors conducive to linkage and expedite development of a model.

References

Alex, N. 1969. *Black in Blue*. New York: Appleton-Century-Crofts.

Downs, A. 1967. *Inside Bureaucracy*. Boston: Little, Brown.

Garnham, D. 1975. "Foreign Service Elitism and U.S. Foreign Affairs." *Public Administration Review* 35 (January/February): 44–51.

Hawley, W.D. 1974. "The Possibilities of Nonbureaucratic Organizations," 371–425 in W.D. Hawley and D. Rogers (eds.), *Improving the Quality of Urban Management*. Beverly Hills, Calif.: Sage.

Janowitz, M. 1960. *The Professional Soldier*. New York: Free Press.

Kaufman, H. 1971. *The Limits of Organizational Change*. University: University of Alabama Press.

Kranz, H. 1974. "Are Merit and Equity Compatible?" *Public Administration Review* 34 (September/October): 434–439.

Lipsky, M. 1972. "Street-level Bureaucracy and the Analysis of Urban Reform," 171–184 in V.S. Ermer and J.H. Strange (eds.), *Blacks and Bureaucracy*. New York: Thomas Y. Crowell.

Meier, K.J. 1975. "Representative Bureaucracy: An Empirical Analysis." *American Political Science Review* 69 (June): 526–542.

Meier, K.J. and L.G. Nigro. 1975. "Representative Bureaucracy and Policy Prefer-

ences: A Study in the Attitudes of Federal Executives." Presented at the Annual
    Meeting of the American Political Science Association, San Francisco.
Mosher, F.C. 1968. *Democracy and the Public Service.* New York: Oxford University
    Press.
Nelson, W.E., Jr., and W. Van Horne. 1974. "Black Elected Administrators: The Trials
    of Office." *Public Administration Review* 34 (November/December): 526–533.
Pitkin, H.F. 1967. *The Concept of Representation.* Berkeley: University of California
    Press.
Reiss, A.J. 1973. "How Much Police Brutality Is There?" 269–288 in S.M. David and
    P.E. Peterson (eds.), *Urban Politics and Public Policy.* New York: Praeger.
Rosenbloom, D. 1973. "The Civil Service Commission's Decision to Authorize the
    Use of Goals and Timetables in the Federal Equal Employment Opportunity Pro-
    gram." *Western Political Quarterly* 26 (June): 231–251.
Skolnick, J. 1967. *Justice Without Trial.* New York: John Wiley.
Stillman, R. II. 1974. "Racial Unrest in the Military: The Challenge and the Response."
    Public Administration Review 34 (May/June): 221–229.

The Impact of Representative Bureaucracies: Educational Systems and Public Policies

Kenneth J. Meier and Joseph Stewart, Jr.

Representative bureaucracy is a core topic of public administration research. Although a representative bureaucracy is supposed to make the administrative arm of government responsive to the public it serves (Kingsley 1944; Levitan 1946; Long 1952; Mosher 1968), a variety of methodological problems (Saltzstein 1979) have prevented scholars from examining whether representative bureaucracies produce policy outputs different from other bureaucracies. Many studies examine the representativeness of bureaucracies in terms of race, sex, or other demographic factors (Meier 1975; Grabowsky and Rosenbloom 1976; Hall and Saltzstein 1977; Cayer and Sigelman 1980; Dometrius and Sigelman 1984; Henderson and Preston 1984). Others studies treat bureaucracies as the dependent variable, examining the determinants of demographic representation (Stein 1986; Mladenka 1989; Kellough 1990a, 1990b). Still other studies, though fewer in number, address the representativeness of policy-relevant attitudes (Meier and Nigro 1976; Rosenbloom and Featherstonhaugh 1977; Thompson 1978; Lewis 1990; Garand, Parkhurst, and Seoud 1991). This study goes beyond previous work to address the neglected relationship between representative bureaucracies and policy outputs and outcomes. What does government do differently if the bureaucracies implementing public policy are more or less representative? Are members of a disadvantaged group "better off" when individuals who share that group's distinguishing characteristic are present in a bureaucracy that affects their lives? This analysis offers an answer to these queries using data from 67 Florida public school districts. Specifically, it examines whether educational bureaucracies with different levels of black representation produce policies that have differential effects on black students. . . .

Data, Measurement, and Methods

Thompson (1976, 215) argues that passive and active representation are linked only when certain key conditions are met. First, the link is more likely when minority officials "deal with issues which have patent ramifications for the well-being of their race." Thus, it can be clear in which instances the bureaucrats are or are not being representative. For example, Thompson notes that minority bureaucrats in the Maritime Administration would be hard pressed to find decisions where they could affect the well-being of the minority community. Second, Thompson argues that the link is more likely to be present where minorities work in close proximity to each other; and, third, where minorities occupy jobs that are discretionary (Thompson 1976, 216–217). Fourth, Thompson says that discretionary jobs at lower levels of the bureaucracy are the most important because they are less likely to be subject to the amount of agency socialization that high-level administrators would be. Although some studies highlight lower level employees' exercising important discretion (e.g., police [Skolnick 1966] and surface mine inspectors [Hedge, Menzel, and Williams 1988]), this position is in contrast to much of the literature, which focuses on policy-making positions at higher levels in the bureaucracy (Meier and Nigro 1976).

The public school systems in Florida are ideal environments in which to study the link between active and passive representation for several reasons. First, these governmental bodies implement policies that are crucial to blacks' ability to earn a living (Duncan 1984, 109–110). This fact and the struggle necessary to achieve the level of desegregation that has been attained leave no doubt that education has "patent ramifications" for the lives of blacks.

Second, data on the representativeness of school personnel are readily available. Each school district reports the racial distribution of its teachers, principals, and other positions to the State Department of Education. The data allow analysis of the effects of employing varying levels of minority educators.

Third, both teachers and principals make discretionary decisions that directly affect the welfare of minority students and, in the long run, the interests of the minority community as a whole. Florida school systems collect a wide variety of data on these decisions. This study looks at two sets of decisions—ability grouping and discipline. Ability grouping is the classification of students according to perceived abilities. This form of grouping is a major issue because the quality of education provided to the higher ranked groups is superior to that provided to the lower ranked groups (Oakes 1985). Racial biases in grouping have been litigated and are the focus of substantial political pressures (Meier, Stewart, and England 1989). The ability-grouping categories used in this study are classes for the educable mentally retarded (EMR), classes for the trainable mentally retarded (TMR), and classes for the gifted. A hypothesis of active representation links higher levels of black principals and black teachers with lower levels of black students in EMR and TMR classes and higher levels of black students in gifted classes. However, because TMR classes are a more "severe" categorization of students, bureaucratic discretion in the placement of students in such classes should be more limited than for EMR classes (Meier, Stewart, and England 1989, 97–98). Thus, the impact of representative bureaucracy is likely to be mitigated for TMR classes.

Discipline, though necessary to maintain an orderly learning environment, is in some cases used to discourage students from continuing to attend school (Fernandez and Guskin 1981). Like academic grouping, racial biases in discipline also have been litigated and are subject to major protests by the black community. Five disciplinary actions are studied here: corporal punishment, in-school suspensions, out-of-school suspensions, expulsions, and referral to courts for prosecution. Active representation should mean that greater black representation will result in fewer black students being disciplined. This relationship might result because black teachers and administrators are less likely to impose discipline in racially biased ways or because black student behavior could change in response to the presence of black role models.

Fourth, this study can determine if representation among management-level (principals) or lower level (teachers) bureaucrats is more likely to lead to active representation. The result allows for a direct test of Thompson's (1976) notion.

Finally, this study goes beyond even previous studies of the impact of representativeness in school systems by looking at educational outcomes. Florida school districts are required to give achievement tests to students in the third, fifth, eighth, and tenth grades (two tests for the tenth grade). Data are available on test scores by race for each of the school districts. Test scores are policy outcomes rather than policy outputs. Policy outputs (distributions in classes, discipline, etc.) can be affected directly by decision makers. Although decision makers try to affect policy outcomes (student performance), they may not be able to because student performance is affected by a variety of factors outside the control of teachers, principals, and even the school system. As a result, representative bureaucracy is not expected to have large impacts on policy outcomes.

This test of representative bureaucracy examines 15 dependent variables in three classes: grouping, discipline, and performance. For each of these variables, it is necessary to compute equity measures. To do this, a ratio is calculated in which the probability that a black student will be assigned to a class, subjected to punishment, or perform at a certain level is divided by the probability that any student at random will be so treated or will so perform. This yields the "odds" that a black student will be in the category under consideration given the overall rate of such categorization in the school system. This ratio is equal to 1.0 when blacks are represented in a category at the same rate as all students in the school system are represented. It is less than 1.0 when blacks are underrepresented and greater than 1.0 when they are overrepresented. To avoid problems created by extreme values, this odds ratio is subjected to a log transformation. Use of this transformation has the added advantage of simplifying interpretation of the coefficients. The parameter estimates can be read as the percent increase in the dependent variable per unit increase in the independent variable (Tufte 1974, 125).

Theoretically, the key independent variable is the representativeness of the teacher faculty (percent of teachers who are black) and the representativeness of the principals (percent of principals who are black). Because Thompson (1976) argues that the impact of representative bureaucracy will be greater as the number of minorities in the bureaucracy increases, we use this percentage figure rather than a ratio that is adjusted by population.

Three control variables are included in all of the models: percentage of adult black population with a high school education, percentage of whites who live in poverty, and the ratio of black to white median income (as a percentage). Prior research has shown each of these variables to be related to racial disproportions in grouping and discipline (Meier, Stewart, and England 1989). They are related for two reasons. First, they indicate the relative level of black economic status, and the educational problems examined here are negatively correlated with economic status (Metz 1978). Second, they indicate potential resources that the black community can translate into political clout, and black political resources are positively related to a reduction in education policies that affect black students detrimentally. . . .

Findings

The first policy used to assess the impact of representative bureaucracy is ability grouping. If representative bureaucracy has beneficial policy impacts, we would expect that representation would be negatively correlated with EMR assignments and TMR assignments (although somewhat less so) and positively correlated with gifted class assignments. Table [4.1] reveals a reasonably consistent pattern. Black teachers are associated with fewer black students assigned to EMR classes (a 1 percentage point increase in black teachers is associated with a .7 percent decline in the EMR ratio) and positively associated with black gifted class assignments (a 1 percentage point

Table 4.1

The Impact of Representative Bureaucracy on Grouping

| | Dependent variable | | | | | |
| | EMR ratio | | TMR ratio | | Gifted ratio | |
Independent variables	Slope	t-score	Slope	t-score	Slope	t-score
Black education	.27	1.92*	−.27	1.28	.14	2.19*
White poverty	−.88	3.25*	−.31	.63	−.04	.31
Black/white income ratio	−.42	2.36*	.34	1.07	−.13	1.73*
Black teachers	−.70	6.14*	−.32	1.26	.32	5.44*
Black principals	−.30	2.93*	−.24	.99	−.05	.81
R^2	.70		.24		.49	
Adjusted R^2	.68		.16		.44	
F	28.12		3.14		10.77	
N of cases	65		56		63	

*$p < .05$.

increase in black teachers is associated with a .32 percentage increase in the gifted class ratio). Although black teachers are associated with lower TMR ratios, the relationship is not statistically significant.

Upper level representation does not fare as well as lower level representation. Black principals are associated with a reduction in the black EMR ratio, but the impact is less for black teachers (a 1 percentage point increase in black principals is associated with a .3 percent decline in the black EMR ratio). Black principals are not significantly related to either TMR assignments or gifted class assignments. For grouping measures, therefore, black representation appears to be more important at the "street level" than it is at management levels. The findings here are fairly consistent with the research of Oakes (1985, 51), who finds teachers having "considerable" input into ability-grouping decisions but does not mention principals as having any direct input.

The results of the analysis for disciplinary measures are shown in Table [4.2]. Black teachers and black administrators are expected to be negatively associated with the black disciplinary ratios. These expectations are confirmed for black teachers. In all five cases, as the percentage of black teachers increases, the disproportionate discipline of black students decreases. The relationship is especially strong for in-school suspensions and expulsions. (A 1 percentage point increase in black teachers is associated with a .92 percentage decline in the black in-school suspension ratio and a .85 percent decline in the expulsions ratio.)

The results for black principals are surprising. In three cases, there is no relationship (out-of-school suspensions, court referrals, and expulsions). For in-school suspensions and for corporal punishment, the relationships are

Table 4.2

The Impact of Representative Bureaucracy on Discipline

Independent variables	Dependent variable				
	Corporal punishment	In-school suspension	Regular suspension	Expulsions	Court referrals
Black education	.46*	−.14*	.08	.17	−.85*
	(3.76)	(.72)	(.71)	(.58)	(2.12)
White poverty	−.59*	.12	.15	2.20*	.61
	(2.57)	(.24)	(.69)	(1.98)	(.65)
Black/white income ratio	−.66*	−.36	−.25*	−.58	−.82
	(4.63)	(1.42)	(1.73)	(1.40)	(1.46)
Black teachers	−.61*	−.92*	−.43*	−.85*	−.49*
	(6.43)	(5.49)	(4.78)	(3.32)	(1.78)
Black principals	.20*	.25*	.04	.06	−.42
	(2.25)	(1.94)	(.43)	(.19)	(1.32)
R^2	.65	.48	.38	.42	.50
Adjusted R^2	.62	.42	.33	.33	.42
F	22.18	8.36	7.23	4.39	6.70
N of cases	65	52	65	36	40

$*p < .05.$

Note: Coefficients are unstandardized regression coefficients. *T*-scores are in parentheses.

positive and significant. In districts with more black principals, black students are more likely to receive in-school suspensions and more likely to receive corporal punishment. Two possible explanations for these findings exist. First, they may reflect the impact of organizational socialization among individuals who have risen to positions of authority within school systems, extended exposure to organizational culture, role expectations, and acquired professional norms that may supplant primary socialization (Kaufman 1971; Meier and Nigro 1976). Principals and their assistants are responsible for administering discipline in most schools, and administrators who are disciplinarians receive public praise (witness Joe Clark of New Jersey). This socialization and climate of expectations may well create pressures for black administrators to adopt the norms of the organization enthusiastically and thus be associated with more punishment for black students (see Rehfuss, 1986 for another example). Second, corporal punishment and in-school suspensions are the lightest forms of discipline covered. By stressing quick discipline of a less severe nature perhaps black principals avoid, or hope to avoid the need for, more severe disciplinary actions such as expulsion or court referral. Although we cannot distinguish between these explanations with the current data, either is plausible.

The analysis using educational performance measures is shown in Table

Table 4.3

Impact of Representative Bureaucracy on Student Performance

Independent variables	Not promoted	Drop-out	Performance on tests, Grade				
			3	5	8	10–1	10–2
Black education	−.03	.85*	−.01	.00	.02	−.02	.04
	(.25)	(3.71)	(.60)	(.05)	(.54)	(.68)	(.07)
White poverty	−.79*	.37	−.02	.04	.10	−.00	.13
	(2.94)	(.80)	(.51)	(.81)	(1.42)	(.07)	(1.26)
Black/white income ratio	−.12	−.93*	−.01	.06*	.00	.01	−.01
	(.86)	(3.57)	(.62)	(2.51)	(.00)	(.48)	(.18)
Black teachers	.05	.29*	.03*	.05*	.07*	.11*	.16*
	(.48)	(1.72)	(1.89)	(2.33)	(2.32)	(5.02)	(3.85)
Black principals	−.33*	−.31*	.00	.02	−.01	−.03	−.04
	(3.34)	(1.80)	(.10)	(1.00)	(.44)	(1.29)	(.93)
R^2	.33	.28	.13	.31	.15	.37	.27
Adjusted R^2	.27	.22	.06	.25	.08	.32	.21
F	5.52	4.68	1.80	5.51	2.22	7.07	4.44
N of cases	63	65	67	67	67	67	66

Dependent variable

$*p < .05.$

[4.3]. Eight measures of performance are used; all are ratios of black performance to performance of all students: students not promoted, students who drop out of school, and performance of students on five standardized tests. The promotion and dropout measures produce results different from any others presented thus far. In both cases, black principals are related to decreases in black non-promotion and dropouts as predicted by the theory of representative bureaucracy. Black teachers are positively related to dropouts and unrelated to non-promotions.

Performance on standardized tests reveals a consistent pattern. Black principals have no impact on the performance of black students on standardized tests. In every case, better representation of black teachers is associated with higher scores for black students on standardized tests relative to all students in the school system. Although the size of the coefficients is not large, we should not expect policy outcomes to be as amenable to bureaucratic manipulation as policy outputs. The pattern of coefficients is also important. The size of the impact of black teachers increases as students go through the school system. (A 1 percentage point increase in black teachers is associated with a .03 percent increase in the black student performance ratio for the third grade but a .16 percent increase for the second tenth-grade test.)

Conclusion

This study examined the impact of representative bureaucracy in 67 Florida public school districts. The test of representativeness of bureaucracy was aided by (a) selecting bureaucrats who have discretion in their actions, (b) using a demographic factor with a lasting impact—race, and (c) selecting policy measures that are directly tied to race so that the relationship between representation and policy would be immediately apparent. The results show that bureaucrats are able to influence not only public policy outputs but also public policy outcomes in predicted ways.

The study also provided a means for comparing the impact of management-level bureaucrats (principals) with street-level bureaucrats (teachers). In general, but not in all cases, street-level bureaucrats show more impacts of representative bureaucracy than do management-level bureaucrats. As Thompson (1976) argues, the impacts reflect the discretion in these street-level positions and the absence of strong organizational socialization to conform to different standards. Management-level bureaucrats are not unimportant, however. They have separate impacts on some policy outputs and permit the discretion that street-level bureaucrats are able to exercise.

References

Cayer, N.J., and Sigelman, L. 1980. "Minorities and Women in State and Local Government, 1973–1975." *Public Administration Review* 40 (September/October): 443–450.

Dometrius, N.C., and Sigelman, L. 1984. "Assessing Progress Toward Affirmative Action Goals in State and Local Government." *Public Administration Review* 44 (May/June): 241–246.

Duncan, Greg J. 1984. *Years of Poverty, Years of Plenty.* Ann Arbor: Institute for Social Research, University of Michigan.

Fernandez, R.R., and J.T. Guskin, 1981. "Hispanic Students and School Desegregation." In W.D. Hawley (ed.), *Effective School Desegregation* (pp. 107–140). Beverly Hills, CA: Sage.

Garand, J.C., Parkhurst, C.T., and Seoud, R.J. 1991. "Bureaucrats, Policy Attitudes, and Political Behavior: Extensions of the Bureau Voting Model of Government Growth." *Journal of Public Administration Research and Theory* 1 (April): 177–212.

Grabowsky, P.N., and Rosenbloom, D.H. 1976. "Racial and Ethnic Integration in the Federal Service." *Social Science Quarterly* 56 (June): 71–84.

Hall, G., and Saltzstein, A. 1977. "Equal Employment Opportunity for Minorities in Municipal Government." *Social Science Quarterly* 57 (March): 864–872.

Hedge, D.M., Menzel, D.C., and Williams, G.H. 1988. "Regulatory Attitudes and Behavior: The Case of Surface Mining Regulation." *Western Political Quarterly* 41 (June): 323–340.

Henderson, L.J., and Preston, M.B. 1984. "Blacks, Public Employment, and Public Interest Theory." In M.F. Rice and W. Jones, Jr., (eds.), *Contemporary Public Policy Perspectives and Black Americans* (pp. 33–48). Westport, CT: Greenwood Press.

Kaufman, H. 1971. *The Limits of Organizational Change*. University: University of Alabama Press.

Kellough, J.E. 1990a. "Federal Agencies and Affirmative Action for Blacks and Women." *Social Science Quarterly* 71 (March): 83–92.

Kellough, J.E. 1990b. "Integration in the Public Workplace: Determinants of Minority and Female Employment in Federal Agencies." *Public Administration Review* 50 (September/October): 557–566.

Kingsley, J.D. 1944. *Representative Bureaucracy*. Yellow Springs, OH: Antioch Press.

Levitan, D.M. 1946. "The Responsibility of Administrative Officials in a Democratic Society." *Political Science Quarterly* 61 (December): 562–598.

Lewis, G.B. 1990. "In Search of Machiavellian Milque-toasts: Comparing Attitudes of Bureaucrats and Ordinary People." *Public Administration Review* 50 (April/March): 220–227.

Long, N.E. 1952. "Bureaucracy and Constitutionalism." *American Political Science Review* 46 (September): 808–818.

Meier, K.J. 1975. "Representative Bureaucracy: An Empirical Analysis." *American Political Science Review* 69 (June): 526–542.

Meier, K.J., and Nigro, L.G. 1976. "Representative Bureaucracy and Policy Preferences." *Public Administration Review* 36 (July/August): 458–470.

Meier, K.J., Stewart, J., Jr., and England, R.E. 1989. *Race, Class, and Education: The Politics of Second Generation Discrimination*. Madison: University of Wisconsin Press.

Metz, M.H. 1978. *Classrooms and Corridors: The Crisis of Authority in Desegregated Secondary Schools*. Berkeley: University of California Press.

Mladenka, K.R. 1989. "Blacks and Hispanics in Urban Politics." *American Political Science Review* 83 (March): 165–192.

Mosher, F.C. 1968. *Democracy and the Public Service*. New York: Oxford University Press.

Oakes, J. 1985. *Keeping Track: How Schools Structure Inequality*. New Haven, CT: Yale University Press.

Rehfuss, J.A. 1986. "A Representative Bureaucracy? Women and Minority Executives in California Career Service." *Public Administration Review* 46 (September/October): 454–459.

Rosenbloom, D.H., and Featherstonhaugh, J.C. 1977. "Passive and Active Representation in the Federal Service: A Comparison of Blacks and Whites." *Social Science Quarterly* 57 (March): 873–882.

Saltzstein, G.H. 1979. "Representative Bureaucracy and Bureaucratic Responsibility." *Administration and Society* 10 (February): 465–475.

Skolnick, J.H. 1966. *Justice Without Trial: Law Enforcement in Democratic Society*. New York: John Wiley.

Stein, L. 1986. "Representative Local Government: Minorities in the Municipal Workforce." *Journal of Politics* 48 (August): 694–716.

Thompson, F.J. 1976. "Minority Groups in Public Bureaucracies: Are Passive and Active Representation Linked?" *Administration and Society* 8 (August): 201–226.

Thompson, F.J. 1978. "Civil Servants and the Deprived: Socio-Political and Occupational Explanations of Attitudes Toward Minority Hiring." *American Journal of Political Science* 22 (May): 325–347.

Tufte, E.R. 1974. *Data Analysis for Politics and Policy*. Englewood Cliffs, NJ: Prentice-Hall.

Bureaucracy as a Representative Institution: Toward a Reconciliation of Bureaucratic Government and Democratic Theory

Sally Coleman Selden, Jeffrey L. Brudney, and J. Edward Kellough

The Minority Representative Role

The goal of this research is to specify the theoretical underpinnings of representative bureaucracy by examining a comprehensive model that includes attitude formation. More specifically, the purpose is to determine factors that lead administrators to assume a minority representative role and the extent to which this role is associated with the active representation of minority interests in bureaucratic decision-making. Drawing on arguments implicit in the literature on representative bureaucracy, we suggest that policy decisions consistent with minority concerns are more likely to occur when public employees assume this conception of their work role. While minority employees can be expected to embrace this role most often and most closely, nonminority administrators may also adopt it as a result of their background or socialization.

By focusing on the minority representative role as mediating between the demographic composition of the work force on the one hand and policy outcomes consistent with minority interests on the other, we are able to offer a more complete assessment of the theory of representative bureaucracy. In addition to race and ethnicity, many other variables likely to influence adherence to the minority representative role are considered. In some circumstances, minority employees with discretionary authority may avoid the minority representative role. Regardless of race or ethnicity, moreover, the attachment of public administrators to the representative role will vary, so that they may not always make decisions and take actions responsive to the minority community. In sum, the model proposes that employees' perception of their work role conditions the translation of demographic (and other) characteristics into policy outputs.

In general, authorities define work roles as sets of behaviors expected of those occupying a particular job or position (Kahn et al. 1964). Role expectations or demands are conveyed to administrators by other persons both verbally and nonverbally; they are also expressed formally through job descriptions, training, and other avenues of socialization. An administrator can encounter multiple role expectations resulting in cross-pressures and conflicts on the job. In addition to these "sent" roles, which consist of expectations and pressures communicated by others, the administrator has a "received" role consisting of her or his perception of the messages sent (Kahn et al. 1964). Ultimately, explain Kahn et al. (1964, 16), it is the received role that is "the immediate influence on . . . behavior and the immediate source of motivation to role performance."

Several scholars have discussed the array of organizational and environmental forces that influence the roles administrators are likely to adopt in public organizations (Henderson 1988; Herbert 1974; Martinez 1991; Murray et al. 1994). Although the article centers on minority bureaucrats, Herbert (1974) recognizes that many of the role dilemmas propounded confront all administrators regardless of race or ethnicity. As an example of the pressures exerted on administrators to assume specified roles, Herbert notes that organizations typically create system demands that reward certain behaviors and sanction others. Employees may be rewarded for "doing as ordered" and sanctioned for diverging from standard practices and procedures. In addition to formal rewards and sanctions, administrators may also feel pressure from colleagues to conform to bureaucratic, professional, or informal norms set by other employees. Henderson (1988) cautions that underlying norms of behavior in organizations can operate to discourage administrators who openly seek to represent minority interests.

But at the same time, some administrators, especially minorities, may feel an intense sense of responsibility to minority communities. According to Herbert (1974, 561), minority communities want public administrators "who will listen to them, who can communicate with them, who care about them." Karnig and McClain (1988, 151–52) describe the role associated with this behavior as one of a "trustee" of minority interests. Trustees bear responsibility for making a positive difference in policy outcomes for minorities and increasing their access to the policy process. The trustee role parallels Mosher's (1982) concept of active representation, which occurs when minority civil servants work to see that the interests and desires of minority groups are represented in policy decisions.

Figure 4.1 **Linkages in the Concept of Representative Bureaucracy**

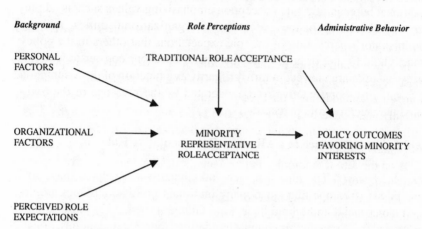

As a result, public administrators may experience cross-pressures to conform to organizational norms emphasizing bureaucratic routine, efficiency, and strict interpretation of rules, while also feeling a need to shape policy decisions responsive to particularized interests. For example, Herbert (1974, 563) maintains that to assume a minority representative role, individuals may have to reject the idea that administrators are and must be "value free and completely neutral," yet he acknowledges that administrators work in bureaucratic settings with established organizational norms, procedures, and reward structures that cannot and should not be ignored. Each individual must decide the relative weights to assign to the various job expectations and demands in conceiving their work role.

The extent to which an administrator adopts a minority representative role will depend on a number of variables related to social background, organizational experience, pressure from other individuals, and the perceived viability of alternative roles. Figure [4.1] presents a model of the formation of a minority representative role perception among public administrators and suggests the potential impact of acceptance of this role on policy outcomes consistent with minority interests. To this point, the literature on representative bureaucracy has not combined the constructs shown in the figure into a model or collected the data necessary to evaluate such a model empirically.

Variables in the Model

According to the model depicted in Figure [4.1], four sets of variables affect adherence to a minority representative role perception: an individual's personal background, organizational socialization, the perceived salience of a traditional bureaucratic role conception emphasizing values such as administrative efficiency in the execution of organizational duties, and the administrator's perception of the role expectations that others in the policy process hold for her or him. Policy actions or decisions consonant with minority interests are viewed, in turn, primarily as a function of the assumption of a minority representative role, moderated by the presence of the traditional bureaucratic role perception.

Explaining Adherence to a Minority Representative Role

Personal Factors. The idea that race and ethnicity will help to shape role perceptions is compelling since many important political attitudes are defined along racial and ethnic lines. Lani Guinier (1994, 137), for example, has argued that "race in this country has defined individual identities, opportunities, frames of reference, and relationships." Political and attitudinal cleavages have formed along racial lines (Carmines and Stimson 1989). Murray et al. (1994) confirm the importance of race in public administration. In their recent survey of minority public administrators, most respondents believed that they should play a strong representational role for minority communities. Earlier work examining policy outcomes has supported the contention that minority employment will further minority policy interests at least with respect to some policy issues. For example, Meier (1993a) and Meier and Stewart (1992) found that the employment of minority public school teachers and principals is associated with fewer disciplinary actions against minority students. Similarly, Hindera (1993a, 1993b) demonstrated that the presence of minority EEOC investigators is positively associated with the percentage of discrimination charges filed on behalf of minorities in EEOC district offices. Based on these findings, we expect that racial and ethnic minorities will be more likely than nonminority administrators to adhere to a minority representative role.

Education is a second personal factor that may influence administrators' role perceptions. Meier (1993b, 26) suggests that "educational institutions, particularly at the post-secondary level, play an important role in the socialization of minorities and women by raising consciousness about the problems facing minorities and women in society." Similarly, this logic could be applied to nonminority individuals. That is, nonminority individuals may also become more sensitized to minority problems as a result of higher education. If so, then administrators with more formal post-secondary education should generally be more likely to assume a minority representative role than those with less education. Only a few studies have examined the relevance of education to representative bureaucracy, however, and empirical findings have been mixed. Daley (1984) found that state government officials with more formal education were more likely to disapprove of policies for "improving the condition of ethnic minorities and women"; whereas, Meier and Nigro (1976) found that federal government executives (GS 16 to GS 18) with more education expressed more support for improving the conditions of minorities. The association between level of education and adherence to a minority representative role is reexamined in the present analysis.

The type of higher education institution attended by an administrator may also influence the individual's perception of work roles. Rosenbloom and Kinnard (1977), for instance, found that minority administrators who had attended historically black colleges believed that they were more effective at facilitating the entry of minorities into high level positions in the Department of Defense. Historically black colleges and universities may inculcate a shared sense of identity or purpose that will carry over into perceived work roles. For this reason, we expect that administrators who have attended these schools will be more sensitive to minority interests and will more readily adopt a minority representative role.

Research has also identified age as a significant demographic variable in studies of bureaucratic attitudes (Daley 1984; Meier and Nigro 1976; Rosenbloom and Kinnard 1977). Typically, younger employees have worked for government for shorter periods and, therefore, have experienced less socialization to organizational norms and values. Moreover, they are not as removed as older employees from their childhood experiences and roots. But although age is related to organizational socialization factors, such as years in government service, it also taps a slightly different dimension (Daley 1984). Individuals of the same age cohort have experienced similar historical events that have shaped their "generation" (e.g., World War II, the Vietnam War, the Civil Rights Movement, and the Persian Gulf War). These factors complicate the relationship between age and work role perception.

A 1976 study, for instance, reported evidence that older bureaucrats were less supportive of policies aimed at improving the conditions of minorities (Meier and Nigro 1976). Similar research published the following year found that younger minority managers felt a stronger responsibility to help other minorities (Rosenbloom and Kinnard 1977). In the 1980s, however, Daley (1984) reported that older administrators were more supportive of a representative bureaucracy and of increasing efforts to achieve this goal. Given that many older administrators in the mid-1990s came to maturity during the time of the Civil Rights Movement and the struggle for racial equality in the 1960s, we expect that age will be positively associated with attachment to a minority representative role.

Political party identification should also be linked to attitudes toward the representation of minority interests. Lipset (1992) noted that the debate over hiring preferences for minorities has in recent years sharply divided the two major political parties, with Republicans generally opposed to such programs and Democrats favoring them. Indeed, affirmative action has become a significant issue in numerous political campaigns, and the Republican leadership of Congress has recently advocated efforts to eliminate such policies (Holmes 1995). Given the current debate over affirmative action and minority preferences in general, we expect that the closer an individual identifies with the Republican party, the less likely she or he will be to assume a minority representative role.

Organizational Factors. Since socialization is an ongoing learning process that continues once an individual enters an organizational setting, and because agencies can create an environment or culture emphasizing organizational loyalty and commitment, socialization to the organization may weaken the link between the demographic background of administrators and adherence to a minority representative role when the organization's mission or culture does not emphasize minority interests (Meier and Nigro 1976; Romzek and Hendricks 1982). Meier (1993a, 397) suggests that when administrators have spent the time necessary in an organization to attain a position of power, they "often have been subjected to many years of organizational socialization designed to encourage employees to adopt agency-sanctioned attitudes." If those values do not include active representation, individuals who seek to represent minority interests may be pressured to abandon such activity (Meier 1993a). Early studies of representative bureaucracy by Meier (1975) and Meier and Nigro (1976) found that organizational socialization was often a more important predictor of bureaucratic attitudes than were social origins and background characteristics of civil servants.

Three indicators of exposure to organizational socialization are the amount of formal agency training received by the administrator, the length of employment in the current position, and the length of government employment in general. Based on earlier research, we anticipate that each of these variables will be negatively associated with adherence to a minority representative role. In the empirical analysis, should the hypothesized negative effect of organizational socialization overwhelm the effects of attitudes and values stemming from administrators' personal backgrounds on the assumption of this role, the potential for representative bureaucracy would be weakened substantially. The theory of representative bureaucracy presumes that social background characteristics will be reflected in the work attitudes and behaviors of bureaucrats.

Another aspect of the organizational setting, the presence of minority coworkers in the work environment, may operate to reinforce the minority representative role. Thompson (1976) maintains that bureaucrats will be more likely to engage in active representation of minority interests when they work in close proximity to and interact more frequently with members of minority groups. The employment of several minority employees by an agency may lead to greater comfort and confidence in pursuing policies responsive to minority interests. For this reason we expect that as the number of minority coworkers in the office increases an administrator will be more likely to assume a minority representative role.

Acceptance of a Traditional Bureaucratic Role. The concept of merit in public employment provides the foundation from which modern civil service systems have evolved, and central to the principle of merit is the idea of neutral competence. According to Kaufman (1956, 1060), the essence of neutral competence is the "ability to do the work of the government expertly, and to do it according to explicit, objective standards rather than to personal or party or other obligations and loyalties." The ultimate objective is efficiency in administration (Denhardt and deLeon 1993). In fact, in an early assessment of the developing field of public administration, Dahl (1947, 2) observed that the "doctrine" of efficiency "runs like a half-visible thread through the fabric of public administration literature as a dominant goal." Years later, Frederickson (1971, 311) noted that the classic definition of public administration has been the "efficient, economical, and coordinated" delivery of public services. More recently, Ingraham and Ban (1986) have argued that economy and efficiency remain the central values underlying the traditional view of neutral competence.

We believe that administrators who focus primarily on the efficient operation of agency processes—that is, those who observe what we call a traditional bureaucratic role perception—will be less inclined to influence agency outputs in response to the interests of distinct segments of the population. They will be less likely to conceive of their job as a representative of any particular group and will, therefore, be less likely to assume the minority representative role. The trade-off between these two role perceptions closely parallels the classic conflict between equity and efficiency (Denhardt and deLeon 1993). Equity in this case may be served when administrators work to represent the interests of groups that have historically been unrepresented or inadequately represented in the policy process. By contrast, efficiency is enhanced by reliance on standard procedures, objectivity, and impartiality on the part of the administrator rather than a focus on the particular circumstances and needs of selected social groups. While the minority representative role and the traditional bureaucratic role need not be mutually exclusive, it is most likely that minority representation will be suppressed when the traditional view is strongly held (Martinez 1991). We anticipate that individuals who perceive their role in a more traditional bureaucratic sense emphasizing administrative efficiency will be less inclined to assume the posture of a minority representative.

Perceived Role Expectations. When administrators perceive that other actors in the policy process expect them to represent minority interests, we believe they will be more likely to accept the minority representative role (Kahn et al. 1964). Other relevant actors in this situation include management, colleagues, employee organizations, the general public, the minority community, professional associations, and political officials. In contrast, when administrators believe that others expect them to assume more bureaucratically-oriented roles emphasizing impartiality and efficiency, subsequent adherence to a minority representative role should attenuate.

Of course, employees may believe that both sets of role expectations impinge on them. For example, the literature suggests that minority administrators often perceive that they face dual expectations of protecting minority group interests and conforming to more traditional or bureaucratically-sanctioned administrative roles (Martinez 1991; Murray et al. 1994). In this situation, administrators may seek a compromise between the two positions in which they still adhere to the minority representative role but not to the same degree as when they experience no cross-pressure (Murray et al. 1994). The analysis below examines the effects of all three sets of perceived role pressures on the assumption of a minority representative role.

Explaining Policy Outcomes Consistent with Minority Interests. The next major question examined in the model is whether administrators who consider themselves representatives of minority interests will be able to see that those interests are reflected in policy outcomes. Administrators who embrace the minority representative role perception most strongly believe that they should act in favor of policies that address the needs of minority clients, support procedures that increase minority access to government programs, and work in other ways to help insure that minority interests are not overlooked in policy decision-making. As suggested in the literature on representative bureaucracy, this process is one means of providing that bureaucratic decisions reflect the diversity of attitudes, opinions, and perspectives in the population (Krislov and Rosenbloom 1981). The model in Figure [4.1] proposes that to the degree that administrators hold these beliefs, specific policy outcomes under their control are more likely to be formulated in such a way as to ensure the protection of minority interests.

Adherence to the more traditional bureaucratic role perception should also have a direct effect on policy outcomes. Because this perception of the administrative role stresses the efficient implementation of agency programs and policies, administrators holding this view will be concerned primarily with objectivity and neutrality, rather than equity-based issues. When administrators operate from this perspective, we expect that policy outcomes favoring minority interests will be judged less important and, consequently, will be less likely to occur.

Methodology

The Research Setting. The focus of empirical analysis is the Rural Housing Loans program of the Department of Agriculture's Farmers Home Administration (FmHA). Since the FmHA is not normally thought of as an agency with a mission emphasizing minority representation, despite the direct relevance of its programs to minority communities, it offers a rigorous test of the viability of the theory of representative bureaucracy. In fact, the history and organizational context of the FmHA suggest, as noted earlier, that the representation of minority interests may be suppressed at the agency. The Department of Agriculture itself is one of the more poorly integrated organizations within the federal government and has been among the slowest to expand employment opportunities for minorities and women (Kellough 1990a, 1990b). A 1982 study by the U.S. Commission on Civil Rights found that the Department of Agriculture and, specifically, the FmHA had "failed to integrate civil rights goals into program objectives" (U.S. Commission on Civil Rights 1982, IV). The report noted that the FmHA had "a reputation for discriminatory lending" (U.S. Commission on Civil Rights 1982, 63). An earlier report by the Commission was also critical of the FmHA's limited distribution of housing loans to African Americans and suggested that FmHA staff training and minority outreach programs were unsatisfactory (U.S. Commission on Civil Rights 1979). From the perspective of the county supervisor, the potential conflicts between the role demands of participation in the FmHA's hierarchy and those of representing minority interests may create friction, dissatisfaction, and inefficiency (Romzek and Hendricks 1982, 75). As Romzek and Hendricks (1982) explain, in an agency whose mission and culture does not embrace minority involvement, acceptance of organizational norms and values will likely decrease representative bureaucracy. Thus, if the theory of representative bureaucracy is found to operate in this agency, then one might expect it to operate as well in other organizations with cultures and historical patterns of behavior less antagonistic to minority interests.

To conduct a valid empirical test of a theory of representative bureaucracy that poses a connection between demographic backgrounds of administrators and policy outcomes, Meier and Stewart (1992) argue that the three conditions must be met. First, the public administrators who are the subjects of the analysis must have a significant amount of discretion in the decision-making process. Second, this discretion must be exercised in an area that has important implications for the group or groups to be represented. As Meier (1993b, 10) explains, a wide variety of socialization experiences are not "relevant to public policy disputes and thus are unlikely to reveal a representational linkage." The third condition necessary for an empirical assessment of the theory is that the administrators are able to be associated directly with the decisions they make.

County supervisors from the Farmers Home Administration meet all three criteria. FmHA local supervisors exert considerable discretion in making loan eligibility decisions for the Rural Housing Loans program (Hadwiger 1973; Wyatt and Phillips 1988). Created by the Housing Act of 1949, this program was designed to provide very low to moderate income residents in rural counties the opportunity to secure government-backed loans for housing purchase and repair. FmHA local supervisors are responsible for reviewing loan applications, interviewing applicants, and selecting recipients of rural housing loans. In making these determinations, moreover, county supervisors receive no direct oversight from district office staff and minimum attention from state office personnel (Pennington 1994). In addition, the redistributive nature of the housing loans and the history of discrimination in the private mortgage lending industry substantiate a profound minority interest in this program. One often-mentioned cause of the racial disparities in mortgage lending is the employment practices of the lending institution. A recent study of Milwaukee area commercial banks and thrifts shows that the likelihood of an African-American applicant being approved for a mortgage increases as the proportion of African-American employees increase in financial institutions (Squires and Kim 1995). Finally, because the loan decisions are the sole responsibility of local supervisors, these outcomes can be linked to specific individuals.

Data Collection. To collect information for an empirical test of the model presented in Figure [4.1], a mail survey was distributed to FmHA county supervisors in the southern region of the United States in 1994. The initial mailing included a questionnaire, cover letter, and postage-paid return envelope. Two weeks following the initial mailing, a follow-up letter was mailed to respondents, and a final reminder letter was sent three weeks after the follow-up.

Responses were received from 234 individuals, 61% of the sample. Of this group, 184 had complete data on the items included in the analysis. As highlighted in the model presented in Figure [4.1], the survey queried FmHA local supervisors concerning their personal background, organizational context, and role perceptions. The FmHA Freedom of Information Office provided Fiscal Year 1994 data on the number of rural housing loan eligibility decisions in each local office awarded to whites, African Americans, Hispanics, Native Americans, and Asians by the supervisor surveyed. Demographic information about the specific areas served by the FmHA field offices came from the 1990 U.S. Census.

Operationalization. Table [4.4] displays all variables used in the analysis. . . . In the first part of the model, the dependent variable is the extent to which FmHA county supervisors perceive their work role as a representative of minority interests. Eight questions were used to gauge the supervisor's attitude toward assuming this role [The text of these items is in an appendix not included here]. In the second part of the model focusing on policy outcomes, the dependent variable examined is the percentage of rural housing loan eligibility decisions in a county office awarded to minority applicants. Ordinary least squares regression is used to estimate each equation.

Because rural housing loan eligibility decisions will be awarded to minorities in part as a function of demand for such loans by minorities in a particular area, the equation examining this variable introduces minority economic hardship in the area as a control variable. The assumption is that minority hardship will serve as a proxy measure for demand for FmHA loans from the minority community. By controlling for demand in this manner, the analysis will gauge more accurately the extent to which county supervisors engage in active representation in awarding loans and publicizing the program. Prior studies examining policy outputs have also used various combinations of area demographic characteristics as control variables (Meier and Stewart 1992; Meier 1993a; Hindera 1993a, 1993b). Due to the high intercorrelations among the important demographic indicators of minority economic hardship, we employ an index developed by the Brookings Institution to construct the hardship variable.

Findings and Discussion

Findings from the empirical analysis lend considerable support to the linkages hypothesized in the model between demographic representation, the assumption of a minority representative role, and the realization of policy outputs consistent with minority group interests. Table [4.5] presents results from the regression analysis in which adherence to the minority representative role perception by FmHA county supervisors is the dependent variable. Overall, the variables included in the model can account for 31% of the variation in minority representative role perceptions.

From the standpoint of representative bureaucracy, the most important finding in Table [4.5] is that minority status, as hypothesized, exerts a strong influence on adherence to the minority representative role. Minority FmHA

Table 4.4

Operationalization of Dependent and Independent Variables

Dependent variables
  Minority representative role acceptance (index 1 scaled 8 to 40)
  Percent of eligibility decisions favoring minorities (scaled 0 to 100%)

Independent variables
  Personal factors
    Race/Ethnicity:
      (0 = white)
      (1 = minority)
    *Education**
      (1 = High school diploma)
      (2 = Some college)
      (3 = Bachelor's degree)
      (4 = Some graduate school)
      (5 = Master's degree)
    Type of education
      (0 = not educated at a traditionally all-black college or university)
      (1 = educated at a traditionally all-black college or university)
    Age
      (1995–Year of birth)
    Party identification
      (1 = Strong Democrat)
      (2 = Moderate Democrat)
      (3 = Independent)
      (4 = Moderate Republican)
      (5 = Strong Republican)

Organizational factors
  Number of training programs attended in past year
  Years in current position
  Years of federal service
  Number of minorities working in county office

Perceived role expectations
  Expected by stakeholders to work in favor of the delivery of public program services in a manner that increases minority access (Index 3 scaled 0 to 8). Stakeholders are district and state management, general public, minority community, nonminority colleagues, minority colleagues, minority employee organizations, professional associations, and local political officials.

  Expected by stakeholders to implement programs consistent with departmental procedures (index 4 scaled 0 to 8). Stakeholders are district and state management, general public, minority community, nonminority colleagues, minority colleagues, minority employee organizations, professional associations, and local political officials.

  Expected by stakeholders to implement programs in a manner that increases minority access and to implement programs consistent with departmental procedures (Index 5 scaled 0 to 8). Stakeholders are district and state management, general public, minority community, nonminority colleagues, minority colleagues, minority employee organizations, professional associations, and local political officials.

Role perception
  Traditional role acceptance (index 2 scaled 3 to 15)

Minority demand for loans
  Minority economic hardship (index 6 scaled 0 to 100). It is designed to control for expected "demand" or "share" of rural housing loans eligibility decisions favoring minorities.

*No respondent indicated that she or he held a doctorate or law degree.

supervisors are much more likely than nonminorities to perceive their role as a representative of minority interests. Crucial to the theory of representative bureaucracy, race and ethnicity appear to influence the attitudes and role perceptions of government employees regarding minority representation.

A number of other personal factors also are influential. For example, the level of formal education of the local supervisors apparently exerts a significant negative effect on acceptance of the minority representative role perception. As education level increases, respondents are less likely to see themselves as representatives of minority interests. This finding contradicts the results of the early study by Meier and Nigro (1976) suggesting that administrators with more education will be more responsive to the needs of minorities, but it is consistent with Daley's (1984) later study of state government officials. We believe that the negative relationship between educational attainment and perceiving oneself as a minority representative may occur, in part, because education is related to personal ambition. For example, Henderson (1988) found that more educated public administrators are generally more ambitious. In the context of the FmHA, ambition may be driving both employee educational attainment and reluctance to actively represent minority interests. Given the recent history of the FmHA with respect to racial issues discussed above, those who seek to advance in the organization (i.e., those who are ambitious) may be hesitant to take on the minority representative role. If that is the case, then such a pattern of behavior would help to explain the negative association between education and acceptance of a minority representative role. Unfortunately, we have no direct measure of administrators' ambition to allow a test of this hypothesis.

Other personal factors associated with the minority representative role perception are age and political party affiliation. Older administrators are more likely to see their role as that of a minority representative, a finding compatible with the generational hypothesis offered earlier. Because older employees experienced the Civil Rights Movement and the struggle of African Americans and other minorities to achieve legal and political representation and social equality, they may be more receptive to this role. Also as hypothesized, acceptance of the minority representative role perception declines as allegiance to the Republican party increases. Strong Republicans are much less likely to perceive their role as a representative of minority interests than are Democrats. This finding comports well with previous research on bureaucratic attitudes (Daley 1984; Thompson 1978).

With respect to the variables tapping organizational socialization, as expected, years in the federal service are negatively associated with assumption of the minority representative role. As tenure in the federal government increases (for those in our sample this measure is effectively the same as years in the FmHA),

Table 4.5

Regression Model for Minority Representative Role Perception

Independent variables	Unstandardized coefficient	Standard error	Standardized coefficient
Personal factors			
Minority	4.47**	1.39	.32
Education level[a]	−1.01*	0.51	−.13
Age	.20**	0.08	.27
Party identification	−.96**	0.43	−.16
Attended traditionally all-black university	1.20	1.48	.08
Organizational factors			
Years in federal government	−.22**	0.10	−.28
Number of days in training	−.01	0.03	−.02
Years in position	.01	0.07	.02
Presence of minority colleagues	−1.97	0.88	−.16
Perceived role expectations			
Expected to increase minority access to programs	.83**	0.28	.24
Expected to implement programs according to departmental practices and increase minority access	.87***	0.26	.32
Expected to implement programs according to departmental practices	.26	0.21	.13
Traditional bureaucratic role perception	−.31*	0.15	−.14
R^2	.31		
Adjusted R^2	.26		
F	5.85		
Number of cases	184.00		

* Significant at .05.
** Significant at .01.
*** Significant at .001.
[a]A two-tail significance test is used for education since a directional relationship was not hypothesized for that variable. For all other variables included in the equation, a one-tail test is employed.

administrators are less likely to adopt this role. The other two measures of organizational socialization, days of training and years in the supervisor position, are not related significantly to the minority representative role.

Contrary to our expectation, the presence of minority coworkers in the FmHA local office is associated negatively with adherence to the minority representative role. The exact dynamic underlying that relationship is not clear. To clarify the relationship between working with minority coworkers and work role perceptions, future research must examine larger organiza-

Table 4.6

Regression Model for Percentage of Eligibility Determinations Awarded to Minorities

Independent variables	Unstandardized coefficient	Standard error	Standardized coefficient	Unstandardized coefficient	Standard error	Standardized coefficient
Traditional bureaucratic role	-.11	0.56	.01	.13	0.56	.01
Minority representative role	2.72***	0.25	.63	2.68***	0.27	.62
Minority hardship index	.51**	0.19	.16	.49**	0.19	.15
Minority				1.47	3.82	.02
R^2	.43			.43		
Adjusted R^2	.42			.41		
F	44.57***			45.64***		
Number of cases	184.00			184.00		

* Significant at .05.
** Significant at .01.
*** Significant at .001.

tional units with more minority administrators in supervisory and nonsupervisory positions than the FmHA presents.

The variables measuring the perceived role expectations of the FmHA county supervisors substantiate the relationships hypothesized by the model. To the degree that the supervisors believe that important actors in the policy environment (such as agency management, colleagues, employee organizations, the general public, the minority community, professional associations and political officials) expect them to increase minority access or in other ways represent minority interests, they are much more likely to accept the minority representative role. In fact, even when county supervisors perceive that they are expected *both* to implement programs according to departmental practices and to increase minority access to programs and therefore seek a compromise between these two positions, they are still likely to adopt the minority representative role perception. By contrast, the belief on the part of these administrators that other actors expect them only to implement programs consistent with departmental procedures has no bearing on their assumption of a minority representative role.

Finally, the results in Table [4.5] confirm the hypothesized negative relationship between attachment to a traditional bureaucratic role perception and acceptance of the minority representative role. County supervisors who adhere to a more traditionally-defined bureaucratic role where efficiency is the primary objective are not as likely to perceive their role as a representative of minority interests.

Table [4.6] presents results from the second part of the model examining the effect of the minority representative role perception on policy outputs consistent with minority interests. The findings strongly suggest that to the degree that the FmHA supervisors perceive their role as minority representatives, they will work to see that minority interests are reflected in the implementation of public programs. In Table [4.6], the dependent variable in the regression analysis is the percentage of loan eligibility determinations awarded to minorities by the local supervisor. Even when the demand for loans from the minority community is controlled statistically through the inclusion in the model of the minority hardship index, adherence to a minority representative role perception by local FmHA supervisors significantly increases the proportion of eligibility decisions favoring minorities. As anticipated, assumption of the traditional bureaucratic role perception is negatively associated with the percentage of eligibility decisions to minorities, although the coefficient does not attain statistical significance. The equation can account for 43% of the variation in loan determinations.

Because the concept of the minority representative role introduced here recognizes that nonminority bureaucrats may also have been socialized to represent minority interests, we modified the equation to include a variable for race/ethnicity of the local administrator. The findings are also reported in Table [4.6]. The model performed almost exactly as before: race/ethnicity did not attain statistical significance. As a result, the indications are that adherence to the minority representative role exerts an influence on administrative behavior above and beyond race.

Conclusion

In an early examination of the construct, Krislov (1974) argued that to test the theory of representative bureaucracy, scholars would need to examine relationships between demographic characteristics and work attitudes and between those attitudes and administrative behaviors. This study has modeled both linkages and evaluated them empirically. Results confirm hypotheses derived from each linkage.

From the perspective of representative bureaucracy, the finding that race and ethnicity exert a strong influence on an administrator's view of his or her role is of critical importance. The relationship demonstrated here between minority status and acceptance of the minority representative role by local supervisors of the FmHA indicates that race and ethnicity make a significant difference in administrative perceptions. Socialization to the agency or the public service more generally does not overwhelm the importance of role perceptions or background characteristics in structuring bureaucratic attitudes. In turn, adherence to the minority representative role perception is positively associated with policy outcomes consistent with minority interests. When administrators see themselves as representatives of minority interests, policy outcomes responsive to those interests are more likely to be achieved.

Considered together, these results significantly reinforce the notion that the representativeness of a public agency can affect bureaucratic responsiveness to identifiable segments of the citizenry. The study thus substantiates research findings by Hindera (1993a, 1993b), Meier (1993a), and Meier and Stewart (1992) linking passive and active representation in other settings. This study adds to our understanding of one mechanism by which active representation occurs, namely the administrative role perception.

Furthermore, the relationship observed between minority employment and the active representation of minority interests holds interesting implications for policy and political questions beyond the issue of bureaucratic responsiveness. Personnel policies requiring equal employment opportunity and affirmative action, for example, may take on additional significance in view of the connections found here between race/ethnicity, bureaucratic attitudes, and policy outcomes.

This research lends new insights into the theory of representative bureaucracy. The results indicate that while demographic or "passive" representation of minorities in government agencies is associated with the adoption of the minority representative role, it is this role, rather than race or ethnicity, that is related significantly to decisions consistent with minority interests or "active representation." To the degree that public administrators view their work obligations in this light, the research suggests that bureaucratic power can complement democratic principles by helping to ensure that all interests are represented in the implementation of public policies and programs. The crucial intermediate linkage is the minority role perception. If adoption of this role can have a democratizing effect on bureaucracy, what steps might be taken to foster it in public organizations?

Two avenues seem open toward this goal. First, public organizations can attempt to establish a culture in which employees are expected to increase access of minorities to services and programs. In this study, even when administrators perceived dual expectations to adopt this stance as well as to implement programs according to department practices and procedures, they were still more likely to assume the minority representative role conception. By contrast, inculcation of a traditional bureaucratic role emphasizing economy and efficiency was associated negatively with the minority representative role. The second avenue, likewise a primordial vehicle for socialization, is the educational system. Master's degree programs in public administration or affairs, through which many government managers and aspirants pass, should expose this audience to the variety of job roles that they may assume as well as their likely implications for decision-making, other workplace behaviors, and the representation of interests that might otherwise be slighted or excluded from consideration. If government organizations do not impart such a message through the expectations they set in the workplace, educational programs in public administration may yet establish the legitimacy of the minority representative role perception.

As always, bureaucratic discretion must be applied with care to balance several values. Mosher (1982, 15) cautions that "active representation run rampant within a bureaucracy would constitute a major threat to orderly democratic government. The summing up of the multitude of special interests seeking effective representation does not constitute the general interest." Resolving the tension between an emphasis on bureaucratic impartiality on the one hand and representativeness on the other may not be easy. No matter what accommodation might be reached, Krislov and Rosenbloom (1981,197) insist that representative bureaucracy should be considered an "augmentation of, not a substitute for, traditional constitutional restraints" on bureaucratic action. We believe that a useful balance can be achieved when representative bureaucracy operates to promote equity, that is, when active representation works to facilitate the consideration of the views of all interested parties in the policy process. In the context of minority representation, this position would mean that efforts are made to ensure that minority interests are not ignored in circumstances where those interests need to be heard and might otherwise be disregarded.

References

Carmines, Edward G., and James A. Stimson. 1989. *Issue Evolution: Race and the Transformation of American Politics.* Princeton, NJ: Princeton University Press.

Dahl, Robert A. 1947. "The Science of Public Administration: Three Problems." *Public Administration Review* 7: 1–11.

Daley, Dennis. 1984. "Political and Occupational Barriers to the Implementation of Affirmative Action: Administrative, Executive, and Legislative Attitudes Toward Representative Bureaucracy." *Review of Public Personnel Administration* 4: 4–15.

Denhardt, Robert B., and Linda deLeon. 1993. "Great Thinkers in Personnel Management." In *Handbook of Public Personnel Management*, ed. Jack Rabin, et al. New York: Marcel Dekker.

Frederickson, H. George. 1971. "Toward a New Public Administration." In *Toward a New Public Administration: The Minnowbrook Perspective*, ed. Frank Marini. Scranton: Chandler.

Guinier, Lani. 1994. *The Tyranny of the Majority: Fundamental Fairness in Representative Democracy.* New York: Free Press.

Hadwiger, Don F. 1973. "Experience of Black Farmers Home Administration Local Office Chiefs." *Public Personnel Management* 2: 49–54.

Henderson, Lenneal J. 1988. "Urban Administrators: The Politics of Role Elasticity." In *Urban Minority Administrators: Politics, Policy, and Style*, ed. Albert K. Kamig and Paula D. McClain. New York: Greenwood Press.

Herbert, Adam W. 1974. "The Minority Administrator: Problems, Prospects, and Challenges." *Public Administration Review* 34: 556–63.

Hindera, John J. 1993a. "Representative Bureaucracy: Further Evidence of Active Representation in the EEOC District Offices." *Journal of Public Administration Research and Theory* 3: 415–29.

Hindera, John J. 1993b. "Representative Bureaucracy: Imprimis Evidence of Active Representation in the EEOC District Offices." *Social Science Quarterly* 74: 95–108.

Holmes, Steven A. 1995. "Programs Based on Sex and Race Are Under Attack; Dole Seeks Elimination." *New York Times*, March 16: 1A.

Ingraham, Patricia W., and Carolyn R. Ban. 1986. "Models of Public Management: Are They Useful to Federal Managers in the 1980s?" *Public Administration Review* 46: 152–60.

Kahn, Robert L., Donald M. Wolfe, Robert P. Quinn, and J. Diedrick Snoek. 1964. *Organizational Stress: Studies in Role Conflict and Ambiguity.* New York: John Wiley.

Karnig, Albert K., and Paula D. McClain. 1988. "Minority Administrators: Lessons from Practice." In *Urban Minority Administrators: Politics, Policy, and Style*, ed. Albert K. Karnig and Paula D. McClain. New York: Greenwood Press.

Kaufman, Herbert. 1956. "Emerging Conflicts in the Doctrines of Public Administration." *American Political Science Review* 50:1057–73.

Kellough, J. Edward. 1990a. "Integration in the Public Workplace: Determinants of Minority and Female Employment in Federal Agencies." *Public Administration Review* 50: 557–66.

Kellough, J. Edward. 1990b. "Federal Agencies and Affirmative Action for Blacks and Women." *Social Science Quarterly* 71: 83–92.

Krislov, Samuel. 1974. *Representative Bureaucracy*. Englewood Cliffs, NJ: Prentice-Hall.

Krislov, Samuel, and David H. Rosenbloom. 1981. *Representative Bureaucracy and the American Political System*. New York: Praeger.

Lipset, Seymour Martin. 1992. "Equal Chances Versus Equal Rights." *Annals of the American Academy of Political and Social Science* 523: 63–74.

Martinez, Thomas R. 1991. "The Role of Hispanic Public Administration: A Theoretical and Empirical Analysis." *American Review of Public Administration* 21: 33–56.

Meier, Kenneth J. 1975. "Representative Bureaucracy: An Empirical Analysis." *American Political Science Review* 69: 526–42.

Meier, Kenneth J. 1993a. "Latinos and Representative Bureaucracy: Testing the Thompson and Henderson Hypotheses." *Journal of Public Administration Research and Theory* 3: 393–414.

Meier, Kenneth J. 1993b. "Representative Bureaucracy: A Theoretical and Empirical Exposition." In *Research in Public Administration*, vol. 2, ed. James L. Perry. Greenwich, CT: JAI Press.

Meier, Kenneth J., and Lloyd Nigro. 1976. "Representative Bureaucracy and Policy Preferences: A Study in the Attitudes of Federal Executives." *Public Administration Review* 36: 458–69.

Meier, Kenneth J., and Joseph Stewart, Jr. 1992. "The Impact of Representative Bureaucracies: Educational Systems and Public Policies." *American Review of Public Administration* 22: 157–71.

Mosher, Frederick. 1982. *Democracy and the Public Service*. 2d ed. New York: Oxford University Press.

Murray, Sylvester, Larry D. Terry, Charles A. Washington, and Lawrence F. Keller. 1994. "The Role Demands of Minority Public Administrators: The Herbert Thesis Revisited." *Public Administration Review* 54: 409–17.

Pennington, Debra, and FmHA Georgia Rural Housing Loans Program. 1994. Personal interview by first author, June 21, Athens, GA.

Romzek, Barbara S., and J. Stephen Hendricks. 1982. "Organizational Involvement and Representative Bureaucracy: Can We Have It Both Ways?" *American Political Science Review* 76: 75–82.

Rosenbloom, David H., and Douglas Kinnard. 1977. "Bureaucratic Representation and Bureaucratic Behavior: An Exploratory Analysis." *Midwest Review of Public Administration* 11: 35–42.

Squires, Gregory D., and Sunwoong Kim. 1995. "Does Anybody Who Works Here Look Like Me: Mortgage Lending, Race, and Lender Employment." *Social Science Quarterly* 76: 823–38.

Thompson, Frank J. 1976. "Minority Groups in Public Bureaucracies: Are Passive and Active Representation Linked?" *Administration and Society* 8: 201–26.

Thompson, Frank J. 1978. "Civil Servants and the Deprived: Socio-Political and Occupational Explanations of Attitudes Toward Minority Hiring." *American Journal of Political Science* 22: 325–47.

U.S. Commission on Civil Rights. 1979. *The Federal Fair Housing Enforcement Effort.* Washington, DC: Government Printing Office.

U.S. Commission on Civil Rights. 1982. *The Decline of Black Farming in America.* Washington, DC: Government Printing Office.

Wyatt, Nancy, and Gerald M. Phillips. 1988. *A Case Study of the Farmers Home Administration: Studying Organizational Communication.* Norwood, NJ: Ablex Publishing.

Progress Toward Achieving a Representative Federal Bureaucracy: The Impact of Supervisors and Their Beliefs

Katherine C. Naff

More than two decades ago, the Civil Rights Act (as amended) required federal agencies to eliminate the underrepresentation of minorities and women in their work forces. This policy was given additional impetus with the passage of the Civil Service Reform Act in 1978, that called for a civil service "reflective of the nation's diversity" and required agencies to engage in affirmative recruitment for all occupations and grade levels in which minorities and women are underrepresented. Yet despite substantial progress in achieving this goal, Hispanics remain underrepresented in the federal workforce (U.S. Office of Personnel Management 1995), and minorities and women lag behind nonminority men in mid and higher grade levels in the federal workforce (see Table [4.7]).

As will be discussed in more detail below, some authorities have attributed at least some of the blame for the failure to achieve a fully representative federal workforce to inadequate support for such efforts by political leaders and agency heads. The role of federal supervisors in this process has been less studied; yet it is the combined individual hiring and promotion decisions made by supervisors on a day-to-day basis that determine the overall demographic composition of the civil service. This paper examines the extent to which federal supervisors believe in the value of a representative workforce, and the extent to which such attitudes influence their recruitment and consideration of underrepresented minorities. Research conducted during the 1970s suggest that federal supervisors often resisted polices designed to increase workforce diversity (Levine 1974; Milward and Swanson 1979;

From Katherine C. Naff, "Progress Toward Achieving a Representative Federal Bureaucracy: The Impact of Supervisors and Their Beliefs," *Public Personnel Management*, Summer 1998, 135–137, 138, 139–147. Copyright © 1998 by International Personnel Management Association. Reprinted with permission from *Public Personnel Management*, published by the International Personnel Management Association (IPMA), 1617 Duke St., Alexandria, VA 22314; (703) 549–7100; www.ipma-hr.org.

Table 4.7

Percentage of Federal Positions in Each Grade Grouping Held by Men and Women, and by Race/National Origin Group, 1995

	Senior executives	Midlevel (GS 13–15)	Other (GS 1–12)
Men	82.3	76.7	44.7
Women	17.7	23.3	55.3
White	88.5	84.6	68.8
Black	7.0	7.6	19.5
Hispanic	2.3	3.2	6.1
Asian Pacific American	1.3	3.6	3.6
Native American	.8	.9	2.0

Source: OPM's Central Personnel Data File, March 1995.
Note: Figures may not add up to 100%, due to rounding.

Rosenbloom 1984). This analysis updates and extends that research by examining the responses of 5700 federal supervisors and managers to a survey administered by the U.S. Merit Systems Protection Board in December 1994.

Representative Bureaucracy as Federal Policy

The importance of a representative bureaucracy has long been emphasized in much of the scholarly literature analyzing the role of a bureaucracy in a democratic polity (Kingsley 1944; Levitan 1946; Long 1952; Krislov 1967; Krislov 1974; Krislov and Rosenbloom 1981; Hale and Kelly 1989). Among the many reasons a diverse civil service is valued include incorporating divergent talents, skills and perspectives into increasingly complex bureaucratic decisionmaking; demonstrating that diverse communities have access to the policy-making process through these representatives; and confirming that the nation's largest employer and enforcer of its laws has its own house in order with respect to equal employment opportunity.

The concept of a representative federal bureaucracy, officially endorsed by the President's Committee on Equal Employment Opportunity created by President Kennedy in 1961 (Kellough 1992), received additional impetus with the passage of the Civil Service Reform Act in 1978. The Act instituted a number of mechanisms designed to accelerate the progress of minorities and women into higher bureaucratic positions (Kellough 1989). These mechanisms included requiring the Office of Personnel Management (OPM) to establish a Federal Equal Opportunity Recruitment Program (FEORP) to conduct affirmative recruitment for underrepresented occupations and grades and mandating the achievement of affirmative action goals as one basis for evaluating the performance of senior executives. The Equal Employment Opportunity Commission (EEOC) was also given responsibility for overseeing federal agency efforts to achieve representative workforces.

Since 1978, the government's efforts in achieving a representative workforce have been evaluated and have often received poor marks. In an assessment of OPM's role during its first ten years, the U.S. Merit Systems Protection Board (MSPB) noted that "OPM has provided erratic, and at times insufficient, leadership and guidance in the areas of equal employment opportunity. . . " (U.S. Merit Systems Protection Board 1989). The General Accounting Office (GAO), in a 1991 report for the Chairman of the House Subcommittee on the Civil Service, was critical of the EEOC for its inadequate oversight of affirmative employment planning by federal agencies (U.S. General Accounting Office 1991). . .

Others found fault with agency leadership and the apparent failure to hold managers accountable for achieving representative workforces. Researchers during the 1970s and 1980s noted that affirmative employment policies designed to increase the representation of women and minorities were being subverted in many agencies. Such practices included deliberately limiting minority employees to minor roles or nonessential tasks or promising to fill 100 percent of clerical jobs with women (Levine 1974, Rosenbloom 1984, Milward and Swanson 1979).

Milward and Swanson [1979] theorize that inadequate agency support for achieving the goal of a diverse workforce is explained by organizational behavior that is naturally resistant to externally-imposed demands. In the case of affirmative action, they suggest, organizations will minimize the effect of such requirements by shuttling women and minorities into functions external to their technological core. The Department of Labor [1991] found, in its study of the glass ceiling in corporate America, that minorities and women are often steered into staff positions, such as human resources, research, or administration rather than those jobs which affect the bottom line. Without experience in bottom line-related functions, they are derailed from "the fast track to the executive suite."

It is individual supervisors and managers, however, who ultimately make hiring and promotion decisions. The importance of supervisory support for a representative workforce has been confirmed by, among others, former OPM Director Constance Newman, who stated that "real equal employment opportunity will come about only when each and every executive, manager, supervisor and employee is committed to and held accountable for equal opportunity" (Office of the Vice President 1993). The difficulties faced by EEO and affirmative action programs were apparent in 1979 when about one-third of federal supervisors completing an OPM survey expressed agreement with the statement, "compared to other employees hired into or promoted into Senior Executive positions, minorities in this agency are less qualified" (Rosehbloom 1981). This article asks whether attitudes toward increasing minority and female representation have improved, and what impact, if any, do such attitudes have on supervisors' efforts to correct underrepresentation in their work units?. . .

. . . [I]t is important to examine whether opposition to affirmative action and representative bureaucracy on the part of federal supervisors has abated. Has the growing recognition of the need to effectively "manage diversity" increased their support? Perhaps more importantly, does the extent to which supervisors' support (or lack of) for achieving a representative workforce have an impact on their efforts to recruit groups that may be underrepresented in their work units? If there is little support for the goals of a representative bureaucracy and such antipathy does have a noticeable impact on their actions, it may help to explain why the government has failed to achieve its goal of a representative workforce at all grade levels and in all occupations.

Data and Methods

These underrepresentation questions are addressed with responses to a governmentwide survey of supervisors and managers administered by MSPB in December 1994. The survey was designed in part to contribute to MSPB's forthcoming analysis of Hispanic underrepresentation in federal employment. It was mailed to a random sample of about 10,000 supervisors and managers, stratified by grade level, occupational category and race/national origin. A total of 5741 surveys were returned, for a response rate of 61 percent.

The extent to which federal supervisors support the goals of a representative bureaucracy is assessed by examining their responses to three items that included a 5 point Likert (Strongly Agree/Strongly Disagree) scale:

- Selecting officials should be held accountable for achieving a workforce that is as diverse as the available civilian labor force.
- When I am choosing among qualified candidates to hire, I take into consideration whether a candidate is a member of a group that is underrepresented in my work unit(s).
- My work unit would be more productive if it reflected the demographic makeup of the local labor force.

Most surveys examining attitudes toward efforts to increase the representation of minorities and women have asked about affirmative action rather than the concept of representative bureaucracy. While the concepts are clearly linked, research has suggested that the degree of support for policies related to equal employment opportunity is dependent on how the question is framed (Fine 1992). The analysis presented here improves upon previous research by analyzing survey items that ask directly about the value of a representative workforce, rather than about affirmative action policies.

As noted previously, it is also important to assess the extent to which supervisors' support for representative bureaucracy affects their own efforts to recruit minorities and women. Research during past eras suggested that those resistant to such policies find ways to undermine them (Milward and Swanson 1979; Rosenbloom 1984). But do those who agree with such policies actually make an effort to recruit and/or consider applicants from underrepresented groups? While positing such a relationship clearly oversimplifies the variety of reasons for which a supervisor makes hiring decisions (Ballard and Lawn-Day 1992; Thompson 1978), it is nevertheless worth examining the relationship between such attitudes and behavior.

This analysis focuses specifically on the recruitment of Hispanics, the only minority group officially underrepresented governmentwide (U.S. Office of Personnel Management 1995). To ensure that supervisors who failed to recruit or consider Hispanics did not do so because they were unable to hire anyone at all, or because Hispanics are already adequately represented in their work units, only the responses of the 1624 supervisors who meet the following criteria are included in this analysis:

- they have the authority to select or recommend for selection candidates for vacant jobs under their supervision;
- they have recommended or selected at least one candidate for a vacancy within the past three years; and
- they believe that Hispanics are underrepresented in their work units.

The dependent variable is a composite of two questions asking supervisors (1) if they have been personally involved in recruiting activities for Hispanic candidates and (2) whether they have actively considered Hispanic applicants for any job vacancy under their supervision within the past three years. Supervisors who answered "yes" to either one of these questions is coded 1 and those who answered no to both are coded 0.

In efforts to hire Hispanics, two separate models are estimated to evaluate the impact of two different, specific attitudes toward a representative workforce. Since the dependent variable is dichotomous (has/has not recruited or considered Hispanic applicants), logistic regression is used to evaluate the effect of supervisors' attitudes on their actions. In model 1, the primary inde-

pendent variable is the item asking supervisors whether they agree that selecting officials should be held accountable for achieving a diverse workforce.
In model 2, the primary independent variable is the item assessing supervisors' agreement with the statement that their work unit would be more productive if it reflected the demographic makeup of the local labor force. Control
variables include the respondent's national origin (Hispanic or nonHispanic,
other minority/nonminority); sex; amount of experience as a supervisor; college degree attainment; and whether the work unit supervised is primarily
professional, administrative or otherwise (e.g., manual trade, technical or
clerical). These control variables are included as previous research has suggested that sex, race/national origin, education, professionalism and familiarity with recruitment policies are all correlated with attitudes in increasing
minority and female representation (Clayton and Crosby 1992; Jacobson 1983;
Matheson et al. 1994; Kluegel and Smith 1983; Slack 1987; Thompson 1978).

Findings and Discussion

Table [4.8] shows federal supervisors' responses to questions related to the goals
of representative bureaucracy. Since women and minorities tend to be more supportive of efforts to achieve a diverse workforce than men and nonminorities
(Clayton and Crosby 1992), responses are broken out by these groups.

Overall, the results suggest that while a sizable minority of supervisors
support concepts related to the achievement of a representative bureaucracy,
it is, nonetheless, a minority. While most minority supervisors (68.6 percent)
and half of female supervisors (49.1 percent) agree that selecting officials
should be held accountable for achieving a diverse workforce, only about
one third (35.3 percent) of nonminorities and men (39.2 percent) agree with
such a policy. As nonminority men make up the majority of federal supervisors, their attitudes are, in some ways, the most consequential.

Slightly less than half of supervisors (46 percent) also report that they
take underrepresentation into account when choosing among qualified candidates; although, this time the responses of minorities, nonminorities, and
men and women are not so different. It seems that the concern expressed by
many white men that the administration's emphasis on diversity has limited
their opportunities (Bridger 1994; Goshko 1994; Harris 1994; Larson 1994)
is probably overstated.

Finally, there is even less agreement among supervisors that their work
units would be more productive if they reflected the demographic makeup of
the local labor force. Although a greater proportion of minority supervisors
(20.2 percent) agree with this statement than nonminorities (9.4 percent) or
women (10.9 percent), overall this notion finds little support.

While a lack of enthusiasm for concepts related to the goals of a representative bureaucracy is disappointing, what is of more consequence is the extent to which supervisors' attitudes affect their behavior. After all, one can fail to support particular policies but still comply with those for which one is held accountable. Survey results indicate that of the 1624 supervisors who indicated that Hispanics are underrepresented in their work units and that they have been involved in hiring at least one person in their work unit in the past three years, only 42 percent either tried to recruit or considered Hispanic candidates. The question is to what extent did attitudes toward the value of a diverse workforce influence the likelihood that those supervisors actively recruited or considered Hispanic applicants?

Tables [4.9] and [4.10] show the results of the logistic regression models estimated to determine the impact of such attitudes on efforts to recruit Hispanics. Both models are statistically significant and useful for predicting such efforts in the federal workforce.

The results suggest that the impact attitudes have on supervisors' efforts to recruit underrepresented minorities depends on the attitude in question. Whether supervisors believe that they ought to be held accountable for diversity is of no consequence, controlling for all else. However, supervisors who believe that diversity contributes to their own work unit productivity are more likely to recruit Hispanics than those who don't hold this belief. This suggests that organizations making an effort to educate supervisors about the value of workforce diversity and its productivity benefits will be more effective than those simply mandating compliance with EEO objectives.

Nevertheless, the results presented in Table [4.10] suggest that even when supervisors believe diversity contributes to workforce productivity, it does not have a great impact on their recruitment efforts. In this table, covariates are held constant using the characteristics of the "average" supervisor responding to the survey (i.e., the modal response) and varying the level of agreement with the statement, "My work unit would be more productive if it reflected the demographic makeup of the local labor force." The average supervisor is a nonHispanic, nonminority man with one to five years of supervisor experience and a college degree who supervises a professional/administrative work unit. The results indicate that the average supervisor who strongly disagrees with the previous statement would have a 36 percent chance of making an effort to recruit Hispanics. However, one who strongly agrees would have a 50 percent probability of making such an effort. Thus, a belief in the value of diversity only increases the probability that he will recruit or consider Hispanics by 14 percent.

The variable that does have a considerable impact on a supervisor's likelihood to recruit Hispanics when they are underrepresented in his or her work

Table 4.8

Supervisors' Attitudes Toward Representative Bureaucracy (percent responding)

Selecting officials should be held accountable for achieving a workforce that is as diverse as the available civilian labor force.

	Nonminority	Minority	Men	Women
Strongly agree/agree	35.3	68.6	39.2	49.1
Neither	17.4	14.2	16.1	18.8
Strongly disagree/disagree	45.3	13.9	42.7	29.2
N	(4540)	(1095)	(4170)	(1467)
	$p < .001$	$p < .001$		

When I am choosing among qualified candidates to hire, I take into consideration whether a candidate is a member of a group that is underrepresented in my work unit(s).

	Nonminority	Minority	Men	Women
Strongly agree/agree	45.9	46.1	45.8	46.2
Neither	19.6	18.8	19.6	19.0
Strongly disagree/disagree	31.9	30.3	31.8	31.0
N	(4510)	(1074)	(4133)	(1452)
	$p < .01$			

My work unit would be more productive if it reflected the demographic makeup of the local labor force.

	Nonminority	Minority	Men	Women
Strongly agree/agree	9.4	20.2	11.7	10.9
Neither	36.9	32.4	35.0	39.0
Strongly disagree/disagree	43.4	33.1	43.5	35.8
N	(4517)	(1072)	(4135)	(1456)
	$p < .001$		$p < .001$	

Note: Percentages do not add up to 100 because "don't know" responses are not shown.
Source: 1994 MSPB survey respondents.

unit is the supervisor's own Hispanic identity (see tables [4.9] and [4.10]). The same hypothetical "average" supervisor who is Hispanic rather than nonHispanic has a 71 percent chance of making an effort to recruit Hispanics even if he doesn't believe diversity contributes to productivity. This suggests that agencies who want to decrease Hispanic underrepresentation will make the most immediate progress if they . . . can ensure that Hispanics are well represented within their supervisory cadre. This finding is consistent with research on minority employment in cities, which has found that the presence of minorities in positions of authority (e.g., chief executive, city council) contributes significantly to the proportion of minorities employed

Table 4.9

**Effect of Attitudes on Efforts to Recruit Hispanics:
Logistic Regression Coefficients** (standard error)

	Model 1		Model 2	
Selecting officials should be accountable for diversity	.011	(.043)		
My work unit would be more productive is it reflected diversity			.142**	(.054)
Respondent is Hispanic	1.47***	(.254)	1.47***	(.255)
Respondent in nonHispanic minority	−.260*	(.108)	−.239*	(.108)
Amount of supervisory experience	.213***	(.043)	.222***	(.043)
Has college degree	.571***	(.123)	.619***	(.123)
Respondent is female	.146	(.119)	.150	(.119)
Supervises professional workforce	.204	(.119)	.179	(.119)
Constant	−1.69	(.309)	−2.115	(.319)
Chi square	113.21***		120.54**	

$* p < .05.$
$** p < .01.$
$*** p < .001.$

by the city government (Cole 1976; Dye and Renick 1981; Eisinger 1982; Stein 1986).

Whether the supervisor is a nonHispanic minority is also significant, although the coefficient is negative. This means that nonHispanic minorities are less likely to recruit Hispanics, even when they are underrepresented in their work units, than white supervisors. One possible explanation for this finding can also be found in research at the municipal level, showing that an increase in the size of one minority workforce can have adverse consequences for another minority workforce. In other words, when one minority group increases its representation, it does so at the expense of other minority groups rather than at the expense of nonminorities or as a result of a growing workforce. Such intergroup competition often results in strains, sometimes even erupting into riots (McClain 1993; Warren, Stack and Corbett 1986).

In an analysis of data from the late 1960s, Rosenbloom showed that in some agencies increases in employment of other minority groups was correlated with a decrease in the employment of blacks. He warned that such interminority group competition was a potential problem for federal EEO efforts (Rosenbloom 1973). To the extent that minorities are aware of such trends, it is certainly understandable that they would be unwilling to actively recruit from minority groups other than their own.

On the other hand, another interpretation is simply that supervisors from other minority groups are as interested in increasing the representation of

Table 4.10

Probability of Recruiting or Considering Hispanics When They Are Underrepresented in the Work Unit

	Level of agreement with value of diversity		
	Strong agreement	Neither	Strong disagreement
NonHispanic/nonminority	50%	43%	36%
Hispanic	81%	76%	71%

The model used to estimate the probability that a supervisor would recruit Hispanics took the following logistic form:

$P(Act) = 1/1 + exp(-b0 + b1$ (response to statement) $+ b2(RNO) + b3(sex) + b4$(supervisory experience) $+ b5$(degree) $+ b6$(supervises professional/admin work unit))

Where   Sex = male
        Amount of supervisory experience = 1–5 years
        College degree = yes
        Supervises professional/administrative unit

Source: 1994 MSPB Supervisor Study.

members of their group in their work units as are Hispanics. When minorities are few in number in an organization, they face a variety of adverse consequences including exaggerated expectations and extreme evaluations (Pettigrew and Martin 1987). From this perspective, it is quite understandable that supervisors from nonHispanic minority groups may be less willing than whites to hire Hispanics simply because they don't want to pass up the opportunity to increase the representation of their own group in their work unit.

Women do not appear more likely than men to make an effort to increase Hispanic representation, despite the fact that they are generally more supportive of diversity efforts than are men (see table [4.8]). Experience and education do show a positive relationship, suggesting that experience and education contribute to an understanding of the need to achieve a representative workforce, just as they contribute to support for affirmative action policies. The nature of the work unit supervised (professional or not) is not a significant factor.

Thus, it seems that if an agency is concerned about correcting Hispanic underrepresentation, its efforts are best spent on recruiting or promoting Hispanics into supervisory positions, who will, in turn, make an effort to ensure their work units reflect adequate Hispanic representation. An additional, though somewhat less effective strategy, would be to educate supervisors about the value of a representative workforce in enhancing productivity; that belief does have at least some impact on their recruitment efforts.

Implications

Despite fifty years of scholarly treatises extolling the virtues of a representative bureaucracy and nearly twenty years after codification of the value of a diverse workforce in the Civil Service Reform Act, the lack of enthusiasm for the concept among federal supervisors persists. Only a minority of supervisors believe they should be held accountable for achieving a diverse workforce, and an even smaller minority believe their work unit would be more productive if it mirrored the demographic makeup of the local labor force. Less than half of supervisors reported that they take underrepresentation into account when choosing among qualified candidates and only half of supervisors who believe Hispanics are underrepresented in their work units have actively recruited or considered Hispanic candidates. Minorities are disproportionately represented among those who believe supervisors should be held accountable for achieving a representative workforce and among those who take underrepresentation into account when hiring. But, they make up only a small portion of federal supervisors.

This analysis has further suggested that such attitudes do have some impact on the recruitment efforts and hiring decisions of federal supervisors. Clearly, this examination is limited in that it was confined to efforts to recruit Hispanics by supervisors who acknowledge that Hispanics are underrepresented in their work units. Nevertheless, it seems that those who do not believe representation affects the productivity of their work unit are less likely to have tried to recruit Hispanics than those who believe productivity would be affected. Thus, there is value in educating supervisors about the value of a diverse workforce, as long as such educational efforts are focused on the extent to which a representative workforce enhances productivity, rather than emphasizing organizational requirements.

This analysis also shows that while supervisors' attitudes, amount of supervisory experience and level of educational attainment can all affect their willingness to try to improve the representation of Hispanics in their organizations, by far the most important factor is whether or not they are Hispanic themselves. Agency leadership that is concerned with increasing Hispanic representation within the agency will be most successful if it ensures that Hispanics are well represented among those making the hiring decisions, regardless of the degree to which those Hispanic supervisors believe in the value of a representative workforce. To the extent that this is also true for other minority groups and women, it means that a representative workforce particularly at supervisory levels has value not only in bringing a diversity of views and legitimacy to the policymaking process, but is the best means for ensuring that diversity will flourish at lower levels of the organization as well. While a lack of supervisory support for the concept of representative bureaucracy may serve as a barrier to its realization, a greater obstacle may be the dearth of women and minorities at supervisory levels themselves. This analysis provides limited support for both of these explanations, but both are worthy of further exploration. . . .

Success in achieving a representative bureaucracy is no doubt promoted and impeded by a variety of factors working in combination. Without continued analysis of accessories and impediments to achieving a representative bureaucracy and active efforts to put these findings into practice, two decades from now we may still be asking why the federal government has not achieved its goal of a civil service representative of the nation at all grade levels.

References

Ballard, Steve, and Gayle Lawn-Day. 1992. "Affirmative Action in Municipal Government: Anatomy of a Failure." *Review of Public Personnel Management* 12 (May–August): 5–18.

Bridger, C. 1994. "Dorn Denies Job Bias Against White Men." *Federal Times*, October 10.

Clayton, Susan D., and Faye J. Crosby. 1992. *Justice, Gender, and Affirmative Action*. Ann Arbor: University of Michigan Press.

Cole, Leonard A. 1976. *Blacks in Power: A Comparative Study of Black and White Elected Officials*. Princeton, NJ: Princeton University Press.

Dye, Thomas R., and James Renick. 1981. "Political Power and City Jobs: Determinants of Minority Employment." *Social Science Quarterly* 62 (September): 475–486.

Eisinger, Peter K. 1982. "Black Employment in Municipal Jobs: The Impact of Black Political Power." *American Political Science Review* 76(2): 380–392.

Fine, Terri Susan. 1992. "The Impact of Issue Framing on Public Opinion: Toward Affirmative Action Programs." *Social Science Journal* 29: 323–334.

Goshko, J.M. 1994. "Foreign Service's Painful Passage to Looking More Like America." *Washington Post*, April 21.

Hale, Mary M., and Rita Mae Kelly. 1989. *Gender, Bureaucracy, and Democracy: Careers and Equal Opportunity in the Public Sector*. New York: Greenwood Press.

Harris, C. 1994. "Discrimination Against White Men Found: IRS Staffer Blames Diversity Efforts." *Federal Times*, May 9.

Jacobson, Cardell K. 1983. "Black Support for Affirmative Action Programs." *Phylon* 44: 299–311.

Kellough, J. Edward. 1989. "The Civil Service Reform and Federal Equal Employment Opportunity." *American Review of Public Administration* 19 (December): 313–324.

Kellough, J. Edward. 1992. "Affirmative Action in Government Employment." *Annals of the American Academy of Political Science* 523 (September): 117–130.
Kingsley, J. Donald. 1944. *Representative Bureaucracy: An Interpretation of the British Civil Service.* Yellow Springs, OH: Antioch Press.
Kluegel, James R., and Eliot R. Smith. 1983. "Affirmative Action Attitudes: Effects of Self-Interest, Racial Affect and Stratification Beliefs on Whites' Views." *Social Forces* 61 (March): 796–822.
Krislov, Samuel. 1967. *The Negro in Federal Employment.* Minneapolis: University of Minnesota Press.
Krislov, Samuel. 1974. *Representative Bureaucracy.* Englewood Cliffs, NJ: Prentice-Hall.
Krislov, Samuel, and David H. Rosenbloom. 1981. *Representative Bureaucracy and the American Political System.* New York: Praeger.
Larson, Ruth. 1994. "White Men Say Foreign Service Locks Them Out of Top Positions." *Washington Times,* January 14.
Levine, Charles H. 1974. "Beyond the Sound and Fury of Targets." *Public Administration Review* 34 (May/June): 240–241.
Levitan, David M. 1946. "The Responsibility of Administrative Officials in a Democratic Society." *Political Science Quarterly* 61 (December): 562–598.
Long, Norton E. 1952. "Bureaucracy and Constitutionalism." *American Political Science Review* 46 (September): 808–818.
Matheson, Kimberly, et al. 1994. "Women's Attitudes Toward Affirmative Action: Putting Actions in Context." *Journal of Applied Social Psychology* 24 (December): 2075–96.
McClain, Paula D. 1993. "The Changing Dynamics of Urban Politics: Black and Hispanic Municipal Employment—Is There Competition?" *Journal of Politics* 55 (May): 399–414.
Milward, H. Brinton, and Cheryl Swanson. 1979. "Organizational Response to Environmental Pressures: The Policy of Affirmative Action." *Administration and Society* 11 (August): 123–143.
Office of the Vice President. 1993. *Reinventing Human Resource Management: Accompanying Report of the National Performance Review.* Washington, DC: Office of the Vice President.
Pettigrew, Thomas F., and Joanne Martin. 1987. "Spring the Organizational Context for Black American Inclusion." *Journal of Social Issues* 43(1): 41–78.
Rosenbloom, David H. 1973. "A Note on Interminority Group Competition for Federal Positions." *Public Personnel Management* 2 (January/February): 43–48.
Rosenbloom, David H. 1981. "Federal Equal Employment Opportunity: Is the Polarization Worth the Preference?" *Southern Review of Public Administration* 5 (Spring): 63–72.
Rosenbloom, David H. 1984. "The Declining Salience of Affirmative Action in Federal Personnel Management." *Review of Public Personnel Management* 4 (Summer): 31–40.
Slack, James D. 1987. "Affirmative Action and City Managers: Attitudes Toward Recruitment of Women." *Public Administration Review* 47 (March/April):199–206.
Stein, Lana. 1986. "Representative Local Government: Minorities in the Municipal Workforce." *Journal of Politics* 48 (August): 694–713.
Thompson, Frank J. 1978. "Civil Servants and the Deprived: Socio-political and Oc-

cupational Explanations of Attitudes Toward Minority Hiring." *American Journal of Political Science* 22 (May): 325–347.

U.S. Department of Labor. 1991. *A Report on the Glass Ceiling Initiative.* Washington, DC: U.S. Department of Labor.

U.S. General Accounting Office. 1991. *Federal Workforce: Continuing Need for Federal Affirmative Employment.* Washington, DC: U.S. General Accounting Office.

U.S. Merit Systems Protection Board. 1989. *U.S. Office of Personnel Management and the Merit System: A Retrospective Assessment.* Washington, DC: U.S. Merit Systems Protection Board.

U.S. Office of Personnel Management. 1995. *Federal Equal Opportunity Recruitment Program October 1, 1993–September 30, 1994.* Washington, DC: U.S. Office of Personnel Management.

Warren, Christopher L., John F. Stack, and John G. Corbett. 1986. "Minority Mobilization in an International City: Rivalry and Conflict in Miami." *PS* 19 (Summer): 626–634.

Discussion Questions

1. Is passive representation a necessary condition in order for active representation to take place in public bureaucracies? Or, as suggested by the work of Selden et al. (1998), is it possible that those with attitudes favorable to the group in question, regardless of their own social background, can just as effectively represent the diversity of policy preferences in the United States? If so, what does this suggest about representative bureaucracy as a goal for public personnel? Can administrative men represent the policy positions of women in the population? Can whites represent the policy desires of racial minorities? Why or why not?

2. Do you think that members of certain social groups (African Americans, Hispanic Americans, Asian Americans, women, etc.) are more likely than others to think of themselves as representatives of their own social group? Does group consciousness vary according to social background in the United States? The articles included in this chapter seem to suggest passive representation leads to active representation more often for racial minorities than for women. How might you interpret and explain such findings?

3. What factors affect how likely an individual bureaucrat is to feel a special responsibility to act as an advocate on behalf of his or her own social group? Are older bureaucrats more or less likely than younger bureaucrats to adopt an advocacy role? Why?

4. Is active representation more likely to occur in certain governmental departments and agencies than others? Which agencies do you think would be more likely to facilitate active representation? Which would be least likely to do so? Why?

Chapter 5

"Reinventing Government" and Representative Bureaucracy

The Impacts of
Employee Empowerment,
Outsourcing, and Entrepreneurship

The broad "reinventing government" movement that developed in the 1980s and 1990s has important, though contradictory, ramifications for representative bureaucracy. Also known as the "New Public Management," reinvention reforms in the United States, Canada, Great Britain, Australia, New Zealand, Hong Kong, and elsewhere focused on changing the culture of public bureaucracies. Reinventers sought to reorient bureaucracies toward outputs and results and away from inputs and procedures. The U.S. federal version, spearheaded by former vice president Al Gore's National Performance Review, emphasized:

- Creating a clear sense of administrative mission
- Steering more and rowing less, that is, arranging for the provision of public goods and services by outsourcing and other means rather than producing and delivering them directly
- Decentralizing agencies and empowering employees by delegating authority and responsibility
- Replacing regulations with incentives
- Developing budgets based on results
- Exposing administrative operations to internal and external competition
- Searching for market rather than administrative solutions
- Measuring success in terms of customer satisfaction (Gore 1993, 7).

Implementing these strategies would create "entrepreneurial organizations" (Gore 1993, 5).

Reinvention seeks greater administrative cost-effectiveness, but employee empowerment, outsourcing, and entrepreneurship, in particular, bear substantially on representative bureaucracy.

Employee Empowerment

All else being equal, employee empowerment will strengthen the connection between passive and active bureaucratic representation. Empowerment rests on the assumption that rank-and-file employees, including those on the front-lines dealing with the public, have intimate knowledge of an agency's work and problems. Therefore, their participation in administrative decision making is valuable. Hierarchy and efforts to maintain a bright line between those who do the thinking (managers) and the work (employees) should be diminished. Employees should also be allowed to use their judgment to improve work processes and customer satisfaction. There are four corollaries: (1) employees should have greater independence and be subject to less supervision (which translates into fewer supervisors and managers); (2) procedural controls on employees should be reduced; (3) employees should be accountable for achieving results; and (4) when their actions are reasonable and undertaken in good faith, employees should be allowed to fail. As Gore summed it up in the chapter's first selection, "We must move from control to collaboration. . . . We must allow the people to face decisions to make decisions. We must do everything we can to make sure that when our federal workers exercise their judgment, they are prepared with the best information, the best analysis, and the best tools we have to offer. We must then trust that they will do their best—and measure the results" (Gore 1993, 91).

Empowered employees clearly have greater discretion and flexibility in trying to actively represent the groups from which they are drawn. They are less constrained by supervisors, organizational cultures, and red tape. They may be better able to promote customer satisfaction when they deal directly with members of their group among the public at large. And, as the chapter's second selection demonstrates, the public may be better able to deal with them.

In "A Demand-Side Perspective on the Importance of Representative Bureaucracy: AIDS, Ethnicity, Gender, and Sexual Orientation," Gregory S. Thielemann and Joseph J. Stewart demonstrate that people living with AIDS have very strong preferences about who provides them with health services: "A clear majority of each group—at least three-fourths of the African-American and Hispanic respondents and over three-fifths of the Anglos—cared if they received their services from people of their same ethnic group" (1996, 171). Both women and men cared significantly about the gender of the staff. Additionally," . . . it was gays and gay men of color who most preferred someone from their group to deliver the services" (1996, 171).

The implications of Thielemann and Stewart's findings are clear. As Samuel Krislov suggested years ago (see chapter 1) representative bureaucracy can enhance administrative legitimacy and performance. Notably, the "demand-side" perspective echoes Krislov in concluding that "Weberian neutrality is not always advantageous" (Thielemann and Stewart 1996, 172).

Outsourcing

The chapter's remaining selections strongly suggest that outsourcing and entrepreneurship pose problems for bureaucratic representativeness. Eyal Press's article, "Faith Based Furor" dramatically points out that the employees of religious organizations engaged in the delivery of public services do not have the same legal protections as government employees. This is true even when these organizations are publicly funded. Although Press focuses on religious organizations, unlike public employees, those working for not-for-profit organizations or private sector firms have only one *constitutional* right they can assert against their employer—the Thirteenth Amendment's proscription against *slavery* or *involuntary servitude*. Public employees have a wide array of constitutionally protected free speech, association, exercise of religion, privacy, and liberty rights in the public sector workplace that do not apply in the context of private employment. Consequently, in the absence of a statutory or other restriction, private employers are free to discipline or fire workers who promote views to which they are opposed, including those that would provide active representation. Press makes it clear that the publicly funded Kentucky Baptist Homes for Children feels free to employ only those whose professional and personal conduct comports with its brand of Christian values.

Entrepreneurship

Administrative entrepreneurship involves collaborating with the private sector in the pursuit of public goals. A problem, as the chapter's final two selections indicate, is that private organizations may end up doing much of the steering *and* policy making. Yet these organizations and their leadership are not subject to such normal democratic controls as elections, open meetings, freedom of information, and provisions for public participation. Although entrepreneurship is not generally analyzed or discussed in terms of representative bureaucracy, it has the potential to displace or bypass the contributions passive and active bureaucratic representation can make to democratic governance. This is demonstrated most clearly by Felice D. Perlmutter and Ram A. Cnaan in "Entrepreneurship in the Public Sector: The Horns of a Dilemma." They provide a detailed case study of how a city's efforts to obtain private funding for public activities might yield great benefits, but also skew public policy and remove choices from the electorate. They are particularly concerned with questions of equity, due process, weakening voter input on public policy, private donors' pressure on public figures, and government dependence on resources over which it has no real control.

The chapter concludes with a short excerpt from *Privatism and Urban Policy in Britain and the United States* by Timothy Barnekov, Robin Boyle, and Daniel Rich. A far more comprehensive study than Perlmutter and Cnaan's, it underscores their main concern: " . . . it is important to examine closely the idea of leverage that has been fashioned on both sides of the Atlantic. Rather than public authority shaping private decisions, the reverse is often the case" (1989, 227). If entrepreneurship results in public policy being deeply affected or made by private entities engaged in partnerships with government, whither representative bureaucracy?

In considering the implications of empowerment, outsourcing, and entrepreneurship for representative bureaucracy and government, it is important to remember that the New Public Management now dominates much public administrative activity in the United States and abroad. So the book ends where it started with as many or more questions than answers. But it has provided some answers to key questions about the potential for public bureaucracies to be representative and, equally important, explained how the key issues have been framed since J. Donald Kingsley first addressed representative bureaucracy almost six decades ago.

References

Barnekov, Timothy, Robin Boyle, and Daniel Rich. 1989. *Privatism and Urban Policy in Britain and the United States*. New York: Oxford University Press.
Gore, Al. 1993. *From Red Tape to Results: Creating a Government That Works Better & Costs Less*. Washington, DC: U.S. Government Printing Office.
Thielemann, Gregory, and Joseph Stewart, Jr. 1996. "A Demand-Side Perspective on the Importance of Representative Bureaucracy: AIDS, Ethnicity, Gender, and Sexual Orientation." *Public Administration Review* 56 (March/April): 168–173.

Empowering Employees to Get Results

Al Gore

"Take two managers and give to each the same number of laborers and let those laborers be equal in all respects. Let both managers rise equally early, go equally late to rest, be equally active, sober, and industrious, and yet, in the course of the year, one of them, without pushing the hands that are under him more than the other, shall have performed infinitely more work."
—George Washington

"When Nature has work to be done, she creates a genius to do it."
—Ralph Waldo Emerson

Two hundred years ago, George Washington recognized the common sense in hiring and promoting productive managers—and taking authority away from unproductive ones. One hundred years ago, Emerson observed that we all share a common genius, ignited simply by the work at hand. These American originals defined the basic ingredients of a healthy, productive work environment: managers who innovate and motivate, and workers who are free to improvise and make decisions.

* * *

Inside government, bad management stifles the morale of workers. The "system" kills initiative. As Vice President Gore, responding to the concerns of Transportation Department employees, put it:

> One of the problems with a centralized bureaucracy is that people get placed in these rigid categories, regulations bind them, procedures bind them, the organizational chart binds them to the old ways of the past . . . [sic] The message over time to . . . [sic] employees becomes: Don't try to do something new. Don't try to change established procedures. Don't try to adapt to the new circumstances your office or agency confronts. Because you're going to get in trouble if you try to do things differently.

From *From Red Tape to Results: Creating a Government That Works Better & Costs Less: Report of the National Performance Review* (Washington, DC: U.S. Government Printing Office, 1993). Excerpted from chapter 3.

Cutting red tape, organizing services around customers, and creating competition will start to generate an environment that rewards success. Now, we must encourage those within government to change their ways. We must create a culture of public entrepreneurship. . . .

Changing the Culture: Power and Accountability

Companies do not achieve high quality simply by announcing it. Nor can they get to quality by hiring the services of the roving bands of consultants who promise to turn businesses around overnight. They do it by turning their entire management systems upside down—shedding the power to make decisions from the sedimentary layers of management and giving it to the people on the ground who do the work. This rewrites the relationship between managers and the managed. The bright line that separates the two vanishes as everyone is given greater authority over how to get their job done.

But with greater authority comes greater responsibility. People must be accountable for the results they achieve when they exercise authority. Of course, we can only hold people accountable if they know what is expected of them. The powerless know they are expected only to obey the rules. But with many rules swept away, what is expected from the empowered?

The answer is *results*. Results measured as the customer would—by better and more efficiently delivered services. If the staff in an agency field office are given greater voice over how their workplace and their work are organized, then the customer deserves to spend less time waiting in line, to receive a prompt answer—and everything else we expect from a responsive government.

So how do we change culture? The answer is as broad as the system that now holds us hostage. Part of it . . . lies in liberating agencies from the cumbersome burden of over-regulation and central control. Part of it. . . hinges on creating new incentives to accomplish more through competition and customer choice. And part of it depends on shifting the focus of control: empowering employees to use their judgment; supporting them with the tools and training they need; and holding them accountable for producing results. Six steps, described in this chapter, will start us down that road:

First, we must give decisionmaking power to those who do the work, pruning layer upon layer of managerial overgrowth.

Second, we must hold every organization and individual accountable for clearly understood, feasible outcomes. Accountability for results will replace "command and control" as the way we manage government.

Third, we must give federal employees better tools for the job—the training to handle their own work and to make decisions cooperatively, good information, and the skills to take advantage of modern computer and tele-communications technologies.

Fourth, we must make federal offices a better place to work. Flexibility must extend not only to the definition of job tasks but also to those work-place rules and conditions that still convey the message that workers aren't trusted.

Fifth, labor and management must forge a new partnership. Government must learn a lesson from business: Change will never happen unless unions and employers work together.

Sixth, we must offer top-down support for bottom-up decisionmaking. Large private corporations that have answered the call for quality have succeeded only with the full backing of top management. Chief Executive Officers—from the White House to agency heads—must ensure that everyone understands that power will never flow through the old channels again. . . .

Conclusion

To change the employee culture in government, to bring about a democracy of leadership within our bureaucracies, we need more than a leap of faith. We need a leap of *practice*. We must move from control to collaboration, from headquarters to every quarter. We must allow the people who face decisions to make decisions. We must do everything we can to make sure that when our federal workers exercise their judgment, they are prepared with the best information, the best analysis, and the best tools we have to offer. We must then trust that they will do their best—and measure the results.

Indeed, we must let our managers and workers fail, rather than hold them up to public ridicule when they do. Only if they fail from time to time on their way to success will we be sure they are even trying to succeed. Someone once asked an old man known for his wisdom why he was so smart. "Good judgment comes from experience," he said. And experience? "Well, that comes from *bad* judgment."

To transform the culture of our government, we must learn to let go. When we do, we will release the same kind of creativity, energy, productivity, and performance in government service that was unleashed 200 years ago, and that continues to guide us today.

A Demand-Side Perspective on the Importance of Representative Bureaucracy

Gregory S. Thielemann and
Joseph J. Stewart, Jr.

In a polity that relies on representation to achieve a semblance of democracy, the composition of a nonelected arm of government such as the bureaucracy is important. In recent years, public administration scholars have addressed the topic in a number of ways. The well-substantiated premise undergirding this work in each case is that bureaucrats exercise discretion that makes a difference in the bureaucracy's outputs (e.g., Skolnick 1966; Hedge, Menzel, and Williams 1988; Meier and Stewart 1992). This conclusion has held in examinations of higher level bureaucrats and lower level, "street level," bureaucrats, although there is some debate about at which level representativeness is more important (Meier and Nigro 1976; Thompson 1976).

The extant literature can be characterized as supply-side in approach because the focus is either on (1) the degree to which a specified bureaucracy is representative of a larger population in terms of various demographic variables (e.g., Subramanian 1967; Meier 1975; Grabosky and Rosenbloom 1976; Hall and Saltzstein 1977; Cayer and Sigelman 1980; Dometrius and Sigelman 1984; and Henderson and Preston 1984), (2) the forces which make bureaucracies more or less representative (e.g., Saltzstein 1986; Stein 1986; Mladenka 1989; Kellough 1990a, 1990b), (3) the extent to which the policy-relevant attitudes of bureaucrats are representative of a clientele or of the public at large (e.g., Meier and Nigro 1976; Rosenbloom

From Gregory S. Thielemann and Joseph J. Stewart, Jr. "A Demand-Side Perspective on the Importance of Representative Bureaucracy: AIDS, Ethnicity, Gender, and Sexual Orientation," *Public Administration Review* 56 (March/April 1996), pp. 168–173. Copyright © 1996 by The American Society for Public Administration. Reprinted with permission from Blackwell Publishing Ltd.

and Featherstonhaugh 1977; Thompson 1978; Lewis 1990; Garand, Parkhurst, and Seoud 1991); or, most recently, (4) the links between the representativeness of bureaucracy and policy outputs and outcomes (e.g., Meier and Stewart 1992; Hindera 1993). Regardless of the focus, the assumption is that a representative bureaucracy is a good to be provided, the attainment of which will produce a better-served, more-satisfied clientele.

Whether this assumption is true or not is particularly important for individuals for whom interaction with a bureaucracy is literally a life-or-death matter, such as those infected with HIV. After all, who should care less about who provides them with services than individuals whose very lives can be extended and whose quality of life can be improved by those services? Survival time with HIV is correlated with use of services (Rothenberg et al. 1987) and with demographic factors such as race (Seage et al. 1993; Bergner 1993), on which bureaucracies can vary significantly. If clients of HIV service delivery agencies care about the characteristics of those who run and staff the service delivery bureaucracy, and consequently are more or less likely to use the services depending on its representativeness, they exhibit a demand for a representative bureaucracy. Thus, this issue area provides a most stringent test of the importance of representative bureaucracy.

Do those in need of bureaucratically delivered services care whether or not the bureaucracy is representative? If they do, are they more concerned about representativeness at the higher or lower reaches of the organization? The analysis presented here offers an answer to these questions drawing on a survey of persons living with AIDS (PLWAs) in Dallas, Texas. These answers are important because AIDS services delivery impacts the quality of life of the PLWAs by facilitating acceptance of the reality of the disease and providing the basic preventative services that enhance both quantity and quality of life. Recent evidence indicates that basic services such as nutritional counseling (*AIDS Treatment News* 1987, 1989) and counseling to aid in the client's psychological adjustment (Keet et al. 1994) are tremendously important in increasing the longevity of survival. . . .

AIDS and Public Administration

AIDS is now acknowledged to be a multidimensional public policy problem (Griggs 1987) with which public administrators must deal (Slack 1991). Perhaps most important, public administrators have to deal with disagreements over the allocation of resources. The federal funds made available through the Title I HIV Emergency Relief Grants of the Ryan White Act are distributed by local planning councils in eligible metropolitan areas (EMAs), which qualify for funds by meeting an AIDS caseload threshold and by creating a responsive delivery system. These planning councils, the composition of which is determined by local government officials, chosen by and using a loose set of guidelines provided by the HIV Division of the Department of Health and Human Services (DHHS), are required by the act to be responsive to all persons with HIV regardless of any other specific characteristics.

Responsive to Whom? The Changing HIV-Infected Population

The problem of creating representative bureaucracies for the delivery of services for clients with HIV disease is exacerbated by the changing demographics of those afflicted with the disease. As of July 1993, the Centers for Disease Control (CDC) reported a cumulative total of 310,680 adult AIDS cases in the United States and its territories, including 82,946 new cases in the previous 12 months. The report shows a decline in the percentage of cases among gays, a slight increase in the proportion of heterosexual cases, and a dramatic increase in the proportion of women and adolescents contracting AIDS. In addition, the ethnic composition of the cases is changing. Although slightly over one-half of the victims of the disease are Caucasians, there are significant numbers of African-American (31 percent) and Hispanic (16 percent) cases as well (Centers for Disease Control 1993).

The increasing diversity of the cases has led to a desire to increase access to services for minorities and women without reducing services to other clients. One mechanism for promoting responsiveness is to create a planning council that is representative of the EMA's caseload. Because the Ryan White Act is not specific on the means of achieving access or representation, the HIV Division of DHHS has issued guidelines requiring representation for special populations that include gay men, gay men of color, women, African-Americans, and Hispanics. These guidelines require local officials to represent these groups on the council, but interpretation of this mandate has varied across EMAs, ranging from seeing it as a command for representation proportional to the caseload to perceiving that having one individual from a group is sufficient. Some cities, such as Los Angeles, employ sophisticated models of overlapping grids to account for geographic and ethnic diversity as well as sexual orientation. Others, such as Houston, have failed to address these needs and leave appointments to the vagaries of local political forces. In this Texas city, the issue of representation has manifested itself in a manner that reflects concern with race rather than sexual orientation (*Houston Chronicle*, July 28, 1993, A-1).

The uncertain requirements for forming a representative local planning council mean that these bodies are often in the difficult position of having to address the issues of equal access to services and effective staffing of service agencies, while the political nature of their appointments pulls them in another direction. Such a balancing act is possible if clients are indifferent about the characteristics of the service providers. Given limited resources, if a representative bureaucracy is important to the clientele, subpopulations of PLWAs will find themselves competing for funds and services, and public administrators will find themselves caught in the middle.

There is evidence that group competition is on the rise. As increasing attention has been paid to the emerging subpopulations such as women and ethnic minorities, resentment and considerable consternation have arisen in the gay communities. In many ways, the local funding battles resemble those being waged over research dollar allocations in Congress. The funding battles that were originally seen over the allocation of research dollars have now moved into the funding of service providers in local areas.

Diversity is made an even more important issue because AIDS manifests itself differently in different communities. This does not mean that the retroviruses of HIV-1 or HIV-2 exhibit different genetic or biological structures. Rather, because factors related to tolerance of alternative sexual behaviors and of treatment strategies for substance addiction vary by subculture, there must also be variation in treatment and prevention strategies. Thus, effective service delivery may depend on the willingness of AIDS patients to take advantage of available services, and their willingness to do so may depend on who provides those services. It is this demand for a representative bureaucracy that our research explored.

Analysis of the Data

. . .

Race/Ethnicity

Turning first to the question of race/ethnicity, slightly less than one-quarter of both the African-American and Hispanic PLWAs cared if the director of the service providing agency was of the same ethnic group as themselves. . . . However, these proportions are almost eight times as great as the percentage of Anglos expressing the same concern. The magnitude of this difference was unlikely to have occurred by chance. Although it might be argued that Anglos did not express a concern about who runs an agency because they are able to assume (generally correctly) that the agency is run by an Anglo, it is still the case that a definite minority of any ethnic group expresses concern about the race of the director.

When the questions focused on the actual service delivery personnel, however, the proportions expressing concern jumped dramatically, and the differences between ethnic groups disappeared. A clear majority of each group—at least three-fourths of the African-American and Hispanic respondents and slightly over three-fifths of the Anglos—cared if they received their services from people of their same ethnic group. Although the proportions of Anglos expressing this concern remained lower than for either African-Americans or Hispanics, the gap was not so broad as to be statistically significant.

Across all ethnic groups, individuals were far more concerned about who delivered the actual services than they were about who ran the agency. Anglos were approximately 20 times more likely to express concern about the ethnicity of the people with whom they interact than they were about who ran the agency. African-Americans and Hispanics are about 3 times more likely to be concerned about who actually delivered the services than they were about who ran the agency, but this difference would still be expected to occur by chance no more often than 1 out of every 100,000 times.

Sexual Orientation

Another categorization which might be important in the delivery of services to PLWAs is sexual orientation. An even richer picture is revealed by the data [regarding sexual orientation] than [for] the analysis of different ethnic groups. Gay men of color cared most about having an agency director with the same characteristics, with slightly fewer than one-quarter expressing such a preference. This was significantly more than the approximately 14 percent of gays and heterosexuals who expressed such a concern, although it should be noted that the probability of the difference between heterosexuals and gay men of color is only $< .10$.

Concerning the staff, however, it was gays and gay men of color who most preferred someone from their group to deliver the services. The difference between gays and gay men of color on preferences about who runs the agency disappeared. Approximately three-fourths of the members of these two groups expressed a demand for lower level bureaucrats like themselves. Although the same preference was expressed by more than six of ten heterosexuals, the difference between this proportion and those of gays and of gay men of color was statistically significant at the .004 and .06 levels, respectively.

Just as with each of the ethnic groups, PLWAs regardless of sexual orientation cared more about the characteristics of the staff than they did the characteristics of the agency directors. The threefold increase in the proportion of gay men of color caring about the staff's characteristics over the director's characteristics was the smallest increase noted for any sexual orientation category. As with ethnic groups, these differences could not be expected to occur even once in 100,000 chances.

Gender

Finally, women and men can be compared on their preferences. Approximately twice the proportion of women as men preferred someone of their gender to direct the service agency, a difference with a probability < .09. But, as with ethnic group comparisons, when asked about the actual service delivery personnel, gender differences disappeared. For both groups there was an overwhelming preference for staffers of the same gender as the respondent. Women were over 5 times as likely to care about the gender of the staff as they were about the director, and the comparable figure for men was 10 times.

Conclusions and Implications

The findings of this analysis are important for . . . representation theory and . . . bureaucracy. . . . [T]he findings demonstrate a demand for representative bureaucracy, unlike those of previous studies. Although at times a "neutral" bureaucrat may be sought to staff an agency, this study shows that Weberian neutrality is not always advantageous. Representative bureaucracy is important not just because it has important policy implications, that is it enhances the likelihood of effective delivery of governmental services, but because it also is something valuable to citizens who are served by the agencies. A representative bureaucracy can contribute to governmental legitimacy, and, as students of bureaucratic politics know, support by a clientele can be an important source of political clout for public agencies.

The evidence is clear and overwhelming in this study that clientele interest in representative bureaucracy is greater at the level where the bureaucrat and the citizen interact than at the higher levels. Indications are that for the citizen it is at that level that the bureaucracy is reified. Higher level personnel are relatively "faceless bureaucrats"; front-line personnel are the agency to the persons seeking services. . . .

Whether bureaucracies providing services to PLWAs are similar to other bureaucracies is an open question. The demand for and significance of representative bureaucracy will probably vary across agencies and policy areas. But the fact that a demand for representative bureaucracy can be demonstrated in this context, in combination with the evidence that bureaucratic representativeness can make a real difference in what agencies do and what effects they have (Meier and Stewart 1992; Hindera 1993), suggests that developing more understanding of the demand for representative bureaucracy and the conditions under which it exists should be high on the agenda of public administration researchers.

Note

The study is based on a survey conducted in September 1992 of 510 persons living with AIDS in the Dallas, Texas, area.

References

AIDS Treatment News. 1987. January.
Aids Treatment News. 1989. March 24.
Bergner, Lawrence. 1993. "Race, Health, and Health Services." *American Journal of Public Health* vol. 83 (July): 939–941.
Cayer, N. Joseph, and Lee Sigelman. 1980. "Minorities and Women in State and Local Government, 1973–1975." *Public Administration Review* vol. 40 (September/October): 443–450.
Centers for Disease Control. 1993. *HIV/AIDS Surveillance.*
Dometrius, Nelson C., and Lee Sigelman. 1984. "Assessing Progress Toward Affirmative Action Goals in State and Local Government." *Public Administration Review* vol. 44 (May/June): 241–246.
Garand, James C., Catherine T. Parkhurst, and Rusanne Jourdan Seoud. 1991. "Bureaucrats, Policy Attitudes, and Political Behavior: Extensions of the Bureau Voting Model of Government Growth." *Journal of Public Administration Research and Theory* vol. 1 (April): 177–212.
Grabosky, Peter N., and David H. Rosenbloom. 1976. "Racial and Ethnic Integration in the Federal Service." *Social Science Quarterly* vol. 56 (June): 71–84.
Griggs, John, ed. 1987. *AIDS Public Policy Dimensions.* New York: United Hospital Fund of New York.

Hall, Grace, and Alan Saltzstein. 1977. "Equal Employment Opportunity for Minorities in Municipal Government." *Social Science Quarterly* vol. 57 (March): 864–872.

Hedge, David M., Donald C. Menzel, and George H. Williams. 1988. "Regulatory Attitudes and Behavior: The Case of Surface Mining Regulation." *Western Political Quarterly* vol. 41 (June): 323–340.

Henderson, Lenneal J., and Michael B. Preston. 1984. "Blacks, Public Employment, and Public Interest Theory." In Mitchell F. Rice and Woodrow Jones, Jr., eds., *Contemporary Public Policy Perspectives and Black Americans*. Westport, CT: Greenwood Press, pp. 33–48.

Hindera, John J. 1993. "Representative Bureaucracy: Imprimis Evidence of Active Representation in the EEOC District Offices." *Social Science Quarterly* vol. 74 (March): 95–108.

Keet, Ireneus P.M. et al. 1994. "Characteristics of Long-term Asymptomatic Infection and Human Immunodeficiency Virus Type 1 in Men with Normal and Low CD4 Cell Counts." *Journal of Infectious Diseases* vol. 169(6): 1236–1243.

Kellough, J. Edward. 1990a. "Federal Agencies and Affirmative Action for Blacks and Women." *Social Science Quarterly* vol. 71 (March): 83–92.

Kellough, J. Edward. 1990b. "Integration in the Public Workplace: Determinants of Minority and Female Employment in Federal Agencies." *Public Administration Review* vol. 50 (September/October): 557–566.

Lewis, Gregory B. 1990. "In Search of the Machiavellian Milquetoasts: Comparing Attitudes of Bureaucrats and Ordinary People." *Public Administration Review* vol. 50 (March/April): 220–227.

Meier, Kenneth J. 1975. "Representative Bureaucracy: An Empirical Analysis." *American Political Science Review* vol. 69 (June): 526–542.

Meier, Kenneth J., and Lloyd G. Nigro. 1976. "Representative Bureaucracy and Policy Preferences." *Public Administration Review* vol. 36 (July/August): 458–470.

Meier, Kenneth J., and Joseph Stewart, Jr. 1992. "The Impact of Representative Bureaucracies: Educational Systems and Public Policies." *American Review of Public Administration* vol. 22 (September): 157–171.

Mladenka, Kenneth R. 1989. "Blacks and Hispanics in Urban Politics." *American Political Science Review* vol. 83 (March): 165–192.

Rosenbloom, David H., and Jeannette G. Featherstonhaugh. 1977. "Passive and Active Representation in the Federal Service: A Comparison of Blacks and Whites." *Social Science Quarterly* vol. 57 (March): 873–882.

Rothenberg, R., M. Woelfel, R. Stoneburner, J. Milberg, R. Parker, and B. Truman. 1987. "Survival with the Acquired Immune Deficiency Syndrome: Experience with 5833 Cases in New York City." *New England Journal of Medicine* vol. 317 (November): 1297–1302.

Saltzstein, Grace Hall. 1986. "Female Mayors and Women in Municipal Jobs." *American Journal of Political Science* vol. 30 (February): 140–164.

Seage, George R. III, Stephanie Oddleifson, Eileen Carr, Barbara Shea, Laurie Makarewicz-Robert, Minka van Beuzekom, and Alfred De Maria. 1993. "Survival with AIDS in Massachusetts, 1979 to 1989." *American Journal of Public Health* vol. 83 (January): 72–78.

Skolnick, Jerome H. 1966. *Justice Without Trial: Law Enforcement in Democratic Society*. New York: John Wiley.

Slack, James D. 1991. *AIDS and the Public Work Force: Local Government Pre-*

Stein, Lana. 1986. "Representative Local Government: Minorities in the Municipal Workforce." *Journal of Politics* vol. 48 (August): 694–716.

Subramanian, V. 1967. "Representative Bureaucracy: A Reassessment." *American Political Science Review* vol. 61 (December): 1010–1019.

Thompson, Frank J. 1976. "Minority Groups in Public Bureaucracies: Are Passive and Active Representation Linked?" *Administration and Society* vol. 8 (August): 201–226.

Thompson, Frank J. 1978. "Civil Servants and the Deprived: Socio-political and Occupational Explanations of Attitudes toward Minority Hiring." *American Journal of Political Science* vol. 22 (May): 325–347.

Faith Based Furor

Eyal Press

President Bush believes in financing religious charities. But if a group takes government money, should it be able to fire someone like Alicia Pedreira? The first time Alicia Pedreira heard from co-workers that they had spotted her picture in a photo exhibit at the state fair in Louisville, Ky., she was baffled. "I thought: Photograph? What photograph?" Pedreira said recently of the strange sequence of events that began in August 1998 and would soon upend her life. "I had no idea what they were talking about."

At the time, Pedreira was working as a therapist at the Kentucky Baptist Homes for Children, a religious organization that contracts with the state to provide a range of services for at-risk youth. Pedreira liked her job, and she had a sterling reputation among her peers. But she wasn't the chattiest person in the office. On the advice of the man who had hired her, she generally kept her personal life to herself—until, that is, her photograph unexpectedly popped up at the Kentucky State Fair. Taken by an amateur photographer during a 1997 AIDS walk and entered, without her knowledge, in the state-fair art competition, the image depicts Pedreira, who is 37, in the company of a woman with short-cropped brown hair whose arms dangle suggestively around Pedreira's waist. The two women look distinctly like a couple, an impression that Pedreira's tank top—which bears a map of the Aegean Sea with an arrow pointing to the "Isle of Lesbos"—all but announces.

"The minute I heard what I was wearing," said Pedreira, "I thought immediately, I've lost my job." She was right. On Oct. 23, 1998, a few weeks after word of the photograph circulated through the office, Pedreira was fired. A termination letter explained that Pedreira's "homosexual life-style is contrary to Kentucky Baptist Homes for Children core values."

Pedreira was devastated; several of her colleagues were so angry that they resigned in protest. Friends urged her to fight back. Last April, Pedreira and the American Civil Liberties Union filed a federal lawsuit in United States District Court in Louisville, accusing the Kentucky Baptist Homes for Chil-

ment and is the state's largest provider of services for troubled youth, of engaging in religious-based discrimination.

Now, as Congress prepares to consider President Bush's agenda to allow an array of government-financed social programs to be administrated by religious groups, her case is being monitored by proponents and opponents alike of so-called faith-based initiatives. Pedreira's lawsuit may well become the most important gay rights case since *Boy Scouts of America v. Dale* [2000]—although the issues it raises are in fact much broader.

Religious organizations have long been exempted from the provision in Title VII of the 1964 Civil Rights Act that forbids religious discrimination by employers, on the grounds that they would otherwise be forced to act against their beliefs when hiring personnel. But starting in 1996, Congress began passing "Charitable Choice" legislation allowing religious organizations to discriminate while accepting public funds for welfare-to-work and, more recently, drug-treatment programs. And although criticism is mounting, supporters of faith-based initiatives are attaching similar provisions to a host of additional social programs, from crime prevention to hunger relief to housing grants. Recently on "Face the Nation," Stephen Goldsmith, a White House adviser, explained that such organizations will indeed be allowed to discriminate in their hiring practices, but only "on the basis of religion."

What Goldsmith did not say is that religion can often bleed into other categories, like gender, sexual orientation and race. "If you can discriminate on religious grounds, it doesn't take much imagination to discriminate in other ways," said Congressman Bobby Scott, a Democrat from Virginia. Indeed, several courts have ruled that the Title VII exemption would allow Christian schools to fire female teachers who give birth out of wedlock. Others have determined that religious institutions can refuse to hire applicants whose views on abortion differ from theirs. Nor is it clear what courts would say if an organization's religious tenets mandate differential treatment on the basis of race. In theory, an organization like Bob Jones University could receive public funds to hire employees while forbidding them to engage in interracial dating.

Alarmed by the implications, a coalition of civil rights and religious organizations—including the Union of American Hebrew Congregations, the N.A.A.C.P, the Interfaith Alliance and Catholics for a Free Choice—recently sent a letter to President Bush urging him to oppose "government funded" discrimination in any form. "It would be unconscionable," the letter states, "that a want ad for government-supported social services could read, for example, 'Catholics and Jews Need Not Apply.'" But the Bush administration—which in February established a White House Office of Faith-Based and Community Initiatives—is unlikely to change course.

Pedreira lost her job, her lawsuit claims, not on the basis of her performance but because Baptist Homes determined that she violated the demand (spelled out explicitly in its employment forms) that employees "exhibit values in their professional conduct and personal lifestyles that are consistent with the Christian mission and purpose of the institution." When the case comes to trial, probably near the end of the year, Pedreria's legal team plans to raise some pointed questions. If hiring discrimination is illegal with government jobs, why not with jobs paid for by the government? Does the public financing of faith-based programs violate the Constitution, whose Establishment Clause requires government neutrality toward religion? Although Pedreira's case deals with state rather than federal financing—and therefore does not overtly threaten Charitable Choice—her lawyers say it will set a precedent for eventually overturning the law. "Charitable Choice authorizes religious-based employment discrimination in government-funded programs," said Michael Adams, Pedreira's attorney. "This case, if we prevail, will say, 'You can't do that, it's unconstitutional.'" . . .

. . . [I]n published statements the [Kentucky Baptist Homes for Children] has made its line of defense clear. Pedreira was fired, the agency has said in an official statement, not on the basis of religious discrimination, but because "homosexual behavior is not in the best interest of anyone, especially sexually abused and confused children and youth."

From a legal perspective, focusing on Pedreira's sexual orientation is smart. There is no federal statute barring discrimination against gay men and lesbians, nor does the state of Kentucky have such a law.

. . . Bill Smithwick, the president of Baptist Homes, explained the agency's reasoning as follows: "To employ a person who is openly homosexual, living in an adulterous situation, is a chronic abuser of alcohol or drugs, etc., does not represent the Judeo-Christian values which are intrinsic to our mission."

Pedreira's legal team sees this letter and other statements by Baptist Homes employees as clear evidence of religious-based discrimination. "We argue that you cannot take government money and impose those religious beliefs on employees," said Adams, "whether the victim is a homosexual—as in this case—or not."

Whose argument will prevail in court remains to be seen. . . .

At the very least, the policy of Baptist Homes runs counter to the trend in publicly financed employment positions: all federal employees, for example, are now protected from discrimination on the basis of sexual orientation. Allowing government-financed groups to disregard this standard has begun to raise concerns in Congress. "We can't adopt a system here that allows religious groups to meet a lower standard of civil rights protection than non-religious groups," Senator Joseph Lieberman recently said in a statement.

But this is not the only concern. Because courts have interpreted the Title VII exemption to include all the "tenets and teachings" of a faith, the door could be open to a seemingly wide range of government-financed discrimination practices. Consider what would happen if a state decided to contract out services to the Nation of Islam. Catholics, Jews or any other group that runs afoul of the Nation of Islam's teachings might find themselves excluded. . . .

Baptist Homes does not hide the fact that its religious tenets prohibit more than just homosexuality. "We've made it clear as to the values we're looking for in the staff we hire," said Smithwick. In general, he explained, leadership positions at the agency must be filled by Baptists. "It's not just a single issue that brought this whole thing to a head. There are other issues" [such as having children out of wedlock]. . . .

. . . "Our mission is to provide care and hope for hurting families through Christ-centered ministries," Smithwick has said. "I want this mission to permeate our agency like the very blood through our bodies. I want to provide Christian support to every child, staff member and foster parent." If forced to change, Smithwick told me, Baptist Homes would rather stop contracting with the government. . . .

. . . Carl Esbeck, a conservative legal scholar, has written that religious organizations can hardly be expected to sustain their religious vision without the ability to employ individuals who share the tenets of their faith. In a recent article in *The New Republic*, Jeffrey Rosen echoed this view, noting that, after all, many secular organizations that receive government funds, like Planned Parenthood, also hire on the basis of their values. . . .

Though her case is still in the early stages, Pedreira seemed unfazed by the prospect of a protracted legal battle. "My goal is not the lawsuit, it's education," she said. "I want people to know this can happen." In Louisville, where local media coverage has been steady, she has already achieved this objective. "People walk up to me all the time," she said, "and tell me I did the right thing." . . .

For all the gratifying moments, however, Pedreira has also suffered plenty of lows. "I've had people throw trash in my yard," she said. "I've been called a pedophile." And she is still dealing with the aftershocks of a traumatic experience. "I was depressed, and I didn't work for months," she confessed. "I felt lost." Since losing her job, Pedriera has not felt inclined to pursue work as a therapist; at present, she's working as a repair technician for Bell South. "Before, I had hoped to climb the ladder, maybe even direct my own program one day," she said. "But I haven't felt ready to go back to that."

Entrepreneurship in the Public Sector: On the Horns of a Dilemma

Felice D. Perlmutter and Ram A. Cnaan

Private support for public services is not new. Even in ancient Greece and Rome, rich citizens were obliged to underwrite the cost of public activities, albeit primarily festivities. In the American context, private contributions for public purposes have, historically, been limited and primarily of two types. First, are the bequests or special gifts such as art collections, parks, or Andrew Carnegie's support of public libraries; second, are the special ad-hoc contributions for public events such as the 4th of July fireworks.

We are currently witnessing a dramatically new phenomenon: the reliance of municipalities on non-tax dollars to support ongoing public services. This is a critical shift, no longer an occasional or ad-hoc occurrence. Furthermore, a distinction must be made between the earlier gifts, which depended on the initiative of the donors, and supported programs of their particular choice and preference and the current policy. What is now evolving is a deliberate public policy designed to counter budget cuts and to enhance public services through organized fundraising approaches. And the onus is on the public administrator to assume an entrepreneurial posture, one traditionally associated with leadership in the profit-making sector (Peters and Waterman 1982).

Proactive administrators reverse a trend of contracting and government load-shedding. Prior to the contracting era, governments both raised money (through taxation) and provided services. Contracting is characterized by the separation of raising money (by government) and service delivery (by private organizations) (James 1989; Kramer 1992; Salamon 1987; Weisbrod 1977). From the government's perspective, these grants and contracts, federal, state or local, allowed the government to retain its responsibility for service delivery while shifting the provision of these services to nonprofit organizations (Cnaan 1993; Lipsky and Smith 1989). This phenomenon was identified by Bendick (1989) as government load-shedding, a process whereby the role of government in the provision of services was reduced. The new trend of public fund-raising runs counter to contracting. The new policy is characterized by fund raising (not tax dollars) to finance public service provision. Thus we also note a new balance in the field of public-private relationships.

This article presents a case study of effective entrepreneurial leadership in a city agency which successfully expanded its services on the basis of contributions obtained, in cash and kind, from private donors. The article has two objectives. First, a case study presents a description of effective entrepreneurial leadership in the public sector: when faced with political and fiscal pressures, this executive thoughtfully and effectively developed a philosophy and designed a strategy for new public-private relationships. Second, we examine the public policy issues associated with the phenomenon of entrepreneurship as it highlights some dilemmas in the blurring of boundaries between public and private agencies, as the costs of this approach also merit careful consideration (Bellone and Goerl 1992). . . .

Context

As a backdrop to the case study, it is necessary to highlight two distinctive contexts: federal and local. In the last decade, there has been a dramatic shift at the federal level from contracting for an array of services from nonprofit organizations (Ascoli 1992; Billis and Harris 1992; Grossman 1992; Perlmutter 1969; Saidel 1989) to an emphasis on "government load-shedding," a process that reduces the role of the government in the provision of services (Bendick 1989; Cnaan 1993). The consequences on the local level of the shifts in the federal level must be examined, for it is precisely this shift which has led to a view of the public administrator as entrepreneur (Lewis 1984), risk taker, and innovator (Palumbo, Musheno and Maynard-Moody 1986).

Our case study has its locus at the local level in a large urban center, the Department of Recreation in the city of Philadelphia. The leadership and philosophy of the mayor, Edward Rendell, epitomized the new trust in public leadership, that is, privatization and entrepreneurship.

When the mayor was elected in 1991, Philadelphia was in a state of bankruptcy. Rendell campaigned on a platform of fiscal responsibility, coupled with a philosophy of privatization. Because of the increased cost of services, public demand for additional services, reduced state and federal aid, and a declining tax base, the city faced a lower bond rating and was also unable to meet its financial obligations. Consequently, privatization became a key strategy as the administration indeed attempted to engage in load shedding. This engendered much controversy, particularly in the Departments of Human Services and Sanitation where most of the contracting-out strategies were to be implemented.

The Department of Recreation, the subject of our case study, was under a different set of constraints as not only were many programs dramatically cut and the season shortened for tennis, swimming, ice-skating, or basketball, but also the maintenance of the department's physical plants was endangered. In this situation, privatization was to be achieved not through contracting out for services, but rather in the quest for private money to allow for the continuation of traditional programs offered by the department and the improvement of its facilities. The department was already suffering from cutbacks in services and programs when Mayor Rendell was elected; thus, the 1993 budget allocation of $40,020,893, compared to the 1991 allocation of $33,251,062, did not keep up with the cost of inflation for the two-year period. Furthermore, whereas the number of people employed by the department in 1992 was 546, it was projected that in 1994 the number of employees would be reduced to 501.

The new commissioner of recreation appointed by Mayor Rendell, Michael DiBerardinis, was a Philadelphian who had worked for many years as a community organizer, and later as a congressional aide; he was known to be energetic, innovative, and a person with a vision. His vision for the department was comparable with the values and vision of the mayor. Commissioner DiBerardinis assumed office, committed to the provision of a full recreation agenda: for him the challenge was to reinstate past programs and to expand them; he was not interested in merely preventing further erosion. He coupled this with a commitment to Philadelphia and to the local neighborhoods, using this commitment as the basis for his strategy for developing new public-private partnerships.

Methods

Our research was stimulated by an article in the *Philadelphia Inquirer* (Copeland 1993) entitled "Private Money for the Public Good: Donors Lend a Hand to a City Department." This article reported that the Drumcliff Foundation planned to give the Department of Recreation in Philadelphia a donation in an amount between $25,000 and $50,000. In addition, the article noted this department had drawn $500,000 from various other donors. Commissioner Michael DiBerardinis was receptive to a study of the department's development work, with a focus on his philosophy and strategy. A series of interviews were held with the commissioner, with Ms. Carol B. Rice, deputy commissioner for Planning and Development, and Mr. Edward Fagan, who serves as Funding and Resource Development Officer for the department. In addition to these in-depth interviews, data were obtained from participant observation of department meetings and from agency documents and budgets.

Beginnings and Philosophy

When Mr. DiBerardinis took office, he found that the department had completed a strategic planning process with a private consultant. The final plan was limited in scope; it focused on financial issues within the allocated budget and the physical plants owned by the department. Its major finding, and recommendation, was that the department owned too many properties with too few resources to properly maintain them. Clearly this plan was counter to the vision and philosophy of the new commissioner that included reopening all swimming pools for the full duration of the summer, activating summer sports programs of baseball and basketball as well as winter ice-hockey programs, and reopening the many recreation centers around the city. Of critical importance was DiBerardinis' emphasis on the direct involvement of local residents and businesses in these centers; any donor activity would not be an abstract fiscal transaction, but a community investment. Commissioner DiBerardinis instituted a new strategic planning process with a broadened mandate. A first priority was the development of a mission statement which would serve as the basis for any further planning; the charge was also to explore specific means with which to achieve department goals.

The new vision for the department was predicated on the philosophy of a partnership between the city, local neighborhood residents, and businesses in the community. The concept of a partnership required full cooperation and involvement of all the parties in both planning and implementation. It is important to emphasize that the involvement of business, according to this philosophy, was not merely to provide money. As Mr. DiBerardinis noted, "I was predisposed to bring the private sector into the execution of public policies." Thus, all three partners were major players from the outset, not just to be used in a partial or opportunistic manner.

While the commissioner realized he needed to identify new sources of revenues, his strategy required a match of interest and commitment between the donor and the donee. Accordingly, local businesses would be approached for their support of specific programs in the local community in which they had a stake. These businesses would thus be offered a sense of civic responsibility, a chance to impact the life of people in the community, and also to obtain positive publicity for their enterprise. The recognition of a quid-pro-quo was both realistic and effective.

The Implementation Strategy

The implementation strategy developed by the commissioner consisted of several components: (1) the formation of a development unit, (2) the initiation of a process of broad departmental involvement in the development effort, (3) the design of a fiscal management approach, and (4) the development of a long-term proactive process in addition to a short-term reactive one.

The first strategy, a structural one, was designed to form a unit dedicated to development, stimulated by earlier organizational shifts. Prior to DiBerardinis' appointment to office in 1989, the Community Care for Elderly Citizens unit was transferred to the Department of Recreation. The head of that unit, Edward J. Fagan, Jr., was told that the Department of Recreation could cover salaries but any other money would have to be generated from outside. Mr. Fagan rose to the challenge and learned the craft of fund-raising in order to support his unit. When the commissioner articulated his philosophy and his vision of a new partnership between the public and private sectors, within the context of community development, Mr. Fagan volunteered to head this effort for the department as a whole. In April 1992, a unit was established with Mr. Fagan as the Funding and Resource Development Officer for the department.

Second, the department established a new process in which all staff members were actively involved in the development strategy. Thus, staff members were encouraged to identify and contact potential donors in order to maximize the advantage of personal contacts. However, once a contact was made and some interest on the part of the potential donor evidenced, a more formalized approach was pursued. The information was forwarded to the Funding and Resource Development Officer who would do the follow-up in order to maximize the potential relationship with the donor. This follow-up involved the presentation of various opportunities for personal as well as financial involvement in the community.

A third important strategy in the implementation process concerned the management of financial contributions because many contributors were concerned that their money should not flow to the general treasury to be used to finance routine city activities, as opposed to their designated preferences. A clear-cut strategy was implemented to accommodate this concern.

A local nonprofit organization, Urban Affairs Coalition, was invited to administer the donations. Thus it was clear that the money, earmarked for specific programs, would not become part of the general city budget. The nonprofit organization would guarantee that donations would only be used for the program designated by the donating party. Furthermore, the donating parties could write checks to a nonprofit organization, rather than to the city itself, and would receive charitable tax deductions. It should be noted that the Urban Affairs Coalition is a registered neighborhood corporation, and as such, received the higher tax deductions granted to these entities.

The final strategy emphasized a proactive stance with long-term consequences: a new outreach to foundations. In recognition of the monetary potential of foundations, the department is currently putting energy in this direction. Thus, it is submitting proposals to national, local, and state-based foundations. These proposals are important indications of the shift from a short-term reactive to a long-term proactive mode.

The Nature of the Gift

To obtain a fuller understanding of the strategy, it is instructive to have information concerning the actual nature of the gifts and the donors involved. Two aspects must be noted: first, whether the contribution is cash or in-kind; second, whether it is one-time only or ongoing. Both elements are important as one designs a strategy for fund-raising by public agencies. It is of interest to note that the cash gifts tend to be viewed as ongoing in contrast to the one-time only nature of the in-kind contributions. It is also important to note that several approaches have been developed in order to obtain cash. These include the direct support of specific programs, selling advertisements, and charging fees for service. Although most of these approaches are not new, their combined effect and their long-term intention make them a new trend in public administration.

The financial impact of the strategy of seeking private support must be highlighted at the outset. In a one-year period, the various contributions totaled approximately $634,650, representing about 1.59 percent of the department's budget for 1993. Given that this is the result of a first year effort, these numbers are most impressive. The following discussion describes the methods used in obtaining these contributions.

In relation to the first approach, the direct support of specific programs, cash donations are all earmarked for special programs that are at risk of being eliminated or drastically curtailed (see Table [5.1]). The strategy of earmarking the cash contribution serves the function of helping to develop the commitment of the donor to a specific service. Most of the current donors are businesses active in the Philadelphia area. The decision to target businesses was not planned but rather evolved as a result of the department's need to obtain funds quickly. Businesses make quick decisions and can forward funds within a few days.

The second approach to raising cash is related to the department's realization that not all businesses are interested in the partnership concept. The

Table 5.1

Sources and Characteristics of Cash Support for Special Programs of the Department of Parks and Recreation

Funding organization	Supported activity	Actual support ($)	Initiator
Health Partners of Philadelphia	Shooting for the Stars	2,000	Deputy Commissioner
	Pull for Pools	2,000 T-shirts + 5,000	Deputy Commissioner
Union League	Youth summer programs	25,000	Commissioner
Emergency Aid of Philadelphia	Latch-key programs	10,000	Mayor's wife
White Dog Cafe and Philadelphia Citizens for Children and Youth	Swings for recreation centers	9,600	Development officer
CoreStates Bank	Shooting for the Stars	25,000	Commissioner
Coca-Cola	Basketball league	5,000	Development officer
Philadelphia 76ers	Basketball league	5,000	Commissioner
Future Leaders for a Better Philadelphia	Penn Rose playground	1,600	Commissioner
	Philadelphia swimming project	2,500	Commissioner
Hatfield Meats	General recreational activities	5,000	Mayor
Korean deli owners	Basketball league	9,600 + reception	Development officer
Modell's Sporting Goods	Baseball field renovation	10,000	Development officer
Unity Day	Festival for African-Americans	5,000	Commissioner
ComCast	Ice rink	3,000	Development officer
Glad bags	Clean-ups	Rebates for bags ($5,000)	Philadelphia Pride
Cardone Industries	General recreation	2,500	Self-initiated
Caroline Buck Foundation	General recreation	5,000	Mayor
Martz Lines (Logo)	Prize for logo competition	500	Commissioner
Urban Affairs Coalition	Local advisory councils	47,350	Commissioner
	Neighborhood basketball league	3,500	Commissioner

more removed a business is from a specific neighborhood geographical location, the less interested the business is in a particular community. Yet, most businesses are interested in their public image and spend large sums on advertising. Consequently, in 1993/94, the department approached a selected group of businesses and offered them the opportunity to purchase an advertisement in an ice rink where the city league is held. The revenues from the advertisements enabled the department to expand the ice skating season from 9 to 13 weeks and to improve the quality of rink maintenance.

The commissioner's ability to implement his policy, and philosophy, is illustrated in this process. Not only did the department sell advertisements, and raise $25,000 (five times $5,000), but it also challenged the local recreation centers to sell smaller size advertisements and raise $4,000 per center to pay for programs that local residents wanted but the city was unable to finance. This approach again emphasizes the philosophy of partnership.

The third method of raising additional funds for achieving the goals of the department was through fees for service. In the past, all revenues went into the city's general fund. The commissioner had persuaded the mayor to deviate from this traditional approach. Thus, in some programs, such as ice rinks, participants were asked to pay a minimal entry fee. The department reached an agreement with the city which allowed it to raise the entrance fee and to keep two-thirds of the additional revenues. Thus, of every additional dollar raised, the department keeps 66.7 cents for its special programs. Money raised through this method was earmarked to extend programs (such as operating ice rinks for 109 days rather than 77) and establishing a reserve maintenance fund (of $20,000 to $25,000) for facilities use. In addition to cash contributions, "in kind" contributions play an important role in the resource strategy (Table [5.2]). The variety of the in-kind contributions is interesting as it shows its importance in a most tangible manner. For example, Gerrard Roofing Technology provided the materials and work for a new roof for a dilapidated community center building, work estimated at $30,000; Asplendh, a tree-cutting company, made its trucks equipped with high ladders available to the department to fix the lights in all the open baseball and basketball courts, estimated at $6,000; finally, the *Daily News*, a local newspaper, provided ongoing publicity for the department's annual fund-raising run and its pool campaign, estimated at $57,500. Thus, the department saved money and reduced the number of repairs that were needed.

An example of one of the most effective approaches developed by Mr. DiBerardinis is the "Pull for Pools." When the commissioner assumed office, many of the neighborhood pools had been closed, and others had a very curtailed summer season. Consequently the Pull for Pools program focused on raising money to clean and prepare all of the swimming pools for an extended summer season, with a full staffing of lifeguards. An invitational breakfast to potential donors set the tone as the president and CEO of First Fidelity Bank hosted the event; Mayor Rendell and a city councilman participated in the program. The philosophy espoused by all the speakers centered on "a passion for Philadelphia," that living in the city was "more than a bottom line," "that swimming is a vehicle for giving children self-esteem." Not only did the speakers link their comments to the department's mission, but the mayor focused on the importance of a public-private partnership. He saw the contributions as bridge loans until the city could stand on its own feet.

Many contributors were involved in the Pull for Pools program including banks, athletic teams (Phillies and Eagles), and corporations (e.g., Coca-Cola). . . . It should be noted that the Philadelphia Water Department, a governmental unit, contributed services because of its interest in having pools open (if the pools are closed in the hot weather, the children open the fire hydrants and much water is wasted).

What Do Donors Receive in Return?

It is difficult to assess the motivation of the key individuals in the various organizations that support the Department of Recreation. Several interpretations can be offered. Self-interest plays a critical role in much voluntary activity. This plays out in several ways. First, good publicity is given to these donations and, thus, free advertising and good will are benefits to the donor. The company that donated the roof to a community center required, in return, a ceremonial opening with the mayor present and newspaper coverage as it wanted to show off its advanced technology. The company asked, further, that the facility be made available to them for viewing by prospective clients. Other donors wanted their names printed on fliers, posters, or the fields where events took place. In fact, some companies did not want to contribute to a joint project, such as the basketball league, and asked instead for an individual project which they could then use as an advertising tool.

Second, this activity makes possible close contacts with the city and mayor since the mayor and his wife have both shown great interest in its success. Thus, making a contribution to the department and participating in fundraising events provides access to influential figures in City Hall and symbolically provides a diploma of good citizenship to be held for future use.

Third, in regard to community concern, the future of the city is linked with the mission and future of the contributing organizations. The logic underlying this is that a peaceful city, with satisfied residents, is good for the organization; the requested support is not too much to pay. In one case, we were told that the organization decided to support the department to prevent

Table 5.2

Sources and Characteristics of In-kind Support for Special Programs of the Department of Parks and Recreation

Funding organization	Supported activity	Actual support	Estimated value ($)	Initiators
Daily News	Broad Street Run	Technical support	50,000	Old tradition
Zanzibar Club	Carosel House	Charity dinner	Unclear	Development officer
Northeastern Hospital	Local facility support	Programs and supply materials	Unclear	Development officer
Greater Atlantic Health Services	Elderly support	Picnic for the elderly	5,000	Development officer
Gerrard Roofing	Intergenerational party	Food, prizes, etc.	5,000	Development officer
Philadelphia Phillies	Recreational facility	Fixed roof of center	30,000	Self-initiated
Asplendh	Rookie baseball league	14 pitching machines	Unclear	Development officer
	Recreation centers	Trucks to install lights in parks	6,000	Through local electric company
White Dog Cafe and Philadelphia Citizens for Children and Youth	Provided swings for recreation centers	A reception for all participants	1,500	Development officer
Modell's Sporting Goods	Shooting for the Stars	Tote bags, bottles, and baseball tickets	5,000	Development officer
Modell's Sporting Goods	Adopting 18 local centers (around Modell's stores)	Sporting goods	9,000	Development officer
Philadelphia 76ers	Basketball tickets and hospitality	1,200 tickets for pre-season and stadium hospitality	10,000	Development officer
Philadelphia 76ers	Basketball clinics	An ex-player came to 10 sites to teach the game and equipment	Unclear	Commissioner
Representative O'Donnell and Councilman Kenney	General recreation	St. Patrick's day party	10,000	Mayor

Wampler-Longacre Turkey	Kids' day in Penn's Landing	Provided hot dogs and entertainment	3,000	Self-initiative
Power 99 Radio	Assistance in clean-ups	On location entertainment for 6 cleanups	9,000	Self-initiative
Glad Bags	Clean-ups	Rebates for bags	5,000	Philadelphia Pride
Graphic News Inc.	Support for local community center	Art supplies and educational programs	1,500	Development officer
AMPRO Trophies	Sport	150 plaques	1,500	Development officer
AMPRO Sportswear	Sport	Production shirts	1,500	Development officer
Wade Communications	City youth swimming team	Travel and video equipment	9,600	Former administration
Gateway Communication	General recreation	Publicity	Unclear	Former administration
Textile College	Basketball	Dinner and admission to games	Unclear	Development officer
Urban Affairs Coalition	Administrating donations	Bookkeeping	5,000	Commissioner

"Los Angeles-like" riots. Some organizations were already involved in supporting other cultural and recreational activities and the call from the department matched their philosophy and practice. In addition, strengthening the city to prevent its future bankruptcy is viewed as a positive return on the investment. Thus, a small private investment can carry a certain program a long way. For example, the Phillies gave $30,000, not a huge amount, and it enabled 15 leagues to be set up in neighborhoods, or the 76ers and Coca Cola gave $20,000 for a basketball program that reached 2,500 kids. As such, donors see a clear and efficient return for their money.

Finally, it is worth noting that the phenomenon of "noblesse oblige," not usually associated with public sector activity, is likely to be given new meaning in this context. As the department expands its circle of contributors and the scope of their support, it seems likely that many organizations will find themselves expected to assist. Support for parks and recreation could be viewed as part of business responsibility to insure that the business is considered a respectable member of the local business community.

Institutionalizing the Change

The changes which took place in the City of Philadelphia Department of Recreation are very new. Further, they reflect the charismatic leadership of the commissioner. It was recognized that the emerging strategies should be institutionalized to guarantee continuation. Specific actions have been taken in the attempt to ensure not only that private funds will continue to support public recreational services, but also that the partnership concept between businesses and residents will be retained.

First, the strategic plan, which was revised and approved in December 1993, clearly states that the philosophy and practice of partnerships and multiple sources of financing are key elements in the mission statement of the department. Thus, until further major review of the mission statement of the department, this change is an integral part of the department.

Second, a new powerful advisory committee was established to work with the commissioner. This Recreation Development Committee is composed of heavy hitters from various areas such as political parties, corporations, arts and culture, universities, sports, and the general community. This committee has three functions: (1) advocating for the department, (2) raising money for the department, and (3) providing feedback regarding plans and programs.

Third, there was a need for a broad inclusion of many players from the department. Since the executive staff consisted of long-time department employees whose commitment to the new efforts were necessary to bring about change, the top management personnel of the department, a group of about

40 senior managers, were engaged in long-term training. This training focused on the new philosophy and on working with multiple partners. The management group now shares goals and skills to look for new resources to enhance the formal budget.

Fourth, donors are not simply solicited but are matched with their interests. At the same time, the commitment to the department and its program was developed so that even if they would not be aggressively solicited, donors would still be interested in assisting. For example, the Phillies, a professional baseball corporation, was originally solicited to assist with "Pull for Pools" program; this involvement subsequently led to activity more directly related to baseball. The Phillies were asked to assist in maintaining a baseball league and purchased 14 pitching machines to enrich the local youth baseball league. The quid-pro-quo was that along with demonstrating good citizenship, the Phillies were also assuring increased present and future interest in the game.

Fifth, as noted above, in April 1992, Mr. Fagan was appointed Funding and Resource Development Officer and a new unit was established. In 1992–93, this new unit was a one-person outfit, but currently one assistant has been added to the unit and there are plans to add a second assistant. Thus, the unit is more robust and contains individuals who are trained in fund raising and are civil-service employees.

Finally, the department is now in the process of developing grant applications to foundations to fund programs for children. These applications are all long-term projects and, as such, will increase the span of commitment from one year to multi-year projects.

These various strategies, which enhance the department's functioning, reflect the philosophy of the current commissioner. But they also have long-term implications for those who will follow as this administration has built continuity into the process.

Analysis and Implications

This article has focused on the entrepreneurial strategies of the commissioner of a public department in a major urban center. The philosophy of public fund-raising which involved a meaningful partnership with local businesses and residents, proved to be an efficient means to provide services that otherwise would have been eliminated or drastically curtailed.

This case study, interestingly, runs counter to Bendick's notion of load shedding. Underpinning Philadelphia's approach is the assumption that government must provide certain public goods and, if the revenues from taxes are insufficient, it must find alternative sources of funding in order to meet its responsibility. Thus, it is not enough just to raise money and contract with the private sector; it must raise money to provide services. The new entrepreneurial approach is new not only in its use of private money to finance public services, but also in its scope and permanency. From an ad-hoc approach of the past, it shifted to a central position in contemporary public administration. It is our contention that the quest for private donations is the trend that will characterize many successful local governments in the years to come. As long as taxes cannot be significantly raised and services become more costly, entrepreneurial administration will be hailed as the way to go. Thus, the establishment of development units and the solicitation of long-term financial commitments are manifestations of a new trend in public administration, one which will most likely be central in the decade to come.

However, it is of the utmost importance to note that for successful implementation of such a strategy it is essential for the public unit to have a solid infrastructure with a strong public base of support, for it is this public infrastructure that serves as the basis for additional projects. All other resources, both volunteer and financial, must be viewed as supplementary as they make possible an effect that is greater than the sum of its parts. However, this infrastructure is costly and must continue to be funded by tax money.

Thus, we wish to focus attention here on the public policy dilemmas which stem from this approach. While the approach may have achieved its goals, it also warrants a broader and more critical examination.

First, given the phenomenon of load shedding, and given the pattern of public sector withdrawal from service provision, is entrepreneurship an effective means of ensuring that public services are distributed to the citizenry in an equitable manner? The common approach for public services is to serve the needs of all including the needs of the poor and needy. However, if a donor wishes to adopt a community center in an affluent neighborhood and give extra services to its residents, will the city accept this preferential treatment or will it encourage contributions to other less fortunate neighborhoods?

Second, and directly related to the first, the public provision of service has many assumptions. Of great importance are the issues of equity and due process. Will equity be lost if the entrepreneurial leader caters to donor preference? Will citizens lose due process, be able to complain about quality of service, accessibility, and/or discrimination if the source of the funding is private? Although some administrators will take full public responsibility for such projects, others may find it convenient to treat them as expendable and thus avoid due process and accountability.

Third, from the perspective of the donors, fund-raising may be viewed as a voluntary tax; from the perspective of the city, it displaces one source of income with the other. Yet, from a democratic perspective, it raises the issue of duplicity concerning the voters' expressed wishes. Although the voter said "no to increased taxes" and voted to curtail government growth and activity, entrepreneurial city officials, de-facto, were able to override voters' preferences. This may be viewed as paternalism and a breach in the democratic order of government. Bellone and Goerl (1992, 131) highlighted the dangers of entrepreneurial activity in the public sector. They stated that "user fees, redevelopment agencies, off-budget enterprises, investment revenues, tax-increment financing, and development fees can be seen as measures to avoid voter approval and, thereby, increase the autonomy of public officials and public administrators."

Fourth, if the strategy of obtaining private money to support the provision of public services is successful, what are the consequences for the nonprofit sector in a capitalist society that historically has depended on the nonprofit sector to provide many services? Given a limited pot of money and resources, will the support of public sector projects be at the expense of the nonprofit sector? While we are not assuming a zero-sum game in terms of contributions, when there are more players in the fund-raising arena, there will be a smaller share for each player even if the total sum will increase. A private philanthropy may have to chose between funding a basketball program run by the city or a summer sport camp run by a small nonprofit organization. Although both serve children in need, it may be more advantageous to the foundation or the individual donor (enhancing their charitable tax status) to help the city at the expense of the small nonprofit organization. In the long run, it can transform the nonprofit sector as small nonprofit organizations find themselves with less funds or out of operation, a danger already noted by small arts organizations in New York City.

Fifth, what are the implications across the various governmental programs? Specifically, because recreation and education are popular, it is relatively easy to raise money for them, in contrast to less popular programs such as sanitation, social services, or public housing. If public budgets are to be allocated without reference to money raised by departments, some less-attractive departments will be left behind. It is easy to imagine a public fund-raising operation where attractive but nonurgent services get sold to sponsors while less attractive ones do not. Should we worry that skimming off the attractive services will create the image that governments are actually providing adequate services, when in reality essential services are not funded? If, however, fund-raising will be accounted for in the public budget then donors will not find it attractive to support the city as a whole.

Sixth, what are the limits as to who can contribute and is there a fine line that limits potential donors who could use the donations to put pressure on public officials? It is quite possible that bidders for city contracts, or those seeking favors in relation to licensing or zoning regulations, will attempt to gain preference by supporting community projects. Because of the informal nature of these projects, no strict guidelines exist to prevent abuse. Some local administrators may be guided by a short-term view, that is, determined by their potential longevity in office; thus, they may accept contributions from various special interest groups that will later cause tensions and unfair commitments. It is a sensitive issue to tell potential donors that because of their values or preferences, their contributions are unwanted. And yet different public administrators will draw different lines based on their immediate and urgent needs.

Seventh, what will happen if the external support, for whatever reason, ceases? What if the mayor alienates the donors and they refuse to contribute? In the case of this study, does it mean that the swimming pools and the ice rinks could be opened only for a short period of time? The guarantee of continuity is lacking under this model. Money raised through taxation has the advantage of continuity even if it fluctuates. Thus, public services are characterized by their long-term commitment while most private contributions are short term and need to be renegotiated annually. Furthermore, as discussed earlier, in-kind contributions tend not to be renewed. This highlights the reality that voluntary contributions are undependable in terms of on-going maintenance and add a volatile dimension to the public sector.

The quest for public entrepreneurial approaches will undoubtedly become of increasing importance as public revenues are diminished and public services are questioned. There is indeed a dilemma as committed public administrators seek to ensure the provision of services to their constituencies. There are no simple answers to the problems raised. It may be that entrepreneurial efforts in the public sector must be accompanied by citizen boards which are more than advisory in nature. The Philadelphia Department of Recreation, in attempting to institutionalize its initiatives, developed a powerful advisory committee to oversee revenues and partnerships. This may provide an interesting vehicle for control and serve as a model to test the protection needed to ensure equity and due process.

References

Ascoli, U. 1992. "Towards a Partnership Between Statutory Sector and Voluntary Action? Italian Welfare Pluralism in the '90s." In S. Kuhnle and P. Selle, eds., *Government and Voluntary Organizations*, pp. 136–156. Aldershot, UK: Avebury.
Bendick, M. 1989. "Privatizing the Delivery of Social Welfare Services: An Idea to Be Taken Seriously." In S. Kamerman and A. Kahn, eds., *Privatization and the Welfare State*, pp. 97–120. Princeton, NJ: Princeton University Press.

Bellone, C.J. and G.F. Goerl. 1992. "Reconciling Public Entrepreneurship and De-mocracy." *Public Administration Review* vol. 52: 130–134.

Billis, D., and M. Harris. 1992. "Taking the Strain of Change: UK Local Voluntary Agencies Enter the Post-Thatcher Period." *Nonprofit and Voluntary Sector Quar-terly* vol. 2: 211–225.

Cnaan, R.A. 1993. "The Symbiotic Co-existence of Voluntary Organizations and Public Administrations: The Case of Welfare Provisions." Paper presented at the Social Policy Association Conference, Liverpool, UK, July.

Copeland, L. 1993. "Private Money for the Public Good: Donors Lend a Hand to a City Department." *Philadelphia Inquirer*, B1, B3.

Grossman, D.A. 1992. "Paying Nonprofits: Streamlining the New York State Sys-tem." *Nonprofit Leadership Management* vol. 3: 81–91.

James, E. 1989. "The Private Provision of Public Services: A Comparison of Sweden and Holland." In E. James, ed., *The Nonprofit Sector in International Perspective: Studies in Comparative Culture and Policy*, pp. 31–60. Oxford, UK: Oxford Uni-versity Press.

Kramer, R.M. 1992. "The Roles of Voluntary Social Service Organizations in Four European States: Policies and Trends in England, the Netherlands, Italy, and Nor-way." In S. Kuhnle and P. Selle, eds., *Government and Voluntary Organizations*, pp. 34–52. Aldershot, UK: Avebury.

Lewis, E. 1984. *Public Entrepreneurship: Toward a Theory of Bureaucratic Political Power.* Bloomington: Indiana University Press.

Lipsky, M., and S.R. Smith. 1989. "Nonprofit Organizations, Government, and the Welfare State." *Political Science Quarterly* vol. 104: 625–648.

Palumbo, D., M. Musheno, and S. Maynard-Moody. 1986. "Public Sector Entrepre-neurs: The Shakers and Doers of Program Innovation." In J.S. Wholey et al., eds., *Performance and Credibility: Developing Excellence in Public and Non-Profit Organizations*, pp. 69–82. Lexington, MA: Lexington Books.

Perlmutter, F.D. 1969. "The Effect of Public Funds on Voluntary Sectarian Services." *Journal of Jewish Communal Service* vol. 49: 312–321.

Peters, T., and R. H. Waterman, Jr. 1982. *In Search of Excellence.* New York. Harper and Row.

Saidel, J.R. 1989. "Dimensions of Interdependence: The State and Voluntary Sector Relationship." *Nonprofit and Voluntary Sector Quarterly* vol. 18: 335–347.

Salamon, L. M. 1987. "Partners in Public Service: The Scope and Theory of Govern-ment-Nonprofit Relations." In W.W. Powell, ed., *The Nonprofit Sector*, pp. 99–117. New Haven, CT: Yale University Press.

Weisbrod, B. 1977. "Toward a Theory of the Voluntary Nonprofit Sector in a Three-sector Economy." In *The Voluntary Nonprofit Sector*, pp. 51–76. Lexington, MA: Heath.

The Limits of Privatism

Timothy Barnekov, Robin Boyle, and Daniel Rich

Reliance on the private sector for urban economic development often is portrayed as a pragmatic choice; a selection of institutional means to achieve presumably agreed upon social ends. In a privatized system, however, the substance and direction of efforts at urban regeneration, as well as the forms and instruments, must be structured to meet the demands of private investors. These efforts depend largely on what the private sector sees as its priorities and is willing to accept as investment risks. In both the US and Britain, despite periodic proclamations of corporate social responsibility, there is little evidence of sustained business interest in urban social investments. In the US, with the exception of brief excursions into urban social programs in the aftermath of the urban riots in the late 1960s, the business community has been disinterested and uninvolved in urban social programs, generally seeing these activities as the responsibility of voluntary organizations or government. In fact, experiences with social programs convinced many business leaders that they possessed neither the skills nor the incentives to play an active role in the social regeneration of cities. In Britain, despite occasional proclamations of corporate social responsibility, the private sector has been even less involved and their is no record of a sustained interest or even willingness to broadly participate in local public-private partnerships.

For the most part, the activities which the private sector considers as sound investments, and as within their domain of expertise, have been property development projects in areas selected for their commercial potential and profitability. The injection of public powers and resources has sometimes induced the private sector to take a more active role in development projects, but it has not altered the pattern of investment choice. Property development has a place in the process of urban regeneration and sometimes it has mobilized substantial private capital. But even when the physical and commercial face of a city is dramatically changed, general benefits for the community are not necessarily the result. Proponents of property development point to new jobs and increased economic activity but often large segments of the urban population—particularly racial minorities, the poor, and the unemployed—are not among the beneficiaries. . . .

In this context, it is important to examine closely the idea of leverage that has been in fashion on both sides of the Atlantic. Rather than public authority shaping private decisions, the reverse is often the case. US policy experience suggests that what is launched as an effort to stimulate private investment for public purposes frequently becomes a program of private leverage of public funds. The long-term result is the inversion of public and private priorities and the substitution of a private planning system for a public one without the establishment of an equivalent means of accountability—and the cost in public revenues can be substantial. In Britain, this inversion of priorities has been increasingly apparent in the 1980s. Urban policy that originally was conceived to address issues of social and economic dislocation and inequality instead has been used to launch and finance a series of property development projects where success is measured in terms of physical change and the return on private investment. Moreover, what began as public policy— with local government being the natural agents of change—has become a "vehicle for the articulation of private sector interests " (Stewart 1987, 141).

The profit motive may be a powerful incentive, but it is not easily harnessed to achieve publicly defined policy objectives. Experiences with public-private partnerships in urban redevelopment demonstrate this difficulty. In the US, partnerships have often formed the basis for local leadership coalitions that are instrumental in general development planning and implementation. The creation and maintenance of public-private coalitions, however, requires a string of public concessions to business interests and a concentration of public resources on services and development ventures that are priorities of the local business community. Moreover, when a community makes use of local business leadership it often cannot avoid being captured by it. At times this has meant that local governments have turned over general responsibility for the guidance of development to institutions which represent only a small fraction of the community and which operate as private governments, effectively insulated from direct public accountability. . . .

. . .

In addition to its divisive social and spatial impacts, the commitment to privatism has brought forth a narrow vision of the responsibilities of local government. City officials throughout the US and Britain have adopted an approach to local responsibilities that redefines municipal governance as public entrepreneurship. In the chase for technology, tourists, and footloose firms, civic leaders in the US and Britain elevated municipal marketing to a central role of local government. But in the municipal competition that ensues, losers always outnumber winners and the cost of participation is significant. Firms play one city off against another, forcing communities to bid-up the incentives they are prepared to offer. At the same time, the resources available for other facets of urban development more directly consequential for depressed areas and their residents are reduced.

In the spirit of public entrepreneurship, privatism is promoted as if it were simply a technical reform; one which implements "positive work programs" and creates the initiative for "getting things done." This reformist perspective presumes the existence of a community of common goals and values and the possibility of establishing a standard level of municipal services beneficial to all residents, an assumption that is contradicted by experience. In both America and Britain the definition of "positive work programs" is a matter of political dispute, and the zeal for "getting things done" is often a public rationale for the pursuit of private advantage. Turning to entrepreneurship and commercial initiative as a solution to the decline of urban areas represents not only an unjustified acceptance of the private sector's expertise but, more importantly, an imposition of artificial and premature closure on the definition of community interests.

Reference

Stewart, Murray. 1987. "Ten Years of Inner Cities Policy." *Town Planning Review* vol. 58 (no. 2): 129–145.

Discussion Questions

1. Employee empowerment has the potential to advance two historic objectives of American public administration: efficiency and responsiveness. What drawbacks, if any, might empowerment have? Are there types of positions in which you would strongly prefer empowered employees? In which would you not want employees to be empowered? Why?

2. The "demand-side" perspective on representative bureaucracy has myriad implications for both effective public administration and representative bureaucracy. As a general rule, do you think agencies' customers or clients should be served by persons of their own race, ethnicity, gender, sexual orientation, age, and so forth? Why or why not? When is the customer or client's demand for such service most appropriate?

3. Toward the end of their article, Felice Perlmutter and Ram Cnaan list seven potential drawbacks of public entrepreneurship. Which three of these do you consider potentially the most serious from the perspectives of representative bureaucracy? Why? On balance, do you favor the kind of entrepreneurship engaged in by the Philadelphia Department of Parks and Recreation?

4. The Kentucky Baptist Homes for Children and the private corporations discussed in the selection on "The Limits of Privatism" engage in public-private partnerships on their own terms, at least partly as a means of furthering their own interests. Is it reasonable to expect them to do otherwise, that is, to take on responsibility for public service out of pure altruism? Which, if any, examples involving the Philadelphia Department of Parks and Recreation suggest the greatest measure of public spiritedness? What differentiates them from the others? What are the implications for representative bureaucracy?

Index

Federal workforce, 32, 35–37, 45, 155
  supervisors' attitudes about diversity,
    155, 158–165
Fees for service, 196
Female representation. *See* Women
Financing
  private. *See* Public-private relationships
  religious organizations, 186–188
Flexible work schedules, 108
Functional participation, 28
Funding. *See* Financing

Gay rights lawsuits, 185–186, 187
Gender
  attitudes, 90
  health representation, 170, 181
  socialization experiences, 79, 104,
    110–111
  workplace policy preferences,
    104–112
  See also Women
Goldsmith, Stephen, 186
Gore, Al, 169, 170, 173–175
Government load-shedding, 189–190,
  202
Great Britain
  discrimination against women, 5, 16–18
  education system, 13–15
  public-private relationships, 206–208
Griggs v. Duke, 67

Hale, Mary M., 79, 104–113
Health representation. *See* AIDS health
  services
Hispanics, recruitment and
  underrepresentation, 115–116, 155,
  159, 161–165
HIV health services. *See* AIDS health
  services
Housing Act (1949), 143

Ideal type bureaucracy, 4, 6
Internal controls, 84
Irish, 62

J. A. Croson Company, Richmond v., 39
Job sharing, 108–109

Jobs. *See* Employment
Johnson v. Santa Clara County, 38

Kentucky Baptist Homes for Children,
  185, 187, 188
Kingsley, Donald J., 4–5, 12–18, 82, 86
Krislov, Samuel, 5–6, 23–29

Labor. *See* Employment
Lieberman, Joseph, 187
Life experiences. *See* Socialization
  experiences
Lipset, Seymour, 77–78, 80–83
Load-shedding, 189–190, 202
Local government
  affirmative action reports, 64
  AIDS health services, 177, 178–179
  black representation, 33, 63–74
  equal opportunity court rulings, 38–39
  female representation, 33, 52–55, 60
  privatization and entrepreneurship,
    190–194, 207–208
Local governments
  black representation, 66–67
  lack of white interest in municipal jobs,
    66–67, 68, 71

Maximum possible differences, 44
Mayors, black, 64, 66, 68, 72, 74
Measure of variation, 32–33, 44–50
Meier, Kenneth J., 78, 84–94, 115,
  125–132, 137
Merit-oriented reform, 98
Merit systems, 22, 31, 58, 59, 140
Merit Systems Protection Board (MSPB),
  37, 157, 158
*Metro Broadcasting v. Federal
  Communications Commission*, 38,
  39
Minorities
  active/passive representation link,
    120–123, 126
  active representation, 117–119
  attitudes toward representation,
    157–158, 160–165
  discretionary jobs, 122, 126
  employee mobilization, 122

About the Editors

Julie Dolan is assistant professor of political science at Macalester College. Her research interests include bureaucratic and executive branch politics, women and politics, public policy, and Congress. She has published in a variety of journals, including *Public Administration Review, PS: Political Science and Politics*, the *Journal of Public Administration Research and Theory*, and *Women & Politics*.

David H. Rosenbloom is Distinguished Professor of Public Administration at American University (Washington, DC). His work focuses on public administration and democratic constitutionalism. He is a member of the National Academy of Public Administration and was the 1999 recipient of the Dwight Waldo Award for Outstanding Contributions to the Literature and Leadership of Public Administration through an Extended Career and the 2001 John Gaus Award for a Lifetime of Exemplary Scholarship in the Joint Tradition of Political Science and Public Administration.